BEWITCHED, BOTHERED AND BEWILDERED

BEWITCHED, BOTHERED AND BEWILDERED

HOW COUPLES REALLY WORK

Wyn Bramley

KARNAC

First published in 2008 by
Karnac Books Ltd
118 Finchley Road, London NW3 5HT

British Library Cataloguing in Publication Data

A C.I.P. for this book is available from the British Library

ISBN 978 1 85575 650 2

Edited, designed and produced by The Studio Publishing Services Ltd,
www.studiopublishingservicesuk.co.uk
e-mail: studio@publishingservicesuk.co.uk

Printed in Great Britain

www.karnacbooks.com

CONTENTS

ACKNOWLEDGEMENTS AND AUTHOR'S NOTE

I wish to thank my partner, Noel, for his help with technical aspects of the manuscript's presentation and for making sense of my original rough sketches for the figure illustrations. He also put in order my somewhat unorthodox References and Bibliography sections. Most appreciated of all has been his calm intervention whenever divorce threatened in the love–hate relationship between myself and my computer as I worked on the manuscript.

Thanks are also due to Becky Thomas and Lizzie Jones at Faber and Faber Ltd and Jane Cramb at Macmillan Ltd for their advice and assistance concerning copyright permissions.

* * *

Lyric extract on p. xix from "Bewitched" by Richard Rodgers and Lorenz Hart from the Broadway musical *Pal Joey* (1940). Words by Lorenz Hart and music by Richard Rodgers. Used by permission of Alfred Publishing Co., Inc., Van Nuys, CA; and Williamson Music, New York.

Interlude. Excerpts on pp. 60–61 from the "Introduction" to *Oedipus and the Couple* by Francis Grier, copyright © 2005 Francis Grier and

Karnac, London, UK, reproduced by permission of Karnac Books, London, UK. All rights reserved. Excerpts on p. 61 from the novel *The Interpretation of Murder* by Jed Rubenfeld, copyright © 2006 by Jed Rubenfeld, reprinted by permission of Headline Publishing Group Limited, London; and Henry Holt and Company, LLC, New York. All rights reserved.

Chapter Eight. Extract on p. 97 from *Love Is Never Enough* by Aaron T. Beck, copyright © 1998 by Aaron T. Beck, MD and Harper & Row, Publishers, Inc., reproduced by permission of HarperCollins Publishers, New York. All rights reserved. Extract on p. 106 from *Schopenhauer's Porcupines* by Deborah Anna Luepnitz, copyright © 2002 by Deborah Luepnitz and Basic Books, New York, reprinted by permission of Perseus Books Group, Cambridge, MA. All rights reserved. Excerpts on p. 110 from Act II in the play *The Cocktail Party* by T. S. Eliot, copyright © 1950 by T. S. Eliot and renewed 1978 by Esme Valerie Eliot, reprinted by permission of Faber and Faber Ltd, London; and Houghton Mifflin Harcourt Publishing Company, Orlando, FL. All rights reserved.

Appendix I. Excerpts on pp. 231–233 from the novel *Mother's Milk* by Edward St Aubyn, copyright © Edward St Aubyn 2006, reproduced by permission of Pan Macmillan Ltd, London, Oxford and Basingstoke, UK; and Aitken Alexander Associates Ltd, London, UK. All rights reserved. The poem "Baby Song" on p. 234 from *Collected Poems* by Thom Gunn, copyright © 1993, 1994 by Thom Gunn, reprinted by permission of Faber and Faber Ltd, London; and Farrar, Straus & Giroux LLC, New York. All rights reserved.

Author's note

To maintain textual clarity and ease of reading, the therapist has been given a female gender. Where human development is discussed, the subject is assigned a male gender. No gender bias is intended.

All anecdotes and case vignettes are based on real people, but are disguised (or combined with similar cases) to protect clients' identities. Only particular aspects of any case have been selected, to illustrate a specific concept or psychological process. No case has been described in its entirety, so as to further protect confidentiality.

Wyn Bramley was Senior Psychiatric Sister at the Cassel Hospital (one of the first psychoanalytically orientated "therapeutic communities" in the UK). She then moved into Student Counselling. Over a fifteen-year period, she set up and headed the counselling service at what is now the University of Westminster, before transferring to a similar role at University College, London. During this period she qualified (1976) at the Institute of Group Analysis and Family and Marital Therapy (now Institute of Group Analysis), while setting up in-service training programmes, with colleagues, for what was to become the National Association for Student Counselling.

In 1986 she moved to Oxford, working as a trainer and clinician in both the private and NHS sectors. In the mid 1990s she set up and then directed the Master's Programme in Psychodynamic Studies at Oxford University. In 1996 she published two books expounding her non-doctrinaire view of psychodynamic therapy. Pertinent to *Bewitched, Bothered and Bewildered: How Couples Really Work* is her book *The Broad Spectrum Psychotherapist*, published by Free Association Books. Currently, she runs a small private practice in rural Oxfordshire.

CASE EXAMPLES AND ANECDOTES

FIGURES

This book is dedicated to all those couples, past and present,
who have shared their relationship with me,
and to the memory of Robin Skynner.

I'm wild again,
Beguiled again,
A simpering, whimpering child again—
Bewitched, bothered and bewildered am I.

Richard Rodgers/Lorenz Hart [from "Bewitched",
Pal Joey, 1940, my italics]

CHAPTER ONE

Should you buy this book? What's in it?

"The first weeks and months of my life determined the degree to which I now feel secure with my other half." *True or false?*

"I thought I freely chose my last partner, but forces outside my awareness really made ninety per cent of the decision." *Fact or fiction?*

"All couples do secret deals with each other and get extremely upset when the unspoken pact is broken. Furthermore, such deals are shaped by childhood experience." *How come?*

"Many couple disputes, even split-ups, result from partners hating in their partner what actually lies in themselves. To a degree such hatred is usual and normal." *Excuse me, normal?*

"Grown-up jealousy, competitiveness, confidence—or lack of it!—arise from unsorted conflicts in my mind about me, mum and dad, when I was just a toddler." *Er, really?*

"When a marriage breaks up, it is seldom 'six of one, and half a dozen of the other'. There really are givers and takers, saints and sinners. But the saints have their own agenda too." *Well, well. Convince me!*

These statements may sound strange at first. In this book I translate some modern psychoanalytic ideas into plain English. This demonstrates how only depth psychology (one that takes into account unconscious forces) stands any real chance of restoring a seriously ailing couple relationship. Appeals to men and women to be more honest, talk things over, take a holiday, exercise more restraint, be nicer to each other, are mere salves and do not last. As well as the love and commitment both sides have poured into the relationship, the bad stuff, the hatred and disillusion, the sense of injustice and/or betrayal have also to be mobilized and faced before a new and better way of operating can be forged. Couple therapy provides a safe place for this to happen.

It is not just a matter of expressing *negative* emotion, "letting it all hang out". Such unchecked ventilation is positively dangerous. The point is that *all* feelings, positive and negative, overt and hidden, need to be understood in terms of the psychology and the relationship history of the persons experiencing them. Without this no one is communicating with anybody; it is just a shouting match.

This book will not tell you how to do couple therapy, but takes clinical experience out of the consulting room into your reading room, so that the concepts and case studies here described might help you to see better the dynamics of your own current or past relationships. However, the questions raised by the opening statements are far from easy ones, and so the answers cannot be simple. You will have to struggle with some bits of theory, interspersed with stories from the lives of real couples, in order to find what you seek.

So let us begin.

Contrary to the popular view, marriages are conceived neither in heaven nor hell, but in infancy and childhood. This is not to say things were done to a helpless child that subsequently formed its character, and thus we can happily blame the parents for later troubles, including a bad marriage. It is rather that, from birth, an infant very purposefully interacts with mum/mum substitute, making sense of its good and bad experiences long before the capacity for language has arrived. The child develops strategies, assumptions, and defences to protect it from the worst, and to preserve or solicit more of the best. It is these very early developments that shape future partner selection as much as hormones and other determinants.

In the next chapter I discuss further how choice of partner results not just from lust and looks, shared interests, and so on, but out of deep early concerns of which both partners are oblivious, but which, by some radar, they spot and manipulate in each other. Understanding these in yourself and your partner widens options for a new and more fruitful way of relating.

I use the term "couple" and "marriage" interchangeably. By "marriage" I do not mean legalized cohabitation or the consecration of vows before a religious authority. I refer instead to an agreement between two people, legalized or not, that they constitute a unit, a bonded pair.

Consider show business duos, for example: Gilbert and Sullivan, Lennon and McCartney, the Two Ronnies. They each have discrete personalities, but together they add up to more than the sum of the two parts. They become a third element, a marriage. Each relates to this unit ("us") in his or her idiosyncratic way. This third element, this joint personality, so to speak, can at different times and to different degrees enhance or conflict with the relationship they desire to have with each other. So consuming can this marriage become, whether viewed from inside as a participant or outside as an observer, that the two people have often to break out and define themselves separately for a while, reclaim their own identity. Each of the Two Ronnies appeared in shows without the other. Lennon and McCartney split up eventually. It is the same phenomenon in heterosexual and homosexual couples.

The pair does not always permanently part, of course, but there are frequent tensions in many couples' relationships concerning the amount of union/separateness that each desires and needs at different times.

For instance, let's introduce a couple we'll call Nick and Nancy.

Nick may treasure solitude as much as togetherness—absence only making the heart grow fonder—whereas Nancy feels any separateness constitutes a dire threat to the marital unit; out of his sight means she is out of his mind. She grows possessive and afraid for the unit as he becomes resentful. Nancy cannot see that when Nick is alone he carries the security and love inherent in the unit inside him. He does not need her physical presence. This could have been how he felt as a child, confident of his family ties, knowing they were always there in the background, so he could roam far and wide, returning to base in his own good time. Nancy, though, was never sure of her family bonds, for dad left soon after mum was diagnosed with multiple sclerosis. He returned unannounced from time to time, before disappearing again. She never knew when mum would have an attack or go into remission. She could even die.

Alternatively, Nick's mother may have been a rather invasive, controlling sort of woman. He "reads" the lack of confidence and insecurity in his partner, which leads her to be somewhat clingy, as *also* controlling. This he deals with by rebelling occasionally, going off on his own. He feels better then, but she feels worse.

Once Nancy and Nick understand the links with the past, why their needs are so different, they can begin to negotiate and compromise, so as to meet both sets of needs without quarrelling.

Neither partner is right or wrong in these situations, only different, holding conflicting views of what a marriage ought to be. Such conceptions, to a large degree, derive from childhood experiences, this time of the *parental couple*, or lack of same. The point is not so much what the child was told or taught about marriage, as what they *saw and felt* as they were being parented, day in, day out. What did they *make* of what they saw and felt—a vow to be different when *I* grow up perhaps? Or a promise to the self that any partner must be just like dad/mum?

I am not talking here of specific memories or traumatic events, rather of the thousands of subtle, unintentional, and repeated ways in which our attitudes, feelings, and reactions to others, and to our social institutions such as marriage, have been shaped by family experience. As grown-ups, we think we make free choices and informed, rational decisions in our close relationships, but, as with an iceberg, only a tenth of what there is to see and know is actually available to us. Our past conditioning lies under the mental sea, none the less profoundly affecting us.

We make massive assumptions about the interpersonal world, scarcely knowing of what we speak. "At home it was just *like* that. I assumed other families were like that too. I took it as normal. The way the world ran." How often have I heard that from an amazed husband or wife, who has just realized the *otherness* of their partner, the fact that they are not just an extension of themselves, but the child of another, sometimes completely foreign, psychological culture. One party's subjective experience of the same marital

CHAPTER TWO

Finding a mate: what are we looking *for*?

The importance of the first couple

N one of us is born alone. Think about it. We are housed within our mother's womb for nine months and when we have filled that space to bursting we emerge from one couple (for we are housed in our mother's mind and heart as well as her womb) into another sort of couple, the physically separate nursing couple. Ejected from our cosy lodging, we become, without so much as a by-your-leave, part of a new and startling arrangement—not one *inside* the other as before, but one *facing* the other. If all goes reasonably well, this becomes a unit as intimate, binding, and as interdependent as any marriage that is to come later in our lives. Although we are genetically programmed to seek each other out, the attachment arrangements can, none the less, go well or badly. Work is required on both our parts.

Babies are born incomplete, unable to fend for themselves without attention from another human being. If Nature had fixed things so that babies were born as finished human creatures, the birth exit would be way too small and the mother would die. Not good for the perpetuation of the species! So, at birth we are not able to experience ourselves as an independent being. We cannot yet distinguish "me" from "mother", where our toes end and her hand begins. Mum is me and I am her, all one universe without differentiation or ownership. As within the womb, we are one. A complex and sometimes distressing learning process will eventually result in the realization of our separateness.

Meanwhile, the physical growth that had occurred in the womb continues outside it. This post birth period is the most precarious developmental period of our lives, both psychologically and physically. Accordingly, Nature has endowed us with an infantile energy and hope that drives us towards the life-prolonging breast and eventually the mother to whom it belongs. Our very life depends on her staying with us. Our infant selves sense the horror that would ensue if she did not or could not.

When the fires of adolescent sexuality are later lit by hormonal input at puberty, a similar drive towards the other sex occurs. This feels to the young person as desperate and necessary to them as were the pairing and security needs of the immediately post birth infant. However, terror of annihilation in the absence of, failure of, or rejection by the proposed mate accompanies that hope and desire. The very positive function of this terror is to spur us into action, despite the attendant risks, towards this selected *other* and then to cement that attachment. The fear of being abandoned and alone then keeps us tied to that union, while sexual desire drives us toward procreation. By providing bonded parents, this arrangement secures a better chance of survival for the baby still to come.

It is worth noting that severe panic attacks in adulthood can often be traced to this fear of annihilation in infancy. When the sufferer is provided with a historical context, the symptoms acquire meaning, and so are less scary.

Courtship mirrors the original struggle to "make it" with our mums. What was easy or tough in infancy becomes easy or tough during courtship. This is because the human animal stores, then *transfers*, all previous experience to current experience. From that database, one can predict, then negotiate, the course of what is happening to oneself now. Past experiences colour the expectation one has of the present situation—in this case, courtship. Deeply embedded feelings and attitudes—longing perhaps, mingled with fear, anger, disappointment, confident hope, and bold action—are mobilized to cope with the new circumstances. In other words, we all learn and automatically use lessons from our past experiences, even those—*particularly* those—we believe we had forgotten!

Out of that first journey along the birth canal, jettisoned into a loud, bright, strange world, our organism feels the gargantuan impact of the external universe upon us (for we do not yet have concepts to think with, or language to speak). We "decide" there and then, in our cells, blood, nerves, and bone (or so it is now posited by therapists and neuroscientists alike), either to grab the newness of the nipple and get on with it, or fruitlessly to turn away in the hope of crawling back into the safe place whence we had come. One of the most fundamental aspects of our personality—to seize the day or take a back seat in life, is set around that time, as, struggling, suffocating, pushed, shoved, and squeezed, we are flung from our only known place of safety into our first marriage with the nipple (plastic or natural); flung towards the smell, feel, warm receptivity, or cool disavowal of the fellow human who is to be our first and most vital partner. For without her, or an adequate substitute, we die.

Even though our biological lives may be sustained, if this, our first couple, fails, or partly fails, at an emotional, trust, or communication level, traces may be left for another, later marriage to cope with. Our mother, as well as our imaginings and beliefs about our mother (were she biologically so, or a surrogate), has an enduring effect on our self precepts. Are we acceptable to others, worthy of love and care? Are we entitled to feel "OK in the world", a fully paid-up member of the human race? Some call that profound sense that will colour all our relationships in the future "personal confidence" or "ontological security". Early mothering and our response to it (for it takes two to make mothering happen), is the prototype, the blueprint for all later significant emotional attachments.

It is important to recognize that this is not a question of fault, blame, or congratulation. It can, and has been, cogently argued that although heartless mothers and totally uninterested or actively refusing infants do exist, these instances are rare. Similarly, the nursing couple who take to the business like a pair of ducks to water is relatively uncommon. A period of adjustment is the commonest picture. Usually an unfeeding, unthriving baby is as unhappy as its unable-to-feed, worried, and fearful mother. No one is doing anything bad on purpose.

What we need to note here, in order to understand the impact of infantile experience on the subject's future, is the state of relations *between* the couple as well as *in* them. For, even when situational and/or health problems in either party militate against a successful first union, most mothers and infants manage, over time, *to cue one another as to how to treat each other.* A successful way forward is negotiated, albeit through distress, frustration, anger, rejection, and reconciliation, and with a bit of assistance from the midwife. This progression seems to me more reminiscent of the average adult marriage than the perfect and permanent state of bliss that so many new mums, and new spouses, expect of, and for, themselves.

So, next time we yell at our partner "You are just too weak/ cowardly/moody/underconfident/scared to take risks", etc., perhaps we should stop and consider what we know or can guess of their early history. The accusations may be correct, but some appreciation of their origins may temper the need to prolong the attack indefinitely, so allowing a bit of compassion in.

On calming down, we should also take a look at why particular characteristics in our partner are so infuriating. Does it say something about us? Are we seeing and railing against qualities in them that are disowned in ourselves? Is this part of why we made a couple with them in the first place: they could carry the junk we wanted to dump? I shall further examine this idea of relocating unwanted bits of oneself in the partner in later sections of this book. It is one of the central concepts in couple therapy. We may love our partners, but we also *use* them, as they use us, to make ourselves feel better.

What about dad?

Dad (and, to some extent, the rest of the family network), has a critical role in supporting the new mother's efforts to do good mothering. Whatever *practical* child-care is shared between husband and relatives, the function of protecting the nursing couple while they adjust to one another *emotionally* is of paramount importance, and is neglected at the child's future peril. It is not quite acceptable to say so these days, but a mother needs a state of near reverie to adequately commune with and know her child in the early weeks and months. Reverie means neglecting other things for a time. A mature husband picking up most of the tabs need not be jealous of the child. He should feel proud that he is giving his child the best possible chance of a good *first* "marriage". Let him aim to make it the model for the next!

Having said that, the almost sexual intensity of some new fathers' jealousy may send him off the rails for a time. This can be understood, if not condoned. In a sense, he has indeed for a time lost his loved one to a rival. An immature man, who formerly relied on his wife for maternal care (however hidden this reliance), or for constant sexual attention to boost a wobbly sense of maleness, is now bereft and often panics. He cannot see that his partner and child now need him more than ever, but in a new role of support-ing and protecting their getting-to-know-you relationship. He senses exclusion, and reacts accordingly.

The birth of the first child has a huge effect on the couple's bond, strengthening or weakening it; or providing, through a difficult and testing time, a real chance for maturation. A woman may be thrilled by her child or may be haunted by doubts about her adequacy as a mum. She badly needs the reassurance of a loving partner at this time, especially if her own mother is not psychologically available.

This exclusiveness and intimacy in the nursing couple is of para-mount developmental concern, even if it does not seem fair to all parties (since when has life been fair?). During what used to be called courtship, was there not (and is there not still?) a well-worn convention that young lovers, *like the nursing pair*, were allowed all manner of concessions? They were permitted to kiss and cuddle in public (unusual then). They were indulged when they wanted to be alone together a lot. Care was taken to seat them together, to send joint invitations, to humour their tiffs and sulks and bring them back into each other's orbit whenever possible. And when they married, amid many a social and/or religious ritual (this is the old days remember, when ritual was a powerful reinforcer), they were given a honeymoon. Off they would go to some secret destination in order to be alone, to find out more about this new estate (couple-dom) that they had entered. In short, they were given the best chance, *as the nursing couple should be*, to do a good job, to get the marriage on the right footing. Then they could return home with a united wedded front to show their family and friends (whatever the inevitable ups and downs of the honeymoon).

Thus, the temporary but essential requirement for exclusivity in the nursing couple gives dad a vital support role to play. How he fulfils this role, or fails to fulfil it, will have a profound effect on the nursing mother and, hence, on her relationship with their child and his subsequent development.

When the couple cannot part

However, continuing the exclusivity past the appropriate time arouses hostility and destructive envy in the excluded. There is much suspicion that the gratification obtained by mother and infant lies beyond the requirements of healthy development. This is also true of glued-together couples who go on behaving like new lovers long after such amorousness is expected or tolerated. Babes in the wood, they do not know how to be separate adults as well as joined lovers.

We all know grown-ups who, as children, never properly "cut the cord", "left the breast", or are "still tied to apron strings". They are extremely taxing to be married to! And some never marry, having never been able to completely identify with their gender. The "confirmed bachelor" feels uncertain about his masculinity. He fears settling down in the conventional way, with all the traditional responsibilities of producing, providing for, and rearing a family. Or he marries a mother figure *so as to avoid disrupting the continuity of care.*

The girls (for they are still girls) also turn away from growing up, preferring to perpetuate their dependency. Their clinging to a partner at first seems to him a sign of devotion or "feminine insecurity", and he may be touched by this. After a while it exhausts him. He realizes he has become the victim of a manipulative helplessness. When such a woman has a child, there is a risk that the infant's demand for total absorption in his survival needs is just too much. Mother feels "need" almost as much as baby does, and he is competition. Dimly aware of this, she may become guilty and depressed.

Endless learned tomes and popular psychology journalism regales us with the multitude of things that can go wrong in a mother–baby relationship. For the purposes of this discourse, let us assume I am conversing with an intelligent and literate readership. You are well aware that an infant must feel safely held, fed, and warmed, both literally and metaphorically, over a sustained period if he is to thrive. (Odd lapses do not count: no one's perfect.) Should this not happen, he will grow up with all manner of doubts and uncertainties, plus a lack of confidence that reflects these early negative experiences.

Equally, if a mother is so absorbed by her infant that she cannot let the child go, future problems are inevitable. In both cases, compensatory later experiences are possible, but such early imprints on the human system do have a permanent effect, however much they are ameliorated later on. Such is the collective clinical experience of psychotherapists, both in the past and present.

The child inside the adult

In adulthood, partner choice always contains in some form the search for the blissful aspects of early infancy. At the same time, there is hope that the new union will make up for all that disappointed in the old. Needless to say, this aspect of partner selection is quite unconscious. For the infant *organism*, whose advanced brain functions had not yet appeared, *still remembers and has recorded*. That newborn infant, comprising all its experiences of gratification and disappointment, still lives inside the adult, *but outside of his awareness*. There is no *memory* of happiness or pain in the usual sense of that term. Rather, the infant's subjective experiences are etched into the emotional life of the grown-up, so that he does not recognize how his judgement in affairs of the heart is *already patterned*.

As the child begins to walk, talk, watch his parents and siblings, and relate to other children at nursery, new disappointments and pleasures will be added to his memory store—some of which he will later recall, and some of which will go underground. In later life he will seek a mate. Whatever his conscious, buried, or half-buried memories may be, he has not yet realized one vital thing.

One cannot put back the clock, return to the Lost Eden with the new love, while erasing the terrors and frustrations of the old. The day in, day out experiences of living together, loving and learning about, fighting and reconciling with the partner, might teach this humbling lesson eventually. Romance with a capital R, and the idealization of marriage, along with the subsequent bitterness and disappointment, fly out the window as, one hopes, maturity and deeper commitment fly in. Alas, many couples separate at this juncture, believing the source of unhappiness lies in their partner alone.

Birth, then, is the first separation, the nursing couple the first marriage—a coming together of two people rather than being one single organism as before. Birth rends asunder whatever the relationship the pregnant mum and her baby had before. Having an infant inside you is totally different from having and holding it outside you. It is the mother's attitudes and beliefs about mothering, as well as her actual experiences at her own mother's hands, that will shape much of the post birth period.

While inside the womb, more or less acquiescent, the child could be fantasized about, "designed" in the mother's mind. Once the child is born, he will become active, as described above, in seeking or avoiding the nipple and all that it represents. The child is far from passive. If mum has intrinsic self-confidence she will find it easier to "read" her infant's needs and fulfil them. If her own mothering was not so happy, she may struggle and fail to set up the reciprocal cues needed in this the first experiment in communication. Just as in a marital row, the two involved may be desperate to communicate, but somehow miss each other.

A new babe can be demanding, rejecting perhaps, puce in the face, constantly vomiting and soiling; not at all the obliging, dependent, adoring little angel mum had envisaged. The necessary disillusion that bedevils all marriages has set in! How it is dealt with by both parties will determine the outcome.

If the separation and trauma of birth results in an eventual reconciliatory union, rather than a divorce, the infant may be said to be equipping himself already with the necessary, if rudimentary, tools to help an ailing marriage. If the disillusion is overwhelming, even only occasionally overwhelming, then later on the hunt begins for a partner who can mend this awful state of affairs.

Is this too much to ask of a marital partner? In any case, is it possible to heal a partner's wounds? When does a husband or wife become a therapist? If the role ascribed is the role accepted, what— if anything—does the "therapist" get out of the situation? If the role is declined, is the marriage doomed? More will be said about this critical concept of necessary disillusion in later chapters.

Grown-up partner-seeking

Early partners can be pretty alarming to the young lovers' parents, as we all know. The choice made may reflect the need for a social accessory, a choice that bestows status among peers. It could be a craving for regular sex at any price, or someone to shock the parents and thus aid both parties' wish to break away from the ties that bind—two against a hostile world. It may be puppy love that prolongs dependency on mum or dad in another form. It may be hero worship of an older man or woman, an identification with what, one day, the smitten person would like to be. It may be an "illicit" liaison that succeeds in the short term because it concerns an affair designed to settle some ancient triangular score in relation to mum and dad. (This "oedipal situation" will be explained further in Chapter Four.)

The reasons for early choice of partner are endless, but rarely concern marriage in the sense meant in this book. Early choice usually reflects a young person's need to have an assistant, another person who can be used to make them look and feel more accept- able. Meanwhile, the partner chosen is using the chooser in a simi- lar way. No wonder the relationship is short-lived. Sadly, on occasion, even so-called adults are unable to grow out of this normal phase. They make a series of unhappy legal marriages that constitute two separate people trying to complete themselves at the other's expense, rather than a couple in any meaningful sense.

It must be said, though, that all of us do this to some extent. It feels natural, especially at times of great personal insecurity, to turn to our partners and lean heavily upon them. So when does the normal become pathological? It is all a question of degree. Different clinicians draw the line in different places. Therapy is not an exact science, if it is a science at all.

When a person eventually feels ready to make a serious, ideally lifelong, commitment, the past as well as the present is drawn more deeply into the selection process. Although the searcher has criteria in mind that are sensible and understandable—looks, intelligence, fair-mindedness, shared interests, and so on, other unconscious variables are powerfully operative at the same time.

In their marvellously informative, funny, and much reprinted book, *Families and How To Survive Them* (1983), the late Dr Robin Skynner and John Cleese talk about choosing a partner in terms of what is "behind each other's screens". Aspects of everyone's upbringing have caused them to deposit certain difficult and unresolved issues (shame, anger, or competitiveness, for example) behind a screen in their mind. In front of the screen is the "shop window", the very opposite of what is behind the screen, a denial of or defence against it. Each partner looks in one another's shop window and sees for sale all the qualities they admire and espouse themselves, an ideal version of themselves, in fact. But they also get a whiff (only a whiff) of what is behind the screen. It smells faintly wicked (in the old sense of that word) and fascinates. The book cites the case of a virtuous pair who got together because of lusty sexual feelings behind both their screens. Sharing the reading of an article in the *News of the World*, they can agree together how disgusting it is that newspapers should be allowed to print such filthy stuff.

One can keep up a screen for an evening, or a week, but not a lifetime. Living together upsets the balance of the screen and it starts to teeter. What the couple first adored in each other becomes the source of all their recrimination and blaming. Roughly translated, this means "I hate and reject in you what I secretly and unknown to myself despise in me."

The upside of this partner choice ("I want you because you seem to be like me") is that by having one another's number, so to speak, and with a bit of mediation and protection from loss of face, such couples can come to understand one another's games and manoeuvrings pretty quickly and so do some repair work. Also, when working well, the couple represent—at least in their shop window—the very best of one another. This can be an inspiration in times of self-doubt, for the mirror that is one's partner shows such a reassuring image.

Then there is the "I choose you because you offer something different from what I am used to" scenario.

Hattie and Henry

Hattie had lived for eleven years with Henry, a gentle, rather passive person who praised and admired her all the time. This was so different to her father, who had been a mean and nasty man who always undermined and criticized her.

At first she blossomed, but eventually the old tie to Dad reasserted itself. She gradually came to lose respect for Henry, found herself acting cruelly towards him, as her father had to her. Henry became "her other half" in more senses than one. He stood for the disowned, bullied part of herself. She could now give her father (Henry) a dose of his own medicine, while getting rid of her own despised submissiveness towards her father by *depositing it in her husband.* Henry now incurred all the loathing she had felt for herself, as a young girl too afraid to fight back.

In therapy, this couple were aided to see both their histories in a new light. Henry's own father had been very timid, so he had been unconsciously attracted to the hidden fury behind Hattie's screen. He had wanted to "borrow" that quality in her, fearing he had "no guts" of his own. At last he could get good and angry, if only by proxy. Hattie could not explain it, but she always felt he engineered situations where her anger would erupt—"as if he got off on it", as she put it.

Hattie had selected a gentle man (on the surface) to offset her father, but that gentleness only filled Henry's shop window. In the back room lay much hatred of *his* father, whom he felt had failed to teach him how to be a proper man. It thrilled as well as frightened him to see his wife railing at him the way he could never in million years have railed at his father.

Over the years, Henry's patient submission to her tempers so stirred up Hattie that she felt she might physically attack him. Yet, although she loved him still, she could not understand why she treated him so badly. Her guilt deteriorated into depression. Her GP saw the couple strife, and referred them both for a couple assessment.

When both these partners named and claimed their own cruelty, understanding its origins in themselves and each other, great improvement occurred. Hattie helped her husband to find a better post and build up his confidence, rather than scorning his lowly job and lack of ambition. Henry learned to stand up to Hattie openly rather than "winding her up" with his "wimpiness", as she described it. (He had thought he was calming her down, with his appeasement!) "Our rows are clean and up-front now," Hattie said at the end of therapy. "They used to be me hysterical, and him all saintly. This is much better."

The message to the prospective partner is often: "you must make up for all my traumas, plug the gaps I still have in my development, *so I don't have to continue to grow any more*. Living with you I should-n't need to. You will grant me peace". Oh dear! This kind of selec-tion means the pair is in trouble before they have even moved in together. In therapy they usually arrive battle weary: one partner bitter, disappointed, and critical; the other exhausted, bewildered, and sad, if not by now downright ill.

Similarly, there is the "you are honoured to be a substitute" message. "You must *be* my mum or dad, brother or sister, or gran. You must continue where they left off, so I never have to really leave them." This is an impossible feat to manage, especially if the cherished person is dead and therefore virtually canonized.

Another requirement: "Once, long, long ago (at the breast?) I had bliss, union, no need for words, and life has taken all that away till now. Till now. For I have chosen you to take me in, consume me, contain me, house me". (As Samuel Beckett once said, "Don't touch me, don't talk to me. Stay with me!") A rum basis for a lasting marriage, but it is amazing how many would-be rescuers reply to this flattering invitation.

Sometimes it works, though! I know of several couples where one party has become nurse, or fellow hermit, or practically parent or therapist to the other, nobly giving up their own objectives so to do. But if it works, can it be so truly selfless? Surely the "noble" one is gaining *something*?

Quentin and Queenie

Quentin, a famous scientist on the brink of a knighthood, gave up his career to take care of Queenie, his alcoholic wife. He lost most of his friends over time as the pair withdrew from social life. Eventually, at Queenie's request, he took her to live in a remote hamlet in France where they were completely isolated.

Perhaps he felt that at last he had shown himself good enough for the mother whom he could never satisfy as a child, so was at peace. Perhaps he had wearied of the demands on him for leadership and public appearances, when only pure science interested him, not the glamour of its public face. Perhaps he knew his colleagues would sigh with relief at his departure, for in the cut and thrust of the politics and feuding between institutes, he was hopelessly inept. Perhaps it was a combination of all these things. Whatever, all parties were satisfied and no one lost face.

There is usually a story behind the story of selfless sacrifice, and this was no exception. When Queenie died of cirrhosis of the liver, at only forty-nine, Quentin, only five years older, felt he had lost everything in both the public and private domain. His life was empty. He contemplated suicide.

In the next chapter we shall look at three couples' stories and examine further the motives of the chooser, as well as exploring who is doing the giving and who the taking.

As an adjunct to this chapter, interested readers may like to consult Appendix I (p. 231) before moving on to Chapter Three; but it can be read later, if preferred. Edward St Aubyn opens his novel *Mother's Milk* (2006) with a moving account of being born, from the vantage point of the infant himself. The sense of bewilderment and separation from "home" is beautifully depicted.

In the same appendix I have quoted Thom Gunn's short poem *Baby Song* (1976), concerning the sadness of the birth experience for the infant. Gunn identifies it as *regret*. This poetic notion can be restated in psychoanalytic terms as a deeply unconscious mind–body "memory" of regret, the pain of which is stirred up (but remains outside of awareness) by the arrival on the scene of a likely-looking partner. The possibility of undoing the regret, making up for the rift from mother, overcomes the natural fear of rejection inherent in courtship.

I have no doubt that, sooner or later, the neurochemists will pinpoint the physical location of this regret (or the neural site that gives rise to it), thus demonstrating the evolutionary value of such early sorrow. The urge to repair the breach with mother intensifies the mating impulse, so ensuring continuation of the species. One day we shall be able to claim scientific evidence for the theory. There is more than one kind of truth. However, on balance, I'll take the poetry!

CHAPTER THREE

Partner-seeking as job application

No one likes rejection, so no one applies for a job unless they believe they possess some of the skills needed: they scan "qualifications required" very carefully. When looking for a partner we may long for someone very different to us, just as in job seeking we may pursue something new and challenging. But, at the same time, we want our best attributes and hard-earned skills recognized. In jobs and in love we tend to go for a set-up where we can carry on doing what we are talented at, while getting something fresh and extra out of the new situation, or at least the promise of further in-service training!

As a couple therapist, I have met many a problem that can be boiled down to the man (say) feeling fed up with having to be macho and strong all the time. Secretly, he longs to let his softer, more "feminine" side have expression. His partner then challenges him: why then did he choose her, knowing the kind of strong man she needed? He is flummoxed, for this is a logical question. The answer is that he did indeed wish to show and enjoy his existing talents, but hoped for development in the marital job as well. The wife is feeling threatened by what she sees as his withdrawal of support for her. She does not appreciate yet that perhaps letting her more "masculine" side grow a little could benefit both of them.

Similarly, many women, for reasons to do with their role in the family, have become expert psychologists without a shred of training in the formal sense. They draw needy and troubled men like a magnet. Such women long to have the understanding they extend to others given to themselves. They grow resentful and punitive to their partners who, drugged by the gratification of their needs, cannot comprehend why their erstwhile understanding, gentle spouse has started talking about separation, and is insisting on seeing a couple therapist. For the first time, they have to learn how to "psychologize", to understand *her*. No wonder they find it hard. She has always done it for them before. She is impatient for the "business" (marriage) to expand, their roles to change. The partner feels too challenged by this, talks instead of "consolidation".

The wise applicant knows there is often a "hidden agenda" in the job advert, requirements that for various reasons cannot be set out in print. It is imperative the applicant reads between the lines if they are to avoid being turned down or not even short-listed, thus discouraging them from applying again. Or worse, they get the job, only to find it is more, much more than they bargained for. Though confident of their knowledge and skills before, they now feel redundant, de-skilled. The same is true in finding a partner. Much safer to find a mate where one can feel secure of meeting the remit before trying to extend the work into new areas.

Selecting a mate—both "advertising" for one (sometimes literally) and "interviewing" for one—is even more complicated than applying for a new post because it is a two-way process. Interviewing panels often *say* the same thing: "You must assess us as well as us looking at you." But everyone in the room knows where the power really lies and who is choosing whom.

In partner selection there is equal opportunity to take a good look at one another. This may seem fairer, but it also means that, because there is no written job specification or rules of conduct for interviewing, sussing out a prospective partner can feel very unsafe. Regulations covering job applications may be irritating, but they do afford a degree of protection. In finding a mate, both parties at first feel obliged to keep their true feelings disguised or hidden, making the whole business even more risky. Still, the power distribution between the pair can be worked out later, once they have established themselves as a unit (see Chapter Six, "The couple's joint personality"). The task to hand is ensuring the other person really wants and is fitted for the job!

Two case examples best describe this mutual job appointment process.

Marisa and Malcolm

Marisa "advertised" for a man who would cherish, protect, and indulge her. Her mother had died after a very long battle with cancer and she had become a substitute mum to a large family. Her father had lost all love of, and interest in, life towards the end, leaving all domestic and financial responsibilities to Marisa, who, none the less, studied successfully for a degree. She had never really been able to enjoy a carefree childhood or adolescence. She missed out, too, on a close relationship with her preoccupied father. She felt she had been forced to grow up too soon.

Malcolm had been a sickly child with a home tutor and a loving close relationship with his mum, who stayed at home to care for him, safe in the knowledge that her husband, a company director, would provide for them. The marriage seemed a happy one. Malcolm's rather sheltered life made him fearful of "the liberated type of woman", as he put it, adding that all the same he had had no direct experience of them. Very creative and able, he now ran an illustrating business from home, a housekeeper looking after his practical needs. Middle-aged now (a father for Marisa?), his parents dead, he sought a wife to pamper and adore, someone feminine and sweet like his mother.

We can already see the problems piling up for this couple, who have not even met yet!

Marisa fell madly in love with her artist, who did indeed spoil and pet her as she had long desired. He enjoyed showering her with affection and showing her off at artistic gatherings. He often painted her, although he was not a portraitist.

It was five years later that the troubles, bubbling under the surface for some while, finally erupted. Marisa had become increasingly irritated by Malcolm's total inability to decide anything, or organize anything, using his undeniable charm to get everyone else to look after him. More and more, Marisa took over the role of organizer, too ashamed to allow others to witness his inadequacy, and increasingly angry that all she had escaped from at home seemed now to be catching up with her.

From Malcolm's point of view, his once gentle wife had become a bully and nag. He could no longer muster the tender feelings with which he had once brimmed over. Both were deeply disappointed.

So what was happening here? Between the lines of Malcolm's "advert" was a requirement that, although he wanted a sweet, gentle wife, she must also (like his mother) be totally capable and fix everything for him without troubling him for a decision. (Interestingly, Marisa's decision to come and see me was made a month after the housekeeper, who had to some extent taken over the maternal organizing role, left to get married.)

Marisa had sincerely sought a protector and cherisher, but underneath she was terrified to give up her role as the capable one. She may not enjoy it, but it was a role in which she knew she excelled and without it she felt exposed and insecure.

In therapy, Marisa complained bitterly that she had been "forced" to take up the reins of capability again and blamed Malcolm for being so inept. There was truth in this, but I could sense in her the relief and return of self-esteem at once again being at the centre of the action, indispensable. He blamed her for conning him into seeing her as a gentle doe when in fact she was a raging lioness. Both felt angry, misunderstood, wrongly accused, and were considering splitting up.

If they had altered their respective "adverts" in the first place, they may have chosen better. Marisa could have asked for protection in her mate *but also some degree of management ability*, so that she would not be robbed of her skill base entirely, but would be relieved of most of it. Malcolm might have more openly sought not only the pretty, soft aspects of his mother, but also her steel, her decision-making talent.

In fact, the couple did very well. Both eventually accepted they could not demand and expect to appoint the perfect candidate, designed solely to satisfy them. Malcolm (helped by his now more patient wife) began to organize bits of their lives and take decisions. Marisa backed off from her constant criticism and scorn, which allowed his old loving feelings for her to surface. With their expectations lowered to realistic levels, and because each owned the *full* rather than censored content of their respective job specifications, their affection rekindled. Instead of waiting for one another to "produce the goods" and then criticizing the other for failing, they now agreed to educate each other about their respective needs, and agreed too (difficult this!) to *be* educated by the other.

Annabel and Alistair

Annabel's overt talent was for being happy and having a good time. Alistair was a trainee airline pilot when they met and loved to travel. They had a busy and exciting first few years, then settled down to parent their three children, all of whom had recently married or moved out or gone on their young persons' travels. Annabel looked forward, in her late forties, to having an exciting *reprise* of the early years. But Alistair "crashed", as she termed it, lapsing into melancholy and moodiness for no apparent reason. Then one day he announced he wanted a year's separation and to go away on his own. There was no other woman. Annabel was devastated and insisted they sought help.

Both partners had originally *consciously* sought a lively and colourful consort to complement their own love of life in the fast lane. But between the lines, much else was written into their respective job specifications, which came out only in therapy.

Alistair was indeed a very extravert and lively character. Though not bipolar in any psychiatric sense, he had always been a boy with mood swings, impulsive and irrepressible one minute, gloomy, almost morbid the next. His school reports were full of compliments concerning his leadership abilities and his popularity, but they commented too on his moodiness and spurts of verbal aggression to other children, whom he could reduce to tears with his cutting comments.

Alistair's parents were so significant by their absence from our three-way discussions that I tentatively enquired about them. Both had died in a car accident, and he had spent his first year being passed from relative to relative, until he eventually settled down with his maternal grandmother, who was kind and loving to him, trying hard to make up for his terrible loss. His sister vanished to some aunt in Scotland and he rarely saw her. When both children grew up there was virtually no contact either.

Annabel described her family (four brothers and a sister, two parents) as immensely warm and loving, the only cloud on the horizon being her father's intermittent depressions. Sometimes he would have a short spell in hospital, other times he would take to his study and be looked after mainly by Annabel, with whom he had a very close relationship. When he could talk to no one else, he would communicate through and with her.

Annabel's first fiancé committed suicide. Her father's sister attempted it twice.

It seemed to me that Annabel had an understandable rage to live after being exposed to so much depression. The faster she lived the less likely that "the cloud on the horizon" would catch up with her. Her "advertisement" for the job of spouse was worded accordingly, not realizing that men who live fast are probably, like her, in flight from something bad.

Accordingly, she was horrified when Alistair hit mid life and one hell of a depression. He was dumbfounded that she called it depression, roundly denying any such thing. He just wanted some "time out".

Annabel was dismayed and furious that the spectre of depression had come again to haunt her. Had she not chosen this man precisely because he seemed so well, so full of beans? He was supposed to rescue her (the skill *not* mentioned in the advert!) once and for all from "all that".

For his part, Alistair, while overtly seeking a wife as adventurous as he, had ably read between her lines, sensing that here was someone "good at handling depression".

And he was right. As therapy progressed, it became clear to us that the only reason Alistair had not broken down before now was that Annabel had always been attuned to his every shift of mood. There was no need to verbalize this; she was probably not even aware of it herself. She "automatically" accommodated his needs, just as she had with her father. She would talk or listen when he needed it, shut up or go away when he craved solitude or was in a black mood, cook his favourite nursery food when she sensed he needed it, and send him off on various mini adventures when she felt he needed to get away. She had kept him healthy.

Far from feeling understood and nourished by this, Alistair now felt controlled and spied on, infantilized. All he could think of was getting away.

Eventually, Alistair did break down completely. He recovered with the help of drugs and loyal friends, who housed him in the roughest times, when he could not bear his wife's presence. As he regained his equilibrium he began individual therapy, with a view to at long last dealing with the awful childhood loss, which not even the most perfect spouse could be expected to tackle.

They are still together as far as I know (no news is usually good news), but the point of this illustration is to show again how what is being overtly sought is frequently not the whole story. There is an unconscious, as well as deliberate, matching of couples at selection time. In this instance, each party was drawn to the other by their shared need to ward off depression. This is what lay between the lines of both their "adverts".

Precisely because what is censored in the "job advertisement" is *unconscious*, it is pointless advising mate-seekers to "tell the truth". At this stage they do not know the truth. Yet, time and again, I am amazed at how couples divine what is between each other's lines and choose pretty well, as did Alistair and Annabel. They had thirty years of happiness before problems struck.

The lover and the lovee

When looking for a long-term partner, some people see themselves in the role of employer and concentrate more on what the "applicant" might do and be for them, while others worry and ponder about whether they will suit the prospective partner/employer. The latter are willing to make all manner of adjustments to secure a better "fit", whereas the former are seeking "the right one for me", someone so right, in fact, that the need for any accommodation does not arise. Let us now leave the analogy of job seeking and take up partner selection from a fresh angle.

As far back as 1914, Sigmund Freud was thinking about partner choice. The person who makes an "anaclitic" choice (I call them the lov*er*) has a temperament inclined toward nurturance and protection. This individual likes and is good at meeting people's emotional needs and is accordingly empathic.

A "narcissistic" choice is made by a person who sees *him or herself* as the object of another's love. This person I call the lov*ee*. Here, a partner is chosen who represents the ideal self, the person one would wish to be. Or the partner is selected so as to recapture a part of the self that seems to have got lost and can now be restored. Or the choice may be someone seen as a copy of the most important person in the subject's life, someone so close they were experienced as an indispensable part of the self rather than as a separate person. Whichever, the chosen one *must* be expert at loving them in the particular way they need to be loved; must, indeed, become a part of them, an extension of the self.

What is being sought here is a frustration-reliever and comforter, a mirror to reassure the person of their own "all-rightness". Someone who will be a second parent, a soul-mate, a better-half, a right arm: someone to complete the person. The partner is required to think the way they think, feel pain and pleasure the way they feel it. In short, they must be so attuned that the brutal communication we call language is mostly unnecessary.

Such wished-for fusion is, of course, an extreme example. Like any other kind of personality, narcissistic people show varying degrees of narcissism. There is narcissism in us all, or we would not survive. An extreme narcissist, though, would never recognize such a symbiotic wish consciously, would be highly affronted and dismissive if it were pointed out to him, but he would certainly feel very unhappy in the absence of that wish's fulfilment.

Such people can be very charming, charismatic even, but are privately wedded to controlling others in order to have their needs met. Equally narcissistic is the overtly meek, self-abnegating person, whose tactics are none the less aimed at compelling others to come up with the emotional goods. Deeply discontented inside, they are always on the hunt for the impossible, and so are doomed to disappointment.

These people are well camouflaged, so not easy to spot. They often make serial legal marriages, all of the partners eventually unable to meet the narcissist's demands. Either partners leave, exhausted by the neediness, or are sacked for not being good enough. However, I do stress again that these are extreme examples.

The lover may, so far, sound like the virtuous one, but it does not quite work like that. The need to protect often covers resentment that yet again they are forced to deny their own needs in favour of someone else's. Once again they are in the "one down" position in their closest relationship. Sometimes, the care-giving hides an appeal once made (fruitlessly) to parents: "Look, I am modelling for you how to love me. See how easy it is. Come on, love me back, put me first for once".

Empathy is an admirable quality, but too much of it can be suspect, a fact of which the empathic one in a couple (the lover) can become painfully aware as the exhausting years roll by. The giver now feels exploited rather than appreciated. The lovee's need is now seen as greed or selfishness and the relationship begins to crumble. Thereupon the lovee feels deprived and hard done by, grows sulky and complaining.

Such a couple can be helped if neither are so burdened by developmental deficits that they cannot take responsibility for, and then struggle to re-own, what crazy hopes they had deposited in each other when first they chose each other. To accomplish this, these hopes and demands must be made conscious and shared.

Paradoxically enough, once they are conscious, very many couples are more able to provide for each other—if only to a degree—some of the missing, longed-for emotional supplies. If the spouses can accept these less than perfect gifts and feel genuine gratitude, the marriage will improve. Without the former mutual blame, love has room to grow.

There exists everywhere, then, narcissistic and empathic characters, all of whom might be said to reside easily within the psychologically "normal" bracket. They tend to pair up together. Extreme examples are used here for illustrative purposes only.

The pairing is not always so clear-cut. One might imagine an extreme lover collecting "orphans" as partners, and only being content when allowed to be the sole dispenser of care-giving. But stop. Such a man or woman's partner is kept infantilized and thus controlled, helpless, and unable to leave. This saintly partner could be viewed rather as an inverted narcissist, who ensures that with compulsive care-giving, supplies of gratitude, love, and attention will always be readily available.

In the same way, the narcissist, instinctively if not consciously aware of his or her own needs, can supply to another person great (apparently selfless) concern and can indeed become indispensable to the recipient, who has no idea that a return is required. Should the return not be forthcoming, the concern dries up. Like a drug addict, a pronounced narcissist will do, or be, anything to gain the supplies on which they depend. Where supplies are scant, relations will be avoided.

Blake and Bonnie

Blake was "sent" to me by Bonnie, his live-in partner of four years. She was a busy buyer in a large department store and could not take time off work to accompany him. In any case, she felt the problems were his, as, apart from his recent gloomy moods, she thought things were fine.

Blake had always loved his parents, insisted his childhood had been boringly normal. But as time went on he was able to take off the rose-coloured spectacles. His mother had been brought up from birth to sixteen in a strict, but kindly children's home run by nuns. Everything was done by the clock: bathing, eating, studying, relaxing. When she grew up, her one ambition was to rear the perfect family. The house was full of child-rearing books and the timetabling routines continued. Blake's father spent much time in the garden shed or down the pub, but was always back on the dot for tea or lunch. He never crossed his wife in anything.

Father and son conspired in the myth that they constituted an ideal family, never challenging mother. They sensed her brittleness so tried to protect her by obeying her every instruction.

Blake grew up to be a solicitor. He joined a successful law firm where he found himself always doing wills for little old ladies, rather than the more interesting, aggressive stuff. His colleagues ribbed him that he was so sensitive and patient that this sort of client always asked for him by name. He should be flattered.

As Bonnie's career swiftly took off, Blake found himself doing the shopping and cooking, then the ironing and cleaning, after a full day's work. At first he was proud of his partner and glad to help, but gradually he started feeling exploited.

Being so busy did not stop Bonnie from continuing to buy his clothes, booking him in at the gym, telling him when and where to get his hair cut, and what books to read. She texted or e-mailed him several times a day. At first this attention pleased him, but eventually he began to resent it.

On the face of it, Blake was the lover, caring for his mate, home, and his clients in a selfless way. But, sadly, his inability to ventilate his growing grudge against Bonnie left him totally dependent on her for psychologically nurturing supplies. As with his fragile mother, he was terrified of challenging Bonnie in case she, too, might break down in some unmendable way.

Eventually Bonnie was persuaded to join us in the therapy sessions. It soon became clear that she was as dependent in her way as Blake. Under her confident exterior she was scared stiff that she might lose Blake, so checked up on him endlessly, tracking his every move and suffocating him with gifts and good advice. She had rules and regulations about how an acceptable man and consort should be, as firmly fixed as Blake's mother's rules concerning the perfect family. Both women could only entertain two positions. If the family/partner were not perfect, then they were a complete disaster.

Bonnie resented Blake's lack of perfection and so tried to groom (bribe?) him to her specifications. She felt this approach would avoid a row (her own rowing parents had divorced). Though he had yet to face it, Blake was furious at her taking advantage of him, but could not fight back for fear of some dire consequence. And, as he wasn't very "with it", her sartorial and other advice was genuinely useful. So he put off being angry more and more.

Bonnie would have argued that it was she who did all the caring and making things happen, she who was not appreciated enough. If Blake had been really empathic, she would not need to tell him what to do, what to wear, what restaurants to go to. He would just *know*.

This co-dependent couple were both quite narcissistic, cleverly manipulating one another to get their respective needs met. Neither would stick up for themselves and battle it out. Both wanted the other to divine their needs and provided a few heavy hints to help out. Bonnie was so preoccupied with the meeting of her own needs that she failed to recognize Blake's gloom for the major hint it was.

Both partners acted the lov*er* to cover their true desires as a lov*ee*.

Great care must always be taken with psychological labels. They are convenient descriptive tools, but they are just labels.

CHAPTER FOUR

How your infancy affects your marriage: separation and triangulation

Starting to separate from mum

G radually it dawns on baby that he is indeed a separate entity to mother. Sometimes his needs—food, warmth, cuddles, respite from a wet bottom—are congruent with her ability to meet them. At other times they so conflict with her psychological and physical schedule that the friendly intimacy—indeed fusion—to which he had grown accustomed is no longer predictable. A dry, powdered bottom can no longer be relied on, at least for a while. It is all a bit hit and miss these days. At first baby is rather miffed.

If supplies do not magically arrive when they are merely wished for, someone else that is "not me" must be doing the providing. Oh heck, I am not the World and the World is not me, it is outside me: I do not rule it, I am not the only one in it, and I cannot control it. Such frustration and loss of omnipotence is helpful in that, provided a modicum of the "I am OK in the world" sense is being gradually established, the curious infant can now seek compensation for this elsewhere. Exciting new learning is available all around. This can fill in the time until mother is once more available. He learns to tolerate her absence, so long as it is not too long.

If baby does not believe she will become available again (based on previous experience), then he will not seek elsewhere for compensatory experience, but remain stuck in "solitary confinement". He undergoes either despair or the mother of all panic attacks until she does return. Although seemingly recovered from later, these experiences will, none the less, flavour all his future key relations, especially in adult marriage, which so replicates this, the first marriage. If a couple comes for help agreeing that the problem is one side's intense possessiveness and/or need to control the other, the reason for it is often linked to such early terrors. The affected person must ensure abandonment cannot happen again. The other partner, once pleased by such evidence of love, can no longer endure the restrictions placed upon them, the constant demand for guarantees or proof of loyalty.

If, on the other hand, the infant senses that absconding mum will be back—it is only a matter of time—then there is in the meantime much fun to be had, sliding about on his bottom or belly, for instance. Baby feels independent doing this, feels strong. Until now only the pleasures of dependence had captivated him. He needs to redress the balance if he is to grow up healthily, able to depend and be depended upon, taking pride and pleasure in both states.

And anyway, dad (and the dog, and possibly siblings) now begin to loom large as playmates and sometime care-givers. But also comes the uncomfortable awareness: what was once just one ("I am the universe and the universe is me"); became two ("me and my bliss-providing mum"); and this has now become three (or more). Where will it all end? Will I be nobody? He has to share precious mum with these folk, who do matter to him, but who cannot help but be a threat, possibly rivals—especially this dad bloke. The fact that mum also loves and values this guy, so to please her he must also please *him*, only makes life more complicated.

In later years, it will become apparent to anyone caring to look, how these developmental events and their handling by all parties, *including the toddler himself*, affect a marriage. (For the infant is not a jug into which adults pour "stuff" that he passively receives. This is one of the grossest misconceptions about psychoanalytic thinking. The child may at first be without speech or bodily control, but he is none the less extremely active and powerful, for all that. Ask any mother!)

The infant struggles valiantly towards survival, as all creatures are programmed to do. His capacities for accommodation, communication, and the giving of heart-melting incentives to his beleaguered mother are amazing, as are his enraged demands when life-maintaining supplies threaten to disappear. His little organism processes all that is done to him and he reacts idiosyncratically. These reactions will surface again thirty years on, when any partner tries the jug treatment.

Dealing with the triangle

The arrival on the baby's scene of dad and other suitors for mum's attention, coupled with her gradual return to her pre-reverie self, the picking up again of her old interests, precipitates much conflict in the baby, soon to be toddler. Some "taking the back seat" types (see Chapter One) will withdraw from the arena and let dad win hands down, whereas others will fight bravely for their lady, only to lapse into temporary sadness as the realization dawns that the battle has already been lost. Dad and mum are firmly wedded to each other. The healthy child, gentle or fierce in temperament, will soon recover, find other things in life that fascinate and challenge, and will live to find his or her own mate one fine day.

It is the child who never leaves the field and hangs on to one or other parent, trying to prevent them coming together, that in adulthood finds him or herself entangled in seemingly impossible threesomes, as if setting up a stage play where he can return to the past and try one more time to solve the unsolvable.

In conceding defeat to the same sex parent, thus allowing the parents to have their special union from which the child is excluded, the pair is necessarily preserved for continued use by the offspring. He still needs a parental couple to care for him. The attempt to woo one parent from another is but a rehearsal for real courtship later on.

The vital point here is that in handing mum over to dad, or vice versa, and refraining from further attack on the parental couple, the child learns appropriate (as opposed to neurotic) guilt. He develops the beginnings of a *conscience*. He learns to stop grabbing and start sharing. It dawns on him that it is possible for three to co-exist without the cake of love having to be cut three ways instead of two, with him getting less than before. Love expands to meet the need.

These are massive psychological strides. The blatant self-interest of early infancy is now tempered by concern for others and the need to repair any damage he may have inflicted. This is the start of altruistic love rather than narcissistic love, though in us all the latter remains as the foundation layer of our personalities.

Although this turmoil eventually dies down, yielding centre stage to other developmental phases, any "unfinished business" from this time will revisit the adult when he makes his first serious couple relationship. The private and intense world of two, impinged upon by all manner of competing forces inside, outside, and between the contemporary couple, cannot but reawaken old anxieties and conflicts in vulnerable subjects. The degree of vulnerability is the degree to which the person failed to gain satisfactory detachment from the urge to dabble in the parents' relationship.

As many readers will know, this very stormy time is known "in the trade" as the Oedipal stage. In the "Interlude" after Chapter Five, I will tell Oedipus's story.

Fidelity and the triangle

Marital fidelity is more critical to some couples than others. For some, a certain lifestyle and the money to pay for it count more than fidelity. To others, protestations of loyalty and devotion in non-sexual areas are what really counts. For others, the welfare and future prospects of the children are more important than who puts what organ into whose corresponding organ. For example, I have very often heard, "They are just toys. It's me he really wants. Let him have his toys." The husband then says, "I would never leave her; she is my *wife*. The others are playthings, and I keep them well out of her way." Both parties have agreed to share a point of view other couples might find abhorrent, so as to maintain the *status quo*. Neither one sees what it is they might be avoiding, or what it is that the denigrated third party represents to each. Any pain remains denied, even to themselves.

Many of us would find such a marriage untenable. However, peace reigns. A balance has been struck. We may suspect that a big emotional cost is involved, but if the pair are prepared to pay it, who is to say they should conform to our way of going about things? This is their preferred solution to triangulation issues.

So, what about those for whom any infidelity is the end, the very last piece of ash in the marital fire? Under no circumstances must either party be unfaithful for that would mean the death of the marriage. Are these worry-driven marriages any more whole-some than the one above?

Unresolved conflicts at the triangular stage of normal develop-ment (the first admission of dad into the baby's awareness) are responsible for plenty of troubles later on. Many couples sense a dangerous area in their relationship and guard against possible problems by prohibiting all temptation. They failed psychologically to cope with competition the first time round, so the solution twenty or thirty years later is to eradicate all possible competition, rather than try to understand what is giving rise to the anxieties surrounding it. This blinkered outlook is aided and abetted by social mores, the government, and religion; all of whom endorse this pragmatic and rather stupid view of managing a problem by exterminating it rather than exploring and learning from it.

What about the tempted soul, the man or woman fighting to remain faithful despite a powerful pull towards a third party? All these crude, prohibiting measures accomplish is the inculcating of guilt into an already troubled person fighting a desire that might go away, or at least fade, once its antecedents are properly understood and talked out.

The person may become adulterous anyway, even when they are helped to understand; but at least it will be by conscious choice. The responsibility for any consequences then lies squarely with them.

This has to be preferable to a messy extra-marital affair where the actors are blown about like leaves in the wind by ancient forces they do not comprehend and over which they have no control. Contrary to the myth that affairs are exciting and happy episodes for the lovers and sheer misery for the legitimate spouses, my expe-rience is that lovers rarely rest easy and always have troubled consciences. (It has to be admitted, though, that I see people who

come for help. There may well be hordes of conscience-free adul-
terers enjoying themselves outside the confines of my consulting
room! Happy people do not come to a therapist.)

Given that the Oedipal phase is all about tabooed love, it will
surprise no one to learn that the more a third party in the adult's
life is forbidden, the more desirable will that party become.
Artificial constraints only add to the taboo—and the desire. If the
sufferer in the grip of illicit erotic promptings gives in, there may
follow a cycle of guilt and eventually depression, as much about the
necessary deceit and lies as the sexual acts themselves. I make no
case here for or against infidelity, only a plea that its complexity and
roots in infancy be given due weight. Sometimes such understanding by the wronged party can, over time, make true forgiveness
possible.

The honoured, rather than betrayed, spouse rarely gets off
lightly either. Suppose a man is sick with desire for his colleague,
but respects his wife. He knows she trusts him implicitly. He cannot
bring himself to let her down. His wife, meanwhile, is at a loss to
comprehend his dark moods, his lack-lustre performance in bed,
his grumpiness. She may blame herself. And for all we know he
may indeed be punishing her for "forcing" him to give up his
colleague.

One cannot help but wonder about this resented loyalty to
"mummy". As a child his father may have been a poor or rejected
consort to his mum, who greatly favoured her darling boy. He was
smothered with adoration, never able to stand up for his own preferences, and fearful of losing his only attachment (as dad was never
there for him). His father never tried to reclaim his place as
husband, leaving the boy to grow up with a very ambivalent attitude to any woman on whose love and trust he depended. He
needed his women badly, but felt controlled by them.

From a moral or societal perspective, we may praise this man's
decision to stay with his wife. But, from a psychological point of
view, his place in the Oedipal triangle as victor over his father has
not altered one whit. Neither has his *unconscious* fury abated,
concerning his subsequent domination by his mother. His dark
moods and hostility to his wife bear this out. The "other woman"
represented a bid for freedom he should have taken up decades
ago. But, as a child, how was he to know?

I have seen some couples become almost jointly agoraphobic, or separately workaholic so as to banish all leisure time; or "working together at home" in a thinly veiled attempt to avoid risks that are largely imaginary. Neither party has the confidence to trust the other's love and goodwill, or to believe that they could survive if the worst ever did happen. Such deep and unmentionable mistrust arises out of the conviction anchored in toddler experience that he or she could never, never compete successfully in a love triangle. The third party would always win. Or, if the battle was won, the (illicit) prize could never be enjoyed, for the rightful winner would always be there in hot pursuit. It is tragic that, having found love, such anxious and guilt-ridden people dare not embrace it. Instead they hide away, or are always looking over their shoulder.

For more robust couples who fought, properly lost, and came to terms with the Oedipal struggle, voluntary fidelity born of love (not possession) of the other, is the only faithfulness worth having. And they can take on board the small risks that no healthy marriage is without. Should those risks be realized, there will be pain, but not total collapse.

Any unrealistic (not based on evidence) feelings of inadequacy, or fear of failing so not wanting to compete, are to do with the Oedipal triangle. So are opposite anxieties concerning the fear of succeeding—in relation to sex, sport, or in the workplace. Fears about, or avoidance of, being in *any way* successful all represent the taking of mum (or dad) from dad (or mum) and the mayhem of guilt and/or revenge that could ensue. The vain hope of the sufferer is that if there is no third party, no competitor or rival, then there will be no war to wage, where winning and losing seems an equally terrifying outcome. But such an attempt at avoidance causes havoc in marriage.

For the loving and faithful other partner, who naturally longs for the sufferer's success, or is secretly ashamed of the other's unwillingness to compete, such unsubstantiated self-doubt can seem quite crazy, especially when no amount of loving reassurance improves the situation. When the need or demand for reassurance exhausts this puzzled and angry spouse, the couple sensibly think about seeking aid. After assessment, it may be that conjoint work is indicated, or that the one with pronounced Oedipal issues should have independent help.

Some partners, then, become very disappointed and angry with their otherwise extremely able and competent partner, whom they feel is just downright lazy, scared, or not pulling his or her weight. This can at times be a simple and accurate analysis of the situation: the offender needs to shape up; but often the matter goes deep into Oedipal territory.

The one who has powerful but unconscious fears around competition, feeling nagged to death, may agree to accept all the blame and leave the union. They may be sad, but also relieved that the problem of always having to prove themselves has gone away. (Yes, some folk who leave a marriage after years of trying actually feel *better*.) Now that failure has been proved, the sword of Damocles no longer hangs over their heads. It has fallen!

This is a sad, maladaptive solution, though, if the two parties otherwise care for each other. It only leaves the non-competitive person so confirmed in his or her sense of inadequacy that a new marriage will be avoided for fear of repetition. This surmise is correct, unless the problem is helped and understood rather than just ditched.

Absolute fidelity is often demanded as an insurance against these old triangular ghosts. Many marry too young in order to ensure a spurious safety from rivals, grabbing the first partner that comes along. Others fear coupledom will make them vulnerable to these ghosts and never commit properly at all. They break hearts one after another, overtly or implicitly making promises, but the promises are never kept. It is not wilful cruelty, but fear of having to re-run the Oedipal struggle that overcomes their love every time.

Others have a whole series of relationships with already married persons. This person and their mate are the legitimate "parental" couple inside the lover's mind. Having secret and excitingly guilty serial relationships with married lovers is one thing, but marrying them, causing a divorce and then "going public", is quite another. The legal partner of the desired one is quite a protection against feared success in the Oedipal war.

When a person is married and finding the pull towards infidelity too strong to be resisted, the search is usually on for the early renounced parent of the opposite sex. Here is a second chance to taste all that was forbidden before. Even so the marriage is often guiltily returned to, the fear of success being too great.

What happens when an affair changes its status? The pair (both legally married to third parties) decide to forgo secrecy, to leave former spouses and marry each other. This can be a great success once the fallout has cleared. Some of the actors get badly hurt, but at least the new situation is open and honest. For many, however, the act of moving in together with this, their new love, making public their relationship and commitment, kills or dulls their sexual life. The once ardent lover is back where he or she started. Sexual love is no longer the arousing, *forbidden*, infantile experience it once was. The second marriage can become, at least to one partner, as dull as the first. The other partner, perhaps having courageously put aside a disastrous first marriage, and left children, is disappointed to find the sacrifices made are not justified by the happiness hoped for.

In these kinds of circumstances, one of the most painful situations for all concerned is when everyone tries to behave well. A married man (say) wants to do right by his (also married) lover, who now wishes to set up home with him and end her own marriage, which she regards as dead, though her husband wants her to stay. Our married man leaves his distraught wife, but continues to yo-yo between wife and mistress, cruel to both.

This is not because he is trying to have his cake and eat it, but because of the *unconscious* and *unresolved* conflicts of guilt and desire over mum. He wishes to be decent like his dad and so stay with his wife, while yet triumphing over "dad" by stealing his mistress (mum) from her unworthy husband. Of course, he is not at all aware of these conflicts. Unless and until he finds a suitable therapist to help him access them, both women may reject him as an indecisive weakling. He is left with nothing.

In a new partnership, one of the partners—normally a perfectly confident person—may become extremely jealous without any provocation. Almost paranoid, they are certain that the beloved will betray them. What has happened? The jealous one has changed in their self-precept from the status of child but would-be lover to an adult who can be cuckolded. The act of marriage/cohabitation has changed their *identification with their childhood self* to that of "being like my father/mother", i.e., a married adult. After all, did not the now jealous party try very hard, once, to compete with the same sex parent? If *in reality* that parent did indeed allow them to win, they are terrified that in a new marriage, now he or she has *become* the father/mother so to speak, they, too, will be humiliated, degraded, branded the loser.

It is *vital* that children are never allowed to win the Oedipal battle, but that they are good-naturedly assisted to see that they can fight another day, and this time win their own new partner, without the need to share or fight over them. If generational and sexual boundaries are scrupulously honoured by the parents, albeit with tact and humour rather than earnestness and barely concealed anxiety, the girl and boy can eventually properly renounce the opposite sex parent as an object of eroticized love and take an interest in their own generation.

Now, all this sounds very theoretical. Every case cannot be reduced to the neat Oedipal formula described above. For instance, many people make second good relationships after catastrophic or disappointing first ones. But that first mistake, even though rectified perhaps in the second or third marriage, if closely examined, will always have some echo in it of the Oedipal (triangular, mother–father–child) scenario.

Everyone has to go through the triangular phase. There is nothing intrinsically pathological about it. It is the degree of success or failure in resolving those triangular conflicts that predispose a marriage to happiness or pain before the couple have even met. They do not come to their wedding feast with a clean slate, but with two histories that cast shadow or light on the celebrations as surely as the bad and good fairies at Sleeping Beauty's christening.

This is why calling oneself a failure because one's marriage has been dissolved is such nonsense, and very destructive to one's self-esteem. Marriage is not an exam, where effort and study is rewarded and anyone can pass if they work hard enough. I have watched some people in my consulting room with enormous admiration and respect, working and working at their relationship until they were physically and mentally exhausted. As their histories unfolded, it became clear to all three of us that the marriage was all but doomed from the start. The real task at hand was to enable them to accept defeat in as mature and non-retaliatory a way as possible.

Refusal to face unpleasant facts can be as destructive and irresponsible as abandoning a marriage at the first sign of trouble and just "trading in" an old one for a new one. Ending a mutually torturing or deadening relationship can be seen as an achievement. The partners are not responsible for their own or their partner's family and parents, or the social and cultural context into which each were born. As infants, they may have participated in circumstances over which they had no control, trying to make the best of them, but they cannot be held accountable for them.

Lucky people with happy, unconflictual childhoods tend to make happy marriages. It is not your fault if you count among the unlucky ones. You can only accept responsibility for what you have done since the marriage began. If you have tried hard and talked yourself hoarse trying to work things out, then you have nothing to blame yourself for. When your grieving is done, get on out there and try again!

It is important to note, also, that absent, dead, ill, or adoptive parents are very much alive and present in every affected child's mind. When they mature into grown-ups, these inner parents are there still. Indeed, they may be even more psychologically present to the child than is usual, for the "real" mother or father is not around the place in the normal way, so cannot be tried and tested, adjusted to and accepted—the good, the bad, and the ugly, but at least *recognizable*. The missing parent(s) remain an unmodified fantasy. How do you conduct an Oedipal battle with someone who is not there, or who is such a precious and fragile dream that competition with them is unthinkable?

If, as we have seen, the usual way of growing up can result in so many relationship difficulties later, imagine how much harder the routine developmental tasks must be for the child wondering what his dad would be like if he were "all there" and not schizophrenic or alcoholic. How does a child who loves his adoptive mother deal with the fantasies he has about his biological mum (and how does the adoptive mum deal with these—so much easier to not ask the child!) And what of the child whose mum or dad left the family; was it the child who drove them away? This is a very common belief in abandoned children who have no further contact with the parent who deserted them. The consequences for any future marriage for that child are vast.

CHAPTER FIVE

How your childhood affects your marriage: authority, gender, socialization, and adolescence

The sense of authority

Another important piece of toddler development, not so far mentioned, is the acquisition of mastery over bodily functions, along with the joy and misery, pride and shame it can produce. Herein lies the basis for all future attitudes and responses to "Authority", as well as the basis for the future adult's personal sense of dignity and decency. What are appropriate standards of public and private conduct, self-control, self-discipline? These values are actually learned in the nursery, from the manner in which the toddler and his body are treated by the adults.

As baby gains control over bladder and colon, with parents praising him to the skies or turning away in disgust from his productions, he starts to sense he has power. He can control not only his own body, but also the reactions of people around him, by pleasing them or withholding from them that which they seem so earnestly to desire—a clean nappy and its eventual abandonment. But also at this time, shame, secrecy, and self-disgust is learned, along with their opposites—grandiosity, self-admiration, ruthless ambition—according to how the family react to this new phase.

Bladder and bowel training has a profound effect on the toddler who finds pleasure in his body's ability to produce "lumps of gold". He learns not only that giving and withholding "gold" brings power and control over others, but that there is an appropriate and socially accepted way of managing these bodily processes as well as an offensive and unacceptable way. Socialization (a later section of this chapter) and the sense of authority go together, developmentally speaking.

Sensitive parenting/nursery training helps the child feel proud, but not arrogant, when he displays his control. He enjoys his new-found power without the need to exploit others with it. Properly taught, he has no fear of "filth", "germs", or "contamination". He enjoys grooming his body to be clean, but has no need to be obsessive about it.

Unfortunately, some children acquire negative convictions about their body's secretions and excretions at this time, largely due to the responses of those around them whose own upbringing left them with unwholesome attitudes to the body. Such beliefs, if not challenged, may extend to the child's entire self precept: if my *body* is dirty then *I* am dirty, unclean, smelly, unwanted. These children can cover up at school and in social situations, though they may seem rather self-conscious, or unduly scrupulous with their hygiene. Living as a couple in adulthood, though, such preoccupations cannot be covered up indefinitely.

Many sexual difficulties, such as inability to "let go", allowing one's partner rather than oneself to have power or control, are linked to this potty-training era. Aversions to sperm and other bodily fluids can spoil uninhibited sex, as can an insistence on absolute cleanliness. In the consulting room a common lament (from males and females) is, "God, it's like making love in an operating theatre."

Embarrassment and self-consciousness during intercourse is common. There are many reasons for this, but a common one is that the person feels exposed; as if they are sitting on their potty in an open corridor with other children, *being watched*. As orgasm approaches there is a fear that it will not be big enough, or that they will not make it at all, or that the other person (parent?) will be disappointed or critical. It is all such a shaming business instead of a joy.

If the couple have other issues with each other over control and power, the outlook is not too good. But if this is an encapsulated problem, some frank and tender talk can provide a much needed "corrective experience". Small courtesies such as keeping the duvet on and the light off for a bit can be of enormous assistance.

When children grow up, residual painful experiences from this time become hitched to adult concerns. They can develop into regular features of couple quarrels. Consider a man whose parents used shame to discipline his bowel habits. He is highly sensitized to any possible exposure to shame in the present. He loses his job, but is too ashamed to tell his wife and kids, so he leaves the house as usual each morning. Soon he finds his reserves are insufficient to support his family. The burden of shame feels crippling. He resorts to lying about what is in the bank, or borrows heavily. On discovery, his partner berates him for his lies and failure to consult with her. If, for reasons in her own background, she is especially sensitive around issues of reliability and trust, it feels as if he has doubly failed her. There is a crisis here that could end the marriage of two persons who otherwise love one another dearly.

Issues around money and power, being a "control freak", obsessional cleanliness, lack of (or chaotic) creativity, often have their beginnings in this period of development. It should be clearly stated, however, that complicated couple problems cannot be simplistically traced to any given phase of human development in one of the partners. That would be absurd and blaming. One marriage can absorb and even ameliorate a particular partner's old difficulties and hurts. Another couple is ultimately destroyed by the way in which that difficulty plays into their other concerns, needs, deprivations, and longings. It is more a case of luck than fault.

Dave and Diana

Dave is an auditor and Diana a sculptor. They both work from home. Her studio is very messy and rarely cleaned, whereas Dave's office is extremely orderly. In therapy, none of us was able to discover anything about either of their potty trainings, but enough was known about the respective families to make an educated guess as to what their attitudes would have been.

Dave got quite a thrill out of Diana's mess, *so long as it was kept out of the rest of the meticulous house*, where he did most of the cleaning. He enjoyed making love to Diana in her studio on bright cushions smeared with clay and paint. He joked that turpentine was his favourite perfume because it reminded him of freedom and mess and sex.

Diana loved to "liberate" him sexually, but could not have begun to manage the more practical side of her life without his help. He acted as her unofficial agent, did all her tax returns, etc. His tidiness drove her up the wall sometimes. They even resorted to making separate spaces in the house where each could live as they preferred. The kitchen was joint space though, and this caused many a grumble from Dave, who always cleaned up before bedtime. Diana was content, indeed pleased, to let him. Her complaint was that she was not permitted to go into his study/office and create sexual mayhem there as they did in her studio. She felt it was unequal.

But it was the shared bedroom that caused the big rows, one half like a bomb site, the other spick and span. Both fought bitterly to have the whole room their way!

This couple took advantage of their differences, which added spice to their lives as well as the rows. Another couple arguing over cleanliness were thoroughly wretched.

The Greensons

The Greensons had chronic sexual troubles (timidity on his part, occasional vaginismus on hers), and these were blamed on the matter of tidiness and cleanliness versus dirt and mess. He began to feel potent in dark or candle-lit relaxing surroundings, but she had to have bright lights and everything clean as a whistle. There were many arguments about sex that were really about who controlled whom and where the power in the relationship really lay.

These two couples were very different, but neither is better or worse than the other. Both shared issues linked to the so called "anal phase" of development, but, because of all the other factors in their respective personalities and the way these made them relate to one another, the marital drama evolved differently. No one is to blame.

Life events during later phases tend either to compound or modify difficulties in earlier ones. Life at school and other external influences, especially key figures such as relatives, teachers, even TV personalities and fictional characters, as well as peer group relationships, all have a compensating or reinforcing effect.

For example, a child applauded by proud parents after successfully completing potty training is left feeling cock o' the walk. He is much more confidently equipped to face the vicissitudes of the Oedipal battle than a constipated child cowed by such self-consciousness he dare not relax his bowels, never mind square up to dad in a fight for mum!.

Similarly, a chronically worried child who felt mum's attachment to him was far from constant or secure is going to feel frightened rather than excitedly challenged by the demands of potty training. He will be terrified of displeasing the parent(s) and risking further rejection/separation from them. This is especially hard for the child entering this very delicate phase only to find that all manner of play leaders and child-minders are given free access to his bottom. On the other hand, it has to be said that a regular nanny or child-minder, tried and trusted, can often give the child a better training in bowel control than an overwrought, embarrassed, or disgusted mum or dad.

Gender awareness

As the child begins to realize that there are two sexes in the world, he must start the process of working out where he (or she) fits. The girl has an easier time of it, for she is already in the female camp with mother. She is already trained in the mental attitudes and behaviours that fit (in mother's opinion) with a sense of femininity. None the less, in the process of maturing the daughter must still surrender the privileges of infancy and being cared for. Instead, she identifies with mother, thus learning to care for others, and one day her own children, while retaining the love of her mother, who takes pride in seeing the miniature of herself in her offspring.

If the daughter does not later on find her own definition of femininity, whether this agrees with mother's or not, marital disharmony can erupt quite early on. Hubby complains that mother-

in-law is running the marriage and the daughter is but her mouth-
piece. When it is the husband who has unsuccessfully separated
from his parents, and then, given a second chance in adolescence
still has not managed it, it is the wife's turn to complain of in-law
intrusion. Unless, of course, he has married his mum, as is evident
by his choice of partner. The two women can make an alliance and
together cosset/control him. There is a danger here, of course, that
one day he may rebel as he never did as a teenager.

The boy has a tougher time coming to terms with, and feeling
confidence in, his gender. He has not only to give up babyhood,
but has also to join the other camp, so to speak: the world of men.
This is made easier if he already enjoys a warm, friendly relationship with a father whom he can admire, and on whom he can
model himself. If dad is ineffectual, or a bully, cold and humourless,
or simply absent, the young lad is at a loss to know what a male
should actually be like, or what constitutes appropriate male
feelings and attitudes.

If he wishes not to be like his father, who else is there to turn to
but his mother? Yet he senses mum's place in his life must change
if the male tribe is to take him in as one of their own. But what if
he is protecting her from a bad-tempered, shouting dad; or alternatively standing in for an absent dad and fearing that without him,
her devoted son, she will crumple?

Moving away from mum is easier if there is a father whose
example he can't wait to follow. If father fails him in this, the boy
will grow up unsure of his masculinity or even his gender. While
still a child, he may end up with a mum he avoids, for fear of being
dominated and effeminized. He has no one. Being sent to boarding
school could be the last straw for this lonely little fellow.

We can guess that on attaining adulthood such a man might be
found by his wife to be cold and unfeeling, in an attempt to appear
male (unemotional) while at the same time avoiding the risks of being
unmanned by too much intimacy with a woman. Such a stance may
seem a solution to him, but it leaves his wife starving and unhappy.

He might also take a rather different course.

Colin and Celia

Colin and Celia came to see me because she was sick and tired of
his public cruelty to her. He would flirt outrageously with every

woman in the room except her. He would leave her to take care of herself all evening, get her own drinks, find her own coat, etc. He even made disparaging jokes at her expense behind her back. These were relayed to her by loyal friends who thought she should know what was going on.

In the therapy sessions, he behaved in much the same way towards her, although it was somewhat muted. One week he had 'flu and Celia came on her own. She was normally a confident, out-going sort of woman so I was always at a loss as to why she tolerated these insults at all. She regaled me with his latest appalling behaviour. Finally, moved by her plight, I found myself uttering, "Why on earth do you put up with it?"

Her tear-stained face was instantly irradiated. "Oh, but in bed! Whether or not we subsequently have sex, he always curls up like a baby, hangs on tight all night. We have never spent a night apart in twenty years. He could not survive it. Sometimes in bed he cries and tells me so. His flirting hurts, but it is all bluster. He can't wait to get home and have the real thing."

The real thing for Colin, trying desperately to convince the world he was a bit of a lad, was the mothering he had to forgo when his twin brother, slightly brain damaged, got all the nursing and he had to grow up prematurely.

A young man unsure of his masculinity may become isolated later on in life, afraid of women, and so never marries. With luck he will find compensation in a career or vocation and a good circle of friends.

Another risks living with a woman, while terrified or resentful of her real or imagined control over him. She complains that "he blows hot and cold all the time. I never know where I am". If this man never got free from his mother and his father never received him into "the other tribe", how will he ever feel independent enough of his wife to love her as a separate being? At the same time, there is a desperate longing in him for union with a warm loving *other*, like the one he once had before gender demands forced him to distance himself from her. But, because he equates such intense need with loss of his manhood, he can come to push away the very thing his long-suffering partner wishes to bestow, but is not allowed to. The love is available, but he dare not take it.

For women, uncertainty about whether father's interest betokened a healthy admiration of her femininity or something rather more sinister will affect whether and how she relates to men. Equally, if her father showed no interest in her gender, she may feel very under-confident as a woman. It is very hard for dad to get it right!

Mother, too, is important here. If she is rivalrous with her daughter, she may succeed in undermining her self-esteem. Conversely, the daughter thus threatened may feel she has to compete to survive. This causes trouble in female friendships later on. Either way the mother–daughter bond of old is gone.

Socialization

Home cannot be the centre of the child's universe forever. He or she must be educated and socialized into an acceptable and, one hopes, functioning member of society.

The child's first brush with education and interpersonal contact outside the family can be a shock. Whatever the drawbacks of home, at least it is a known quantity. A way of surviving, even thriving, within it has been worked out. Now our little four- or five-year-old has to deal with the scary new fact that all children are *not* equal as far as brains, social skills, and popularity are concerned. Already in the throes of coming to terms with dad's authority in the family, however gently dispensed, the child may also have to deal with being bullied at school, and/or deciding which protective gang to join when none of them seems too appealing but the thought of isolation and rejection is worse.

Mum has authority, too, of course, but dare he call on it without incurring further teasing or worse? He is, after all, struggling to be a little man, not a "mother's boy". What to do? Submit to the bully who may be blurred in his young mind with his father? Traces of the Oedipal contest may still linger in his mind. Does he murder the aggressor, compete with him, run away? How can he be legitimately self-assertive without bullying others, which he has been taught is wrong? How, in short, can he develop his own authority and respect that of others?

Arguments in marriage where either partner is signally failing to meet their career or social potential often relate to this period. A good airing of school memories (but not using them as excuses) can be most conducive to shared understanding.

Fathers are vitally important to their children, girls as much as boys. A girl should feel a princess to her dad, respected and loved for herself, but also as a desirable female. As part of her healthy development, she and dad need to flirt and play, as (copying mum?) she works out how to get the men to pay her due attention. If dad none the less keeps a clear boundary between fitting and unfitting behaviour, she will grow into a young woman comfortable with her own sexuality.

It is essential that both boys and girls witness their parents' uninhibited (but controlled) love for each other, as well as their capacity to fight and make up. This shows the kids that, though sex is not dirty or shameful, it is also a private matter between consenting adults. The post-quarrel cuddle shows, more than any words can, that marital aggression is not dangerous and sometimes can lead to rather a lot of fun.

This is the couple that will be lodged forever in the offspring's mind and unconsciously used as a model to copy, modify, or destroy later.

Adolescence

Next comes the turbulence of adolescence. Or does it? Some youngsters circumvent it altogether as too dangerous to be faced. Earlier phases may have proved hard or distressing in some way. By the time adolescence is reached this young person has given up the fight and will take peace at any price. Such a character may strike the prospective lover as eminently reasonable, patient, gentle. This is due to unwillingness or inability to take life by the reins, rather than wisdom and maturity. The opt-out clause has been taken up. The other partner will be left to take responsibility for all emotional conflict. Not a good recipe for success, unless the partner has a great need to be in charge, to be a *container* (see Chapter Seven, "Imogen's story").

We all remember the sometimes excruciatingly difficult issues that need tackling during adolescence: sex, career, identity, leaving home, college maybe, or travel. And a search for identity: who the hell am I, and what is it all *for*?

In addition, today's adolescents have to cope with an increasingly complex, fast-moving world of technology, conspicuous consumption, and instant obsolescence. There are demands for quick-fix solutions in every walk of life. There is no time to "stand and stare" any more. Our achievement-orientated mentality, backed up by the ever stiffer demands of higher education—succeed or sink—leave little time or energy for the experimentation we old 'uns enjoyed. Such experimentation allowed us to protest at the injustices previously inflicted on us, get things off our chest through our dreadful behaviour, consort and conspire with our peers to boost our sense of importance and society's uselessness. Cleansed, we began revisiting earlier phases of our lives, making good where we missed out or messed up.

For instance, after a few years of "drugs, sex and rock'n'roll", a youngster winning a place at university—rare and special in those days—felt they had at last earned their father's respect. Now they could begin to take healthy pride in themselves, and in their opinions. Disagreements could now be *allowed*, *tolerated*, rather than having to knock down the father or be knocked down by him, as formerly. This Oedipal "adjustment" will stand the youngster in good stead in future couple relationships. Bullying or being bullied is no solution to conflict, and no way to handle parenthood, either. As with dad, both partners need to feel that for all their conflicting attitudes and beliefs, they have equal value and shared access to power.

If we do not allow the young time and opportunities to be healthily horrible for a while, we are gathering up massive social and psychiatric problems for the future. We must grant them space and time to look into their interior resources and their stored pain, instead of pressing them for purely cerebral results. They need to learn how to relate as well as how to accrue qualifications. If we do not create the climate for this to happen, we rob them of their right of self-determination. Academic, scientific, technological, and commercial experts they may become, but adult men and women equipped to meet the stresses and strains of coupledom and raising a new generation? I doubt it.

The abridged Oedipus and Electra myths in plain English

Sigmund Freud took the legend of Oedipus, and that of Electra, to illustrate the psychology of male and female development around the time when the child becomes aware of a third person in his or her life. Until then, the child had only to deal with the twosome, mum and me.

How this triangle is resolved by four to six years old determines the type and degree of conscience and the capacity for repair and atonement in relationships that the emerging adult will have. As described in the previous chapter, guilt, gender confidence (or lack of it), and the readiness or otherwise to engage in heterosexual relations is also profoundly affected by the negotiation of this troubling time, irrespective of, or combined with, genetic predeterminates. The Nurture versus Nature debate continues, but most therapists would agree we are talking not "either/or", but "both/and".

So, first let the story of Oedipus unfold.

Oedipus

Long, long ago, in mythological time, King Laius of Thebes, husband to Queen Jocasta, kidnapped and raped Chrysipp and was cursed by Pelops, the boy's father. This curse bore down on Oedipus, the only son of Laius and Jocasta. When he was born it was prophesied that he would grow up to murder his father and marry his mother. Horrified, the royal pair sent for a servant and instructed him to expose the child on a hillside until he died. To be extra sure they had his heels pierced with nails, so he could not walk to freedom (hence the name Oedipus: in translation, "swollen foot").

However, the slave took pity on the child and gave him to a shepherd who took him to King Polybus of Corinth. The King and Queen had been unable to have children, and so were overjoyed, adopting the child at once and bringing him up as their own.

When Oedipus reached maturity, one night he attended a party given by King Polybus and a drunken guest called him a bastard. Anxious to know the truth, Oedipus journeyed to the Oracle at Delphi and asked about his parentage. In reply the Oracle merely repeated the prophecy.

On his way down the mountain, Oedipus arrived at a bridge where three roads met and came upon an older man in a chariot who demanded that he get out of the way. When Oedipus—a prince after all—refused, the man struck him, whereupon Oedipus killed him and most of his entourage.

Unbeknown to Oedipus, this man was none other than King Laius of Thebes, his own father. Killing in self-defence was permissible in those days, so Oedipus continued his wanderings unhindered. He was unwilling to return to Corinth and his imagined father, Polybus, in view of the Oracle's repeated prophecy. (He had decided the drunken guest was lying; that Polybus really was his father.)

A mysterious creature (the Sphinx) was terrorizing Thebes at this time. Only the man who could answer its riddle could slay it. The riddle went as follows: What goes upon four legs in the morning, two in the afternoon, and three in the evening? Oedipus answered correctly: Man. He is on all fours as a baby, upright as a man, and on three legs (the third a walking stick) in his old age. (We know that Oedipus was on all fours for a long while because of the nails in his feet, and that after the tragedy he was blind and needed a cane with which to find his way. It was as if some part of him knew his fate.)

The citizens were so glad to be rid of the beast that they offered him the throne of Thebes and Jocasta, the wife of the recently murdered King Laius. They married, and, depending on which version of the story you read, they had several children.

Soon the city's jubilation turned to wretchedness as plague after plague besieged Thebes. King Oedipus sent for the blind seer Tiresias, who said to him, "Oedipus, it is you yourself who are the pollutant." Oedipus would not believe him and denounced him as a fraud.

One day, a messenger arrived at the palace to announce that King Polybus had died (of natural causes, unusual in Greek myth). Upon questioning, the messenger confessed that he himself had carried Oedipus as a child to the King of Corinth. Queen Jocasta, realizing the truth, ran to her incestuous bedchamber and hung herself. The marks on Oedipus's feet being the final proof, Oedipus, finding his dead wife–mother, stabbed out his eyes with the pin of her brooch and abandoned his kingdom, leaving it to his two sons and more tragedy to follow.

Electra

I do not find this story nearly so satisfying.

Paris, a Greek noble, kidnapped the beautiful half-goddess, Helen of Troy, to be his concubine. Her husband King Menelaus was incensed with fury and went to King Agamemnon for military help, thus starting the Trojan Wars.

While Agamemnon was away in the wars, his Queen, Clytemnestra, took up with a lover Aegisthus. Both conspired to murder the King on his return.

When the deed was finally committed, Agamemnon's son, Orestes, and his daughter, Electra, were housed in other royal palaces, Electra in Athens and Orestes on Mount Parnassus, befriended by King Strophius and his son Pylades.

By the time Orestes was twenty, he started receiving messages from the Delphic Oracle that he ought to be avenging his murdered father. But he did nothing, until by accident he met Electra, eight or so years after the murder, at their father's tomb, where she still sorely grieved. They recognized one another and planned their revenge. Depending upon whether you read Sophocles, Euripides, or Aeschylus, Electra took part in the bloody double murder or merely connived at it, pushing her brother to do the deed.

After the murder, Orestes went mad and commenced his wanderings, pursued by the Furies, who were bent on punishment.

Although Clytemnestra was adulterous and a murderess, there was no specific curse upon her as there was with Oedipus's father. Electra not only evaded having to put out her eyes, but was actually rewarded by marriage to the Prince Pylades! But Electra's adoration of her father and hatred of her mother was clear. It was the nearest story Freud could find.

Comment

In the introduction to *Oedipus and the Couple* (2005, p. 2) the editor, Francis Grier, comments on Oedipus's parents' own "Oedipal" problem:

> They appear not to have been able to think about the situation; to allow the more difficult and complex relationship to compel them to develop emotional maturity in response to its demands. Instead, they felt driven to drastic action to wipe out the hated threesome. They attempted to avert what they felt to be certain catastrophe by trying to forcibly turn the clock backwards, to go back to their previous twosome situation. In order to do this, however, they had to commit murder, which was their conscious intention when they commanded the shepherd to expose Oedipus on the mountainside. The myth goes on to tell of Oedipus's survival. If we allow ourselves to imagine that their strategy had succeeded, and that the baby Oedipus had actually been killed, we can see that it is very unlikely that Laius and Jocasta's long term plan of returning to an idyllic twosome could actually have succeeded, due to the appalling persecutory guilt from which they would have undoubtedly suffered. Presumably they would have then conspired for the rest of their lives to erect increasingly manic and possibly psychotic defences against actually knowing in depth and owning what they had done.

Grier then remarks on the Oedipal aspect of partner selection:

> At a deeper level, perhaps we are merely employing strangers to stand in for father, mother, brother, sister—those closest family

members we "really" desire incestuously. For some couples the breaking through into consciousness of this underlying phantasy, perhaps through dreams, can be devastatingly shocking, and can be felt to threaten their adult relationships with catastrophe. Often enough, such couples feel compelled to employ extreme defensive measures, such as stopping all sexual contact, or only having sex "illicitly", out of marriage (paradoxically felt unconsciously to be more, not less, "licit", because such relationships would be with persons felt *not* to represent close family members), or getting into a cycle of regularly divorcing and marrying new partners. [*ibid.*, p. 3, original emphasis]

Jed Rubenfeld (2006) also comments on a variation of the Oedipal myth's interpretation, in his exciting novel *The Interpretation of Murder*.

It's the father, not the son. Yes, when a little boy enters the scene with his mother and father, one party in this trio tends to suffer a profound jealousy—the father. He may naturally feel the boy intrudes on his special, exclusive relationship with his wife. He may well half want to be rid of the suckling, puling intruder, whom the mother proclaims to be so perfect. He might even wish him dead.

The Oedipus complex is real, but the subject of all its predicates is the parent, not the child. And it only worsens as the child grows. A girl soon confronts her mother with a figure whose youth and beauty the mother cannot help resenting. A boy must eventually overtake his father, who as the son grows cannot but feel the churning of generations coming to plow him under.

But what parent will acknowledge a wish to kill his own issue? What father will admit to being jealous of his own boy? So the Oedipal complex must be *projected onto children*. A voice must whisper in the ear of Oedipus's father that it is not he—the father—against the son but rather Oedipus who covets the mother and compasses the father's death. The more intense these jealousies attack the parents, the more destructively they will behave against their own children, and if this occurs they may turn their own children against them—bringing about the very situation they feared. So teaches Oedipus itself. Freud had misinterpreted Oedipus: the secret of the Oedipal wishes lies in the parent's heart, not the child's. [pp. 468–469, original emphasis]

(This novel is set in 1909 New York, and is based on Freud's, Jung's, and Ferenczi's visit to America. The visit took place in reality. Many of the characters are historical figures, although the bizarre murder and hero detective are fictional. The key witness Nora—plainly based on Freud's famous case study of "Dora"—has lost her memory. Can the new Freudian psychology come to the rescue?)

CHAPTER SIX

The couple's joint personality

Jack and Jill Johnson live in the same house, sleep in the same bed, dine at the same table most days, and go on holiday together. Yet they are separate individuals with separate characters, different interests, problems, and personal histories. The neighbours, though, regard them as just "The Johnsons", as if they were a single, albeit joint, person. This is the "us" of the first chapter.

"Joint personality" is a bit of a misnomer really, for the couple are much more than the sum of their two selves. They are not merely stuck together like Siamese twins, one plus one equals two; they meld with each other to form a *dynamic system*, the third element, that holds them both in tension within it. Eventually children may come along, and the system enlarges to accommodate them. They, too, will have their unique identities, but will also contribute to the interpersonal force field we call family.

Like each couple, each family has its own characteristics *as a whole unit*. This unit is not static, like a table, say, where the constituents of legs and flat top remain in place, whatever is put on or under the table. Rather do the members of a family grow and change, combining and recombining with each other in all manner of alliances and divisions. They join forces and sink differences in order to defend the family from outside threats, or turn inward to thrash out family issues within its (one hopes) secure walls. A couple or a family then, is a *living system*, not an inanimate object.

Jack has a relationship with himself ("I am this/that sort of a person"). He has, too, a relationship to Jill, and to the entity Jack-and-Jill; in other words, the couple of which he is a component. Jill, too, has a set of attitudes and beliefs, sincerely held, though they may at times appear to contradict one another: to herself; to Jack; and to her-and-Jack as a marital set-up.

For instance, Jill may feel: "I, Jill, am basically an extrovert, pretty able in a practical sort of way—I can make things happen. My Jack, though, is more introverted and academic in temperament, thinks long and deep about things. He reacts to events rather than initiating them as I do." Now, what is interesting is that although this pair are very different they would both agree that "*we, the Johnsons*, are a hard-working, socially responsible, liberal sort of couple, who none the less like to enjoy ourselves". Over the years, without thinking consciously about it, they have constructed a banner for themselves that shows the world what their shared system stands for, even though their contributions to that banner are not the same.

When at lunch with a friend, Jill bubbles and fizzes more than at home. It is as if she reclaims her old, pre-couple personality. Jack, in his way, also returns to his old self occasionally. This is healthy for a couple. Aspects of the self on both sides have to be modified or occasionally surrendered to make necessary compromise possible. But this comes at a price. Separate friendships do much to soften this unavoidable sacrifice.

One of the advantages of splitting up, once the pain has subsided, is the realization that the terrible loss one had incurred included chunks of one's own being that can now be reclaimed, like lost luggage. The partner may be gone, but in many ways one can now be a fuller, not a lesser, person.

Both Jack and Jill have credits and deficits in their personalities that complement or balance one another's, and so between them supply the qualities described on their banner. Jack's capacity for analysis of local social and political issues enables him make a powerful argument for, say, better youth provision in the area. Jill responds by starting up a youth club herself, with a view to then training others for the work. For the pilot scheme, she persuades the rather shy Jack to bring along his guitar and offer lessons to the young folk. She enables him to be more adventurous and confident while he tempers her impulsiveness that sometimes gets her into deep water (of which more later!). Jack and Jill bring different qualities to the project, but the neighbours nod sagely. "There go the Johnsons, doing their social-worky thing again."

Let us look very briefly at the elements of *any* system, before returning to the living system that is "the Johnsons". We will see how Jack and Jill's youth club project altered and destabilized their system at first, and then how the system righted itself. Their marriage was greatly imperilled and it would be easy to blame Jill for her "bad behaviour". Seen from a systemic point of view, however, rather than a moral one, we begin to understand what a strong and protective function the joint personality has.

Behaviour takes place in a *systemic context*, and this context must be studied as much as the individuals concerned if there is to be any healing of couple wounds. One's other half does not act "out of the blue", though to an unobservant partner it may appear so. (Indeed, part of the couple context giving rise to the behaviour may be that the other partner was ever averting their gaze!)

People act not in isolation or spontaneously, but in response to the emotional states stirred up in them by others. They naturally seek the meeting of needs in relational terms with those around them. Some may judge that Jill was at fault, others Jack, for his negligence. But apportioning guilt to one and declaring the innocence of the other would never have saved this couple, whereas their appreciation of what had occurred *within the shared system both had generated* did in the end make for a new start.

The couple as living system

The Americans, with their customary economy of language, would describe a system thus:

$$\text{Input} \rightarrow \text{Throughput} \rightarrow \text{Output}$$

Take the system we call an engine. You put in petrol. The throughput is combustion. The output is thrust and waste emissions. Similarly, consider a biological system, the digestive system for instance. You put food in. The components in the subsystem we call mouth—acids, enzymes, and so forth—act on this input and then shunt it to the next subsystem, the stomach, thence to the small intestine, and so on. Each subsystem has entrances and exits, and components within each operate on the input received. Eventually, we see the whole digestive tract's output in terms of energy, nutrition, and waste products (Figure 1).

All living systems (and *social* living systems such as "family" and "couples" are included) have at least one external boundary, which, under optimal conditions, is stable (but potentially flexible), and at least two openings, one providing entry and one an exit. If you stuff a big Christmas dinner into your system "tum", it stretches to accommodate the extra food. You may feel uncomfortable, but at least the elastic boundary wall of your stomach prevents you from exploding.

If the stretching doesn't accomplish the desired effect then the system will *self-regulate*. That is, it will open its lower end and squirt excess food into the small intestine, relieving the pressure on the overstretched stomach boundary. If you do not partake of any Christmas dinner at all, your stomach lining and other components will ensure that hunger is created and you will reach out for food despite your best intentions. Your eating a little food will restore the collapsed and shrunken boundary to its optimal size and tension.

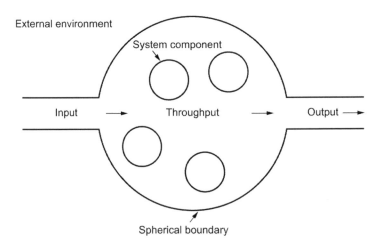

Figure 1. Simple system in a stable state.

Now, events *external* to the system may press on the boundary, reducing the efficacy of the components and their throughput activity. Say that the over indulgent Christmas eater above had a tumour on the outside of his stomach wall. As more Christmas pud is forced in, the wall stretches and thins. The external tumour may then rupture the weakened boundary, and food spills out into the abdominal cavity, causing a medical emergency.

Another would-be celebrant, just returned from a Far East exotic holiday, finds himself unable to "throughput" (digest) at all, due to an amoeba caught from some unwashed fruit. The system is trying to correct itself by ridding itself of the bug, hence the symptoms. This time the pressure on the system is coming from inside.

Like a balloon, the boundary wall of any living system—a fish, a wood, a family, or a nation—changes shape according to the pressure being exerted from within and from without. Unless the boundary is flexible, any pressure on or in the system would result in boundary rupture. Unless this was quickly repaired, all system content would leak away and the system would die.

All living systems have this propensity for self-maintenance. In the same manner, the couple system will adjust to internal upheavals in all sorts of ways, metaphorically taking in, spewing out, stretching and shrinking its boundaries, trying to preserve itself at all costs. The two human components inside the system will move around in the system space, sometimes very far apart, sometimes overlapping comfortably and companionably, sometimes bumping up against each other in anger or intimacy. ("Components" are the permanent fixtures inside the system that act on the Input. The energy they discharge or withhold determines the shape of the boundary at any one time.)

The boundary can stretch or sag, as I will show with the Johnsons, but the system is always attempting to accommodate undue pressure from within or without and to re-establish a stable state. It is this self-regulating tendency that couple therapists attempt to harness in their work.

Simple diagrams will probably illustrate these phenomena more clearly. Some readers by now may feel rather queasy with all this talk of innards and digestion, so let us return to the Johnsons (Figure 2).

Jack reads the evening paper and tut-tuts about the recent spate of vandalism. Jill is interested. They discuss the data contained in

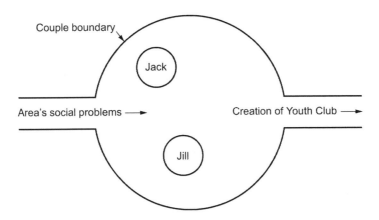

Figure 2.   Social couple system—The Johnsons in a stable state.

the paper while laying out what information each of them has gleaned from other sources about this problem. This is Input. Jack and Jill are the couple system's components applying their brains and experience to this raw data. Their thinking and planning is the Throughput. As a result of all this activity an idea is born, the youth club, with attendant elaboration (the guitar lessons). This is Output.

The plot now thickens! In the search for premises, Jill, the self-confessed up and at 'em one, goes to see the Vicar about doing up a side room in the church hall. A new Vicar, eager to make his mark, has just taken over. He is young, good looking, idealistic, full of plans. Jill is delighted, invites him home to tea, introduces Jack.

What with joint funding, health and safety regulations, purchasing of equipment, and a consultation with the young people themselves, the project—and the visits—seem to be going on forever. Jack leaves the practical stuff to his wife and watches TV in his study while she and the Vicar earnestly pursue their plans.

Jill, fifteen years older than the unmarried Vicar, is flattered by his admiration of her abilities and suspects he is attracted to her. The tea and biscuits gradually become little suppers. The Vicar invites Jill on to more committees. They are spending a lot of time together.

Jack starts getting moody. He trusts Jill, who has always been faithful, and scorns jealousy as a weakness, so he deals with the situation by a mixture of "turning a blind eye" and sulking. Instead of firming up his music skills, as promised, he packs away his guitar (Jill scarcely notices) and spends more time walking the dog, or reading in his study. They are still very much a couple, but the system may be said to be under stress. Figure 3 illustrates what it looks like.

Input is ostensibly the same. Output is a bit slow, owing to the time-consuming suppers, but all the same the club is slowly taking shape. What has changed is the Throughput. The system component called Jack is cowering in a corner of the system, trying to pull its boundary round him like a security blanket. Jill spreads herself along the edge of the couple boundary, available to the Vicar whenever she can be, without actually breaking through the now thinner wall. How much further can it stretch?

Look at Figure 3. Imagine the Vicar pressing further on to the wall of the couple boundary, Jack retreating more to the left, taking his comfort zone (belief that Jill cannot be unfaithful) with him. As Jill leans ever further towards the Vicar's own boundary and he pushes harder, the couple boundary could rupture at the thinnest point, bottom left.

Indeed, after a couple more months, this seems quite likely (see Figure 4). Jack is now thoroughly alienated from his wife, who is almost bursting through the boundary at the other end of the

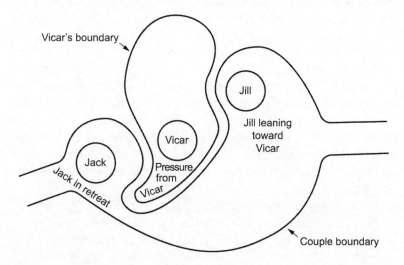

Figure 3.   Social couple system under stress.

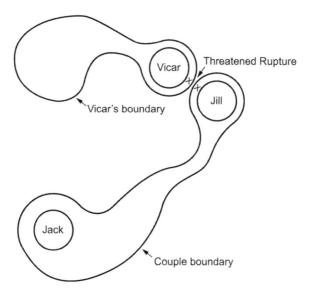

Figure 4. Social couple system—crisis point.

system space, while the Vicar is straining against his system boundary towards her. This is crisis point. The crosses represent the points of impending rupture.

Jill, excited, feeling really appreciated for the first time in what seemed ages, goes to the vicarage for tea one day and makes her physical desire obvious. The Vicar is perplexed, conflicted, wanting her, but aware of his social reputation and his belief in the sanctity of marriage. At his suggestion they sit down to try and talk it over.

Jill now has to face that what she has been pursuing is not a new marriage, or even a regular affair. She has been so infatuated that she has given no thought to consequences. The Vicar has been holding up a mirror to her, showing her how desirable and intelligent she is, despite her age. She has been lonely for a long time, feels old, redundant as a mother. Here is a man (another son?) who has given her back her youth. She should walk away. But she cannot bear to give it up, not yet.

Impulsively, Jill begs: one night, just one night!

The Vicar is shocked, but aroused, too, by her renewed offer of physical intimacy. He does indeed kiss her. As the chasteness of the kiss threatens to turn into passion he pulls back, suggests they— ahem—put the matter before God.

Pray about it? Jill is incensed. Her gorgeous, virile young lover has turned into a coward unable to take responsibility for, or manage, his sexuality at all! This is narcissistic rage, not loss: the Vicar is refusing to comply with her demand that he fulfil her needs. She is far too angry to consider, or even recognize, his internal conflict. In her humiliated and thwarted state she experiences nothing but loathing for him.

Jill is proud, though. To regain composure and self-respect she swallows her fury, pretends that yes, it had all been a mistake. Then she returns home to smash a bit of crockery.

Later, she grudgingly admits to herself that with Jack, whatever his faults, she had never felt the need to compel him in this way. She loved him for himself, warts and all. The Vicar was like her, in his enthusiasm, his rushing about getting things done. Their attraction was to their own image not an *other* person at all. Jill knows she has had a narrow escape.

The evening meetings lessen. No food is served and the practical business is quickly concluded. Meanwhile, Jack senses something is "up"; the game has changed. He comes out of his retreat to start fighting for his marriage. He takes up his guitar again, insists on giving a little demonstration on the opening night.

Seeing Jill grumpily stomping about rather than floating around the place as if in a dream, he feels more able to tackle her about their recent estrangement. She tells him of her deep sorrow at the loss of her children, who have so recently flown the nest. She also confesses her growing boredom within the marriage, how taken for granted she has been feeling. Concerning the Vicar, they both maintain a discreet silence!

The couple system's boundaries gradually restore themselves to their earlier stable state (see Figure 5). All the pulling, tugging, and stretching is now superfluous. The Vicar ceases pressing from the outside. Jill and Jack no longer occupy opposite ends of the system space but are situated adjacent to one another in the middle. Bruised but not beaten, both take a fresh look at each other and agree to start again.

But what if the Vicar had not suffered an attack of conscience at the critical moment? Their consummation would have ruptured his system's boundary, within which, until then, there had only been one component, himself. How to let in a second? For her part, Jill

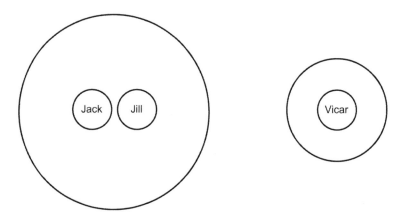

Figure 5. Social couple system—return to stable state.

would have torn her couple boundary with Jack, leaving him floundering and unsafe with a gaping hole in the wall (Figure 6).

We all seek and need carefully constructed, well-maintained living systems in which to dwell safely. It would have been a long time before Jack could either recover or meet someone else, replacing the system on which he had depended for so long.

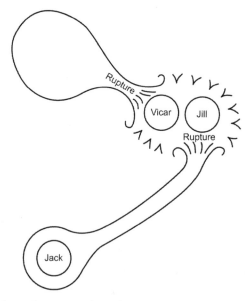

Figure 6. Social couple system—boundary rupture.

When a person is suddenly left, it is not only the beloved that is lost. One's psychological home, traditions, language, culture, a large slice of which the deserter takes with them, is torn apart too. It is a double trauma. The one who "escapes" the system rarely gets off lightly either. Had Jill moved in with the Vicar, it would have been quite a job to repair his boundary, now in need of stretching to accommodate a second component—Jill. What would have to be done about the Vicar's flock, not to mention Jill's avowed humanism and rejection of God? Injured boundaries in human systems do not snap shut to order, but have to be carefully and over time resealed and redesigned to encompass very new arrangements. The Vicar's old boundaries just would not have done.

Later, in couple therapy with Jack, Jill admits that had she and the Vicar finally got together, mutual disillusion would have set in long before either system's boundaries had been repaired. There would have been no secure system to which she could return, for she would have left her and Jack's boundary in a mess, and himself as the other component of their system in a fragile, barely functioning state.

Where the situation permits, a prepared for and negotiated parting is infinitely preferable to a dramatic packing of bags. Thus, boundaries can be controlled, opened or closed by mutual arrangement rather than through violent rupture. This makes them easier to seal afterwards. Like a physical wound, stitching the boundary together is going to hurt, but if the edges are clean, it will mend faster.

In the later figures I have left out the entry and exit points to and from the system to keep the illustration simple. What we are concerned with in this chapter is what goes on *inside* the system. In the early chapters we were more interested in how people choose each other, thus becoming the critical components of a new couple system. These two human components shape the quality of its long-term throughput (married life), just as genes limit what the individual human being can do and be, no matter what marvellous nurturing and educational aids are brought to bear.

In a marriage, the couple can only operate within their emotional and relational potential. But remember that two potentials working together can often achieve more than the sum of each. Most couples operate well below their full joint potential, so much can be done to help them. But once potential is realized, they can go no further. To be blunt, you can't make a silk purse out of a sow's ear. But often you can fashion a very serviceable and satisfying purse from the sow, if the ambition for unrealizable perfection is set aside.

The internal parental couple (another joint personality)

Close your eyes and go back in time. Pick a period in childhood when you believe you have a clear picture of your parents as a unit, a pair. What was the overall quality of their marriage *from your point of view*? Constantly bickering? Formal? Embarrassingly close to each other? Easy-going? Now think about how they managed and taught you (and any brothers and sisters). What kind of a policy, if any, prevailed over discipline, social behaviour, study, sex education, religion, money? Were they united over these policies or at loggerheads? Did one of them leave all this to the other? Could they negotiate, compromise with each other?

Next, try to put yourself in their shoes as a couple. How did they see you? A prince, or princess? A disappointment? A worry? A nuisance? And how did each of them see you in relation to their other partner? If you are male, did dad see you as a fellow male support "agin the women", or as a rival for mum's attention, or did he fail to register you at all? If you are female, did your mother proudly parade you before her friends when you shopped together, or did she keep you in the background, especially when dad was around? Did she take you into her confidence as a fellow female, or keep you at arm's length?

There are no right or wrong answers here. The questions merely serve to remind the reader of the enormous, incalculable extent to which childhood influences of an unspoken and consciously forgotten sort shape the way we establish couples later on. We all have pictures in our mind about our parents. If these were presented to them in their later years, they would almost certainly cry, "Oh no, it was never like that!" We are not concerned here with historical accuracy, or which version is right or wrong, but with the *subjective* experiences, good and bad, of the child yet to grow and make a marriage.

When young, we all observed our care-givers, arriving at our own conclusions even if we do not now remember them. The "parental couple" may consist of mum and gran, or dad and mum sharing, or just mum, or workers in a children's home; but parenting of some sort there must be, for the child to survive. For simplicity's sake, let us look at the conventional (well, once it was conventional!) nuclear family—mum, dad, and child. The child observes his parents with each other, either parent with himself, and thinks about himself as observed by the parents. Who the hell is he if these pictures clash rather than add up to a pleasing whole? In choosing a mate later, without realizing it, he will stick with the one who holds out most promise of happily completing, deleting, or amending the pictures he carries inside.

Quite often, on attaining maturity and a reasonably satisfactory marriage, a person may look back and think, "Despite everything, my own marriage has turned out just like my parents', although we two are a bit further along the road than they managed." It is tempting for therapists to believe (we need more research) that each generation is trying to both "make good" the mistakes of the last, while at the same time paving the way for their own children to travel yet further along the road to marital content. (Certainly, in clinical practice, we see people from families where there has been severe trauma—war, torture, persecution, exile. Almost always the fall-out is passed on to the next generation, in some unspoken hope that it will be metabolized into something easier to deal with.)

Seen from this perspective, an "average" or struggling marriage is cause for celebration, not criticism. To have made it work at all, considering the kind of legacy left by both parental couples, should earn them a gold star. I am reminded of this humbling idea whenever I hear one partner seizing all the responsibility for couple breakdown, the better to beat themselves up. Others, with no ulterior motive, genuinely feel a failure instead of realizing that, given the raw material of the two people who forged the bond, it was a miracle they lasted five minutes, let alone five years.

Tom and Tina

Tom and Tina both wanted a relationship different to that of their parents; indeed, they deliberately sought a partner who would ensure this. After eleven years, they now have a relationship that demonstrates this tendency to carry unresolved problems down the generations via the internal parental couple, only to repeat those problems, but in a less pernicious form. Perhaps their children, still very young, will grow up to get it right at last!

Tom comes from a rather well-to-do, cultured background. His mother had her own private income, and father ran a successful glazing business. Tom suspects mum looked down rather on his father, who chatted endlessly "about nothing substantial" and who did not share her love of horses, county fairs, and Old Masters. Father took Tom and his little brother all over the country while conducting his business. The boys loved it and learned to just screen out their father's prattlings.

As he grew older, six or seven, Tom became aware of his parents' estrangement. There followed terrible quarrels deep into the night, every night. The au pair put him to bed when he would have preferred his mother, but mother was too busy shouting. Dad bellowed back. Despite his protestations—for he longed to understand what was going on—the au pair shut the door and told him he was not to worry. The quarrels seemed to go on forever until, when he was twenty-one, his mother divorced his father. He had, and still now has, no idea what was wrong between them.

Tina comes from a working-class background in rural Scotland. Her father was not an alcoholic, but he drank nightly at his local pub, returning late. His excuse was that he could not face the rows, but Tina's mother claimed his drinking actually caused them. Mother had left school at fourteen but was bright and creative, always pining for a better life and hating Scotland. She longed to move, at least to Edinburgh, but dad would not hear of it, preferring the wild countryside that drove her mad with its gloom. This is all Tina could glean. Neither parent would admit anything was wrong. The rows were so frequent Tina was too ashamed to bring anyone home. The parents stuck together, miserable to the end. As a child, Tina longed to see them divorced. She felt they "ate each other up" with resentment.

Though the two parental couples appear very different, there was much similarity *as far as their children's experience of them* was concerned. Tom and Tina both had bewildered fathers who could not make sense of their wife's pain. Tom's dad used talk and travel, Tina's alcohol and staying out late, to cover this bewilderment. The wife in both cases continued to scream at her husband, never feeling heard. Both mothers had had frustrated artistic leanings and bitterly resented the alleged philistinism of their husband. None of the parental partners ever made significant contact with each other.

Both Tom and Tina's "damage" came not so much from the quarrels themselves, as the fact that they were never, ever, resolved or explained. No one ever made up after a fight, and the fights themselves were a great mystery to both children. There seemed to be no cause for the endless suffering.

Tom grew up swearing he would never endure a marriage like his parents. He became isolated and withdrawn, to protect himself from any temptation to fight. He avoided marriage until he was forty, then met Tina, who seemed to have an uncanny understanding of his interior life. She quietly and gently drew him out of his shell. For a time they were very happy.

Tina grew up to deal with her wounds in an almost opposite way. A quiet, much qualified researcher, she would sit peaceably in any gathering, work-related or social, but the moment there was any debate on any point, however small or big, she would rush in and try to get to the bottom of it, unable to leave it alone until she had satisfied herself that no stone remained unturned in her uncompromising search for "the truth". She often shocked or embarrassed people with her intensity.

When this intensity was finally directed towards Tom, it was agony for both. There had been no especial problem in their marriage, but now even the most routine disagreements, such as what channel to watch, or whose turn it was to go to the supermarket, would be turned into the Spanish Inquisition. At least, that is how Tom described it. Tina's version was that the more she pursued her legitimate desire for the truth, the more he withdrew and often just walked out of the room.

Both partners were suffering terribly for the same reason. Tina was desperate not to be left unheard like her mother, so the interrogations never let up. Tom was equally desperate not to be shouted at like his father, or risk the debasing spectacle of himself shouting back, so he just quit the field. The more he ran away the more she pursued, and vice versa.

They were both loving, intelligent people, so soon came to understand the origins of their hostilities. However, neither could

entirely abandon an entrenched position taken up in order to detox-
ify the effects of their internal parental couples. She *had* to be heard.
He *had* to not hear. Consequently, they still have a few happy
months together, followed by months of Tina rowing and pleading
for contact, Tom quite unable to give her what she so badly needs.
They go for weeks without speaking and in these periods consider
parting.

Sometimes they come for a "top up" session. This affords a little
relief, but not much.

They have done better than their parents. They see that. But is
the happiness they enjoy worth all the distress they have to endure
in the bad times? Who is to judge?

The need to destroy or mend the internal couple

If you still doubt the existence of an internal couple in us all, look
around your friends. How do they react when they hear of the
sudden break-up of a celebrity couple or royal marriage? Or even
another friend's marriage for that matter. Do you suspect that some
of them gloat rather, or adopt a "serves them right" approach, while
others feel a disproportionate degree of sympathy, expressing the
hope that the split is only temporary, even dreaming up ways they
might get together again?

As children we knew grown-up couples did things we were
barred from (why weren't we allowed in the bedroom?). They had
special privileges, like going out on the town half the night, while
we did homework. They had magical powers, too, and could even
make babies. We were forever excluded from these secrets and
denied these privileges. We had to wait, years and years and years,
before we would be permitted to enjoy these benefits.

The most intolerable thing of all was that we had no control over
these two people. They got together of their own accord, without
any help from us, thus making us feel even more helpless, useless,
and shut out. Indeed, this couple had the temerity to go ahead and
actually create (or adopt) us. No permission was sought. Who did
they think they were, *royalty*?

However much we consciously loved our parents, there was
also envy, jealousy, anger, and impotence in our minds and hearts.

In adulthood, this resurfaces whenever we see a couple getting together to share their lives. Guilt over the unconscious wish to smash the couple changes to relief when they disconfirm our capacity to destroy by actually asking us to their wedding.

Alternatively, the requirement that we celebrate the couple's love with them is adding insult to injury. It reminds us that not only did the parental couple exclude us, but we are supposed to be glad about it, too! No fear. At the wedding feast can be heard dark mutterings: "Mark my words, it'll never last!"

It is the same when a couple part. Great sadness at the news reflects the sorrow and wish to atone of the person who once so desired to destroy their parental couple. (But they have probably repressed such wishes because of the mitigating force of the love they had for parents.) The gloaters are still angry with the powerful, envy-inducing pair and rejoice in their downfall.

In marriage, the pair may be able to lay these ghosts to rest. For at long last they have located with, and in, each other all those mysteries in which their parents indulged. They can afford to forgive and forget. Others, though, perpetuate the battle in marriage.

Jon

Jon was troubled by fantasies that sometimes came to him while having sexual relations with his wife. He saw himself driving two stallions, himself standing in a wagon furiously cracking a whip. The horses' backsides would start to bleed as he drove the animals faster and faster. His climax came as the blood began to pour down their flanks. We came to see the dream as his triumphing over the internal couple. He was an adult at last and he could do sex for himself. The pain he inflicted was the pent-up anger for all the afternoons he had had to "go and play outside" while his parents retired to the bedroom.

Some couples, where both partners are burdened by unconscious guilt at the wish to destroy the parental couple, are unable to consummate their bond at all, or have real difficulty in "letting go" and sexually enjoying themselves. Others rejoice in their sexual and procreational activity, now they have "joined the club". They find themselves getting on far better with their parents than before. Some couples cease or drastically reduce sexual activity on having children, as if they fear passing on to them those unbearable feelings of exclusion that they themselves once had to bear.

CHAPTER SEVEN

Imogen's story: three basic modes of couple functioning

W hen the Vicar entered their lives, Jack and Jill of the previous chapter underwent a rough patch in their marriage, but all the same their style of going about things (mode of system functioning) was the most wholesome of the three basic modes seen by therapists in their work. I will briefly present these modes in a moment.

You might ask, why bother with these diagrams and technical terms? Jack, Jill, and the Vicar's story are perfectly comprehensible without them. That is true. But if we are to understand their situation from a therapeutic (helping) vantage point rather than just as a diverting tale, we need some theory.

When reading a novel, we follow the narrative, making heroes and villains according to our prejudices, identifying with those who seem like us, or whom we would like to resemble. It never occurs to us to alter the plot. A clever writer will get us on this or that person's side, will make us weep or laugh. Our emotions are stimulated then manipulated. A couple's story in the consulting room will also have those effects. But the whole point is to understand both the events and the motives behind the manipulations *in a new way*. Then the actors and therapist can intervene in the story, and there can be a change of ending, a happier, more adaptive one, it is hoped.

Theory gives us tools to think with, and protects us from over involvement in one or other of the couple through our identification with them. If the reader is to apply ideas from this book to their own situation, it is important they do so via the theoretical constructs underpinning case examples and not because "Mrs Thing's problem on page so and so sounds like mine." You are not Mrs Thing and your partner is possibly very different to hers, whatever the superficial similarities.

So what was so good about Jack and Jill's way of functioning, if it got them into trouble anyway?

First, a major truth must be accepted and borne. There exists no recipe for couple bliss, no guarantee of success that can be bought, stolen, or earned; no magic amulet to wear against malign forces, no inoculation against break-up. This giving up of hope is very hard to do, the wish in us all for a true panacea being so powerful. It is only when we abandon the pursuit of magic solutions, though, that we can begin to see our selves and our partner straight. We can gradually come to terms with our "joint personality's" potential for—and limits to—growth. No capacity is limitless.

The modes I shall describe are not prescriptions. This is not about the way couples *should* conduct themselves, but about the way they *do*. They have not had any choice in the matter.

Flexible mode

Without choosing it, or even being aware of it, Jack and Jill's marriage had always operated as a *flexible system*. The simple diagrams in the previous chapter show how the couple boundary was pushed and pulled as forces inside the system yanked Jack to one end of it, while Jill strained at the other end, longing to get out. But the system walls generated and maintained over the years held fast—just!—to the point when the Vicar began his withdrawal and Jack his reclamation policy with regard to his marriage. Then the boundary gradually slipped back into its spherical, comfortable position.

In such a flexible system, two equal adults, more or less mature, more or less independent, battle and collaborate their way through their joint lives in a more or less secure setting, created by both, for both, and with serious commitment and investment. Within that system's space, they may at times be far apart, preoccupied with separate careers perhaps, or just rather bored with each other for a while (Figure 7).

At other times they feel very close, not losing their sense of being a separate individual, but actually heightening it by feeling so loved and attended to by the loved one. Their emotional lives overlap and the boundary shrinks to enclose and protect them (Figure 8).

In Figure 9 we see family and other concerns pressing in from the outside, and internal matters pushing out from the inside. The

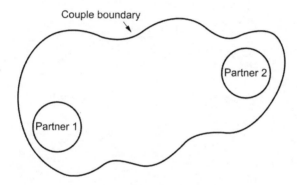

Figure 7.   Social couple system—distanced components.

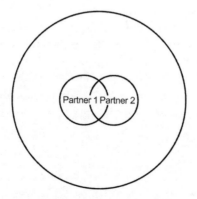

Figure 8.   Social couple system—overlapping components.

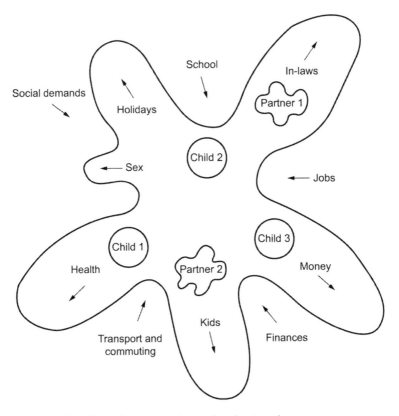

Figure 9. Social couple system—internal and external pressures.

boundary has become very amoeba-like, on the move, wriggling this way and that, constantly adjusting. The system may appear chaotic, but is actually able to compensate for the components' temporary inefficiency or stress. It deploys the boundary to hold in all the turmoil, and keep out the external threats until stasis is returned to and couple attunement re-established. The more flexible the boundary, the more "heat" the family as a whole can stand. Stressed couples can afford to operate as a less than perfect team.

Container–contained mode

I have worked with many couples who spent years avoiding upheaval of any kind, especially angry exchanges, for fear that one harsh word or one different point of view meant imminent divorce. Such a couple cannot negotiate or grow, only maintain sameness, locked in a hived-off world of their own making. This couple mistakenly believes that the safest boundary is a tight, unyielding one upon which no dangerous pressure must ever be exerted, either from within or without.

One partner holds the other inside the self, like a Russian folk doll with a smaller doll safely tucked inside. Jung (1926) called this "the container and the contained" relationship (Figure 10). However, they may change places from time to time, the container becoming the contained.

Serious problems occur when both have a need—which feels like a right—to be contained at the same time. Whose needs are to predominate? The rigid, virtually closed boundary does not allow for compromise, or a fight, or for leaving the system in order to have needs met elsewhere. One or other partner must be quietly forced to contain the other; but on no account must the boundary be disturbed. Getting ill might force one of them to become the container, or making the other feel very guilty or selfish may accomplish this. There is much compulsion—"you *must* contain me"—but with no overt anger. The violence of this struggle for

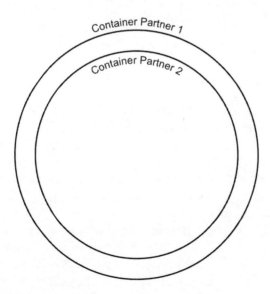

Figure 10. Social couple system—container–contained.

containment by the other would feel like a life and death contest if the two involved allowed themselves to *experience* what is going on. But the violence is driven underground. How long can it remain there?

The person who is most often, or always, contained by the other, happily continues their day to day life unaware of the spouse's growing discontent. That spouse is stuck in the unpleasant role of policeperson sealing off their partner from some dreadful riot. The rabble that must not be allowed in are the undealt-with feelings and conflicts from long ago that the contained person cannot, or will not, face. With a police officer at the door, peace reigns so there is no need. But when the police officer quits his job, the contained person is shocked by the abruptness, the unfairness. Why were they not warned? What have they done to deserve such cruel treatment? The exasperated container blurts out at last: "I have been trying to tell you for years, but you were not listening".

However, if doing the containing suits the person occupying that job, neither party will psychologically grow much but peace will be maintained. I illustrated this in Chapter Two (pp. 20–21) where the scientist took his alcoholic wife to France, remaining well until she died, when he had a breakdown.

Cricket ball mode

The third modality is what I call the "cricket ball" system (Figure 11).

When a cricket ball is stripped of its outer coating, hundreds of tight rubber bands are revealed, making the ball very hard indeed. No gaps lie between these criss-crossed bands. It is never going to change its tough spherical shape, whatever attempts are made to dent it. So dense and solid are its contents there is no chance that energies from within will blow it apart, either. A cricket ball it will forever remain. Good at its specific job, but unable to adapt or modify itself to suit other contingencies.

The strips of impenetrable rubber represent all social, family, and cultural "givens" that hold this type of relationship together. The two people may barely relate at all, and have come together sensing with great relief that neither will disturb the other's self-sufficiency too much. They are happy to lead parallel lives, sharing

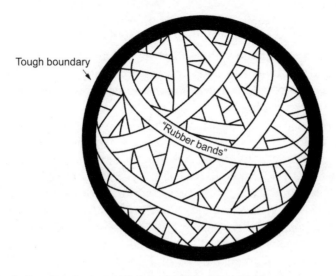

Tough boundary

"Rubber bands"

Figure 11. Social couple system—cricket ball.

domestic duties and scrupulously meeting joint social/religious/ professional obligations, while not having to share anything of their interior world, their psychological privacy, with the other.

We see another version in the immature, irresponsible pair who are virtually "fostered" by relatives. Auntie does the finances and gran cooks. Child-care is divvied up between sisters. Uncle mediates in the fights, or harbours one of the couple until tempers between them have cooled. Without such stalwart supports (rubber strips) the whole system would collapse. This tough outer boundary to some extent makes up for the weak components at the centre of the system.

Other young couples may feel damaged and hurt by earlier experiences at the hands of their families and rush into what they think is a retreat: a home and babies of their own. Playing at happy families grows boring, but the tribe members rally round and between them supply the necessary rubber bands. Somehow the couple holds, and occasionally they even grow up.

Sadly, there is also the young pair who, in the first flush of passion, rush into living together. In an orgy of destructive envy they invade the parental bedroom (metaphorically speaking), demonstrating gleefully that anything the grown-ups have ever done, they can do better. This is not adult relating, but an enactment of accumulated hidden hatred that, none the less, produces babies. Sometimes, a cricket ball system hurriedly assembled by dedicated friends and relatives can keep the young family together long enough for the couple to mature and find each other as persons rather than co-conspirators.

Many people who grew up in foster homes or war zones seek in marriage all they feel they have missed. They plan for, and carefully construct, a model family that has all the ingredients in place—house, money, children, holidays, jobs, the right schools; but often there is very little love, intimacy, or laughter within the system because the parties have not developed enough trust in the world and in relationships to ever really give themselves to another. The marriage as an institution will almost certainly survive, bound together by carefully constructed obligations, duties, roles, and conventions. There is also the determination by the parties to find an identity and maybe some healing in the vocation of spouse and parent. Yes, the institution will last, but what about the couple *relationship* and its effects on any offspring?

Individuals who have either been passed from carer to carer, or who have survived repeated social trauma, have never experienced the comfort and safety of secure but flexible family boundaries. When they discover as adults that they are now allowed to make their own, they tend to make them very tight and inflexible indeed, as if to ward off the terror of the uncertainty and isolation they felt when young. The "rubber bands" of rules and regulations, routines and duties, plus the absolute requirement within the system space to *always be a successful family* can make for lots of problems in the next generation.

In the cricket ball system, the two components may be a great team for all practical purposes, the model parents even, but for one reason or another lack the trust to make that special bond with each other that the children pick up on their radar, carrying it with them into their future relations with partners. It is this lack that makes the "rubber bands" so needful. The boundary takes over some of the function of the components. If the parental intimacy that glues the family together is in short supply, a boundary as strong as a cricket ball will ensure the children at least feel that the system is safe, predictable, and durable (even if a bit stifling). It also serves to keep the couple locked together, too busy with maintaining their happy family image to stop and look at each other as man and woman and face the barrenness. No one can get out of this fortress of a system, so they may as well make the best of it.

I must stress again that we are not talking absolutes here. Few people are incapable of any trust or intimacy at all. The degree of "cricket balling" will indicate the degree to which the capacity for flexible functioning has been hindered by the couple's respective earlier experiences.

It should also be stressed that many haphazard or downright inadequate parental couples have been held together by just this cricket ball solution. Give a wholesome flexible boundary to some families and they would immediately take advantage of the free movement offered by wrecking the whole system, to their own detriment. Some extended families and some social/care agencies (unsung heroes all) have provided "the rubber strips" to couples that have enabled their children to reach adulthood and make relationships infinitely better than their parents. So we should not divide systems and their boundaries into good ones and bad ones.

As described earlier, some people can only function in their job as partner or parent if they are protected by a "container" from having to acknowledge disturbing parts of themselves. Such a person could not do the required fighting and making up, the continuous negotiating, the insisting on separateness while enjoying and soliciting union, that are everyday occurrences in the flexible system of the Johnsons. Such complex activity would stir up all the demons from which the "contained" person is being sealed off.

Let us not be tempted to make rash value judgements. Boundaries cannot be imposed or chosen. They evolve to serve and preserve the system they enclose. Any boundary has to be better than no boundary!

Imogen' story—Imogen and Iain

What do you make of Imogen's life in terms of boundaries and systems? Think about this as you read on. Given her family circumstances, how much choice did she have? How much choice do any of us have in our marriages?

Imogen's Hungarian parents exiled themselves to England after the 1957 invasion of her country by the Russians. She was two years old, her brother four. There was a large extended family, all political activists. Uncles and one set of grandparents emigrated to the USA in the same year, and the other grandparents went to Australia. Her brother went with them, though she never found out why.

Throughout her childhood her parents kept up with the home country, their compatriot friends, and their politics, as if expecting one day to return, but they never did. Imogen did well at school, but was rather lonely, aware that she was different in some way to the other children. Still, she made superhuman efforts to get along with them. She grew into a real beauty with a gift for languages. At eighteen she began her degree in languages at London University.

She remembered her mother being very low in the first few years after leaving her native land. Her father quickly got involved with political groups, leaving the two women together. Imogen acted as companion/nurse despite her tender years. She recalls her father "behaving as if he were some sort of ambassador, forever travelling Europe, carrying messages and addressing big conferences." She supposed she must have loved him, but she and her mother scarcely saw him.

By the time she went to secondary school her mother had recovered, joining her father's activities and travelling with him. Imogen brought herself up with the help of the occasional au pair.

Coming of age, and now an independent student, Imogen was clear what she wanted from life. First, a family of her own that she would keep together come hell or high water. Next, an unassailable place in English society with no revolutionary activity to worry about. She wanted nothing to do with politics and the dangerous outside world. In a word, she longed for security.

At a student party she met Iain, who was studying land management at a nearby college. He was something of a loner. She admired his self-reliance, the way he kept to the edge of the party crowd, watching them and joining in where needful, but never losing self-control. He seemed quietly confident for his age (nineteen), somewhat aloof and mysterious (like her father?). Imogen assumed that still waters ran deep.

Iain's parents ran an estate in Gloucestershire. He was very keen on horseracing, crosswords, and playing the stock market. He had no close friends, but his exquisite manners and public-school charm ensured he got along with anyone he met. He seemed to stand for old-fashioned conservative British values, or so Imogen imagined, as she fell passionately in love. They both left college without completing their courses and married as soon as was practicable.

Five children followed in rapid succession. All went to private schools and were given every possible advantage. Iain appeared the perfect father at first, driving them wherever they wanted to go, attending parent evenings with Imogen, taking them on adventure holidays and to Disneyland.

During these first ten years it very slowly dawned on Imogen that her husband, for all the outward show, was a stranger. It was as if he merely imitated husbandly behaviour, acted as father, host, gentleman farmer, but could never actually *be* any of these things. Sex was intermittent and half-hearted; he seemed bored by the glittering parties and houses to which they were regularly invited, though he bought her beautiful clothes and jewellery. He seemed always to be filling time, and was quite grateful to be given a project—take the boys to football, or whatever. The only time he got excited was when his racehorse won him a trophy (someone else fed, trained, and groomed the animal), or when he pulled off a clever deal on the stock market (though he had no need of the money).

Iain refused to admit there was a problem, and accused her of imagining things. He left her alone for longer and longer periods until she became quite depressed. She suggested splitting up in the hope this would shock him into doing something about the marriage, but he just said "don't be stupid" and walked out of the room. Neither pleading, nor shouting, nor threatening would make him discuss their relationship. *He* was quite content. Any problems must be hers.

Imogen felt the children were too young to weather a divorce, so she now took herself in hand, gave up complaining, and started studying. Within a few years she became a professional translator at conferences. She developed her own circle of friends, insisted on her own short holidays as well as the family ones. Iain showed no interest in her work or her friends, but neither did he complain about them.

Despite being a non-believer, Imogen then rejoined the Catholic church of her forebears, and became known for her dedication to committee work and for fundraising for Third World projects. She immersed herself in this busy world of new friendships and work, Iain taking on more and more domestic responsibilities. He never enquired as to her whereabouts so long as she remained in phone contact. He developed an absorbing interest in computer technology. In short, they were leading separate lives under the same roof.

To all intents and purposes, the marriage had settled down. There were no more quarrels, but no intimacy either. Imogen thought this the best solution for the children's sake.

Despite her busy life, her loneliness and restlessness grew until the inevitable happened. At one of her conferences she met Rex, an archaeologist widower, and plunged into an intense love affair.

She negotiated nights away, claiming she needed regular breaks from her hectic schedule. Iain complied. He must have guessed something was going on, but ignored all the tell-tale signs and carried on as normal. At times he would gaze at her sadly, as if regretting that they had not done better, but at other times she seriously wondered if he were not relieved by her absence.

Rex was forever travelling to the Far East on digs, or attending international conferences, so it was difficult for the lovers to meet. When they did, Imogen believed paradise had come to her at last. She felt fulfilled for the first time in many years.

After a year of dividing her energies between her children and her lover, she began experiencing familiar feelings of dread and doubt. Rex was passionate and considerate in all things, but very definitely had a life of his own. He hated parties, beach holidays, and poetry, all of which were centrally important to Imogen. She began to feel the old loneliness.

Rex's wife had died very young of a rare blood disease. Imogen suspected that he had walled himself off from any other further emotional involvement, but at first proudly thought that she alone had managed to break through his defences. As his timetable allowed them less and less time together, she saw now that, though very much in love with her, part of him remained frozen. He was unlikely ever to make the kind of commitment to her and her children, about which she had fantasized.

Eventually the affair became quarrelsome, and finally it ended by mutual agreement.

Imogen converted her grief into renewed energy towards the family. She was forty-two. The oldest son had left home, the other four were teenagers. They now became her central project: she showered them with attention, advice, presents. The family as a whole visited prospective colleges or gave parties for her son's friends, to whom Imogen became a confidante/auntie. Family holidays once again became the norm. Previously a homebird, Imogen discovered the pleasures of travel, plunging into this as she had into everything else.

At forty-seven, the old sadness is back. There will be another lover, I have no doubt, especially as the children leave home. But what about her carefully constructed cricket ball system? Could she just walk away from it? She has all she dreamt of as a young student—family, and a secure and respected place in her social/work/church community. She is wanted and admired as much as her parents ever were, albeit in a different way.

In an odd way, too, she remains "married" to Iain. She insists the relationship is dead, but hangs on to it none the less, dismissing him waspishly as her sixth child. All the same, without him the whole edifice of respectability and security crumbles. She needs him to play his part, as she needs the identity she has twice rebuilt after so much disappointment.

Is there a part of Imogen that is still trying to get Iain to *notice* her, as her busy father never did? How long will she wait? If a warm and committed man arrives on the scene, will she be able to abandon her fortress? Had she pressed on with Rex, would he have come round in the end?

We cannot be sure of the answers. It is plain, though, that here was family displacement that much affected the child, even at only two years old. She lost her country, her brother to relatives abroad, and her mother to depression in the early years (though by mothering her mother she managed to derive a bit of nourishment for herself). Her father was lost to political idealism, rapidly followed by the desertion of her mother, who clearly preferred her husband to the child.

On becoming an adult, is it any wonder Imogen made an early marriage, determined on building for herself all that she had missed in childhood? Her quite conscious aim was to contrive a container–contained marriage. Iain was chosen to be the one who would hold her inside him, protect and cherish her, keep her safe, while she turned inward, away from the fearsome world of tanks and revolutions to make her ideal family nest.

Far from guarding the nest, Iain turned out to be the contained, while Imogen was forced to do the containing, or leave.

I believe Iain was probably diagnosable as Asperger's syndrome, an autistic-like disorder at the milder end of that spectrum, where the person is unable to empathize, stand in another's shoes, and experience something genuinely akin to what they are feeling. There was little evidence that he was capable of change. He could neither love her properly nor leave her. He adhered to her like a sticking plaster, but could not peel himself away and relate to her as a separate person.

When it became clear that he would not or could not discuss the marriage, Imogen's response was to try to make the best of it. Fearing she may become ill as her mother was, she wilfully turned away from her sadness and set about turning her marriage into a cricket ball system. As the second component in the marriage, Iain was excellent for all practical purposes, but emotionally useless to this passionate and needy woman. How insulted she must have felt at his total disinterest and lack of pride in her achievements.

With Rex she once again sought containment, and he failed her. But is it reasonable or realistic to require another person to compensate for all previous unmet needs? Rex had his own traumatic experiences to deal with and was not offering containment to anybody. The best he could cope with was a part-time relationship fitted around the one thing that was secure and predictable in his life, his work.

Perhaps the story will end happily, perhaps not. Once independent of her children, might Imogen begin to deconstruct her marriage rather than maintaining it as a lie? Is it Iain she cannot leave, or the fortress they have together built and held against all odds, including a serious extramarital relationship? Could she tolerate not being contained, not containing the other (where at least you run the show, so are safe), and not having the cricket ball system to bolster her?

To risk the flexible system feels just too dangerous for some people.

CHAPTER EIGHT

The couple's life cycle. The early years: Forming and Norming

The couple system goes through a life cycle just like any other living organism. In this chapter I will borrow a catch phrase from group therapists. They see their therapy groups (and indeed any group—family, football team, church, army) as progressing through *Forming, Norming, Storming*, and *Performing*.

How does this apply to the pair bond? Well, we have already seen most of the *Forming* process in Chapters Two and Three. Individuals seek one another out for many reasons, not least in the hope that the partner chosen will repeat an earlier good parenting experience, since lost, or that they will make up for a traumatic or inadequate experience by providing the missing ingredients, or healing the trauma. Whether such aims are healthy or realistic depends on the degree to which the elected partner is unconsciously *compelled* by the chooser to fit their requirements. The chosen one has his or her own needs left over from childhood. If these are not allowed for by the chooser, the forming couple will not last, or will commit to each other only to face bitter disappointment.

Intermittently, couple members can and should parent one another, in much the same way they would loan their car if the partner's had dodgy ignition. But if the demand is for full time care (the ignition is never repaired) at the expense of adult to adult relating, the marriage is in serious trouble. Forming may never progress to the establishment and then embedding of Norms. I have seen couples who have lived together for thirty years still fighting over what a Norm should, often *must*, be. The position of each partner pressing the other to meet unrealizable needs remains stuck. Neither can give and both feel entitled to take, much aggrieved by the other's "lack of love".

Couples also Form in order to bring out the best in each other. One partner may accurately sense that the other is further along some particular road that they, too, wish to travel. Or that qualities weak or absent in the self are abundant in the partner. Combined, their respective weaknesses and strengths make a satisfactory whole, an "us" from which they can both derive self-esteem, and a feeling of completeness.

Seeing the other's complementary quality enables the "lacking" person to learn from their spouse, thus expanding each party's repertoire for relating. One may be good at "talking turkey" for instance, for "laying cards on the table", but sometimes offends; the other may be diplomatic and tactful, but often too cautious. Put them together and they make an ideal negotiating team. If they can learn from each other as well, then even apart they broaden their skill base. She becomes more like him, he like her.

The risk here is that envy of the partner's talents, or the talented one lording it over the lacking one, will spoil the collaboration and not allow for the genuine humility necessary for learning. An overly competitive couple will use, or rather *abuse,* their best developed qualities to acquire dominance. Fierce quarrels break out over just those character traits that first brought them together. Will Forming lead to Norming in this case? Or to parting?

There is no cut-off point between the phases in the cycle. Forming flows into Norming as the couple gradually come to realize that, for the time being at any rate, they are not going to split up. This may be signalled by moving in together or getting engaged, but that is an *event*, an outward manifestation of a *process* interior to the couple.

Once two people live together, all manner of sociological Norms come into play that they may never have thought about. These are different and less complex than the private Norms they set up between themselves in the early years, but are no less problematic for all that. It is not politically correct to say so, but clinical experience as well as ordinary social observation confirms that, while there are exceptions to every rule, certain commonly held assumptions about the different genders are actually true.

The pioneering American father of cognitive behavioural therapy (CBT), Aaron T. Beck, deftly summarizes these in his book *Love Is Never Enough* (1988). I will give a pair of examples:

Men: "If she wants to tell me something she will tell me without my asking."

Women: "If I don't ask, he'll think I don't care." [Beck, 1988, p. 104]

Beck discusses how conversational styles differ, men interrupting more, making declarations of fact more often than feeling, delaying a response to their partners until she has finished and then "getting their oar in"; whereas women tend to *listen* more, adjusting their view and reaction as they go along. Men resent the female's emotionality and propensity for changing positions, which they perceive as weakness. Women resent what they regard as men's authoritarian stance and their inability to forget their own stance *pro tem*, so as to absorb another's.

Research referred to by Beck shows that girls use words as a bridge, boys as a weapon.

Almost three quarters of American women prefer to discuss personal problems with a girlfriend, whereas most men talk sports and politics with their male friends, reserving personal problems for their partners.

In couple exchanges, men look for clarification of a problem, then its solution. Women are looking more for a sympathetic ear, an understanding of how having that problem must feel. If the sympathy is forthcoming they can bear not having a solution and then begin to work round the problem.

Regarding marriage/coupledom, to paraphrase Beck:

Men think: "Our relationship is not working so long as we keep talking about it."

Women think: "Our relationship is working so long as we can talk about it."

These are generalizations, of course. Beck's sensible book was first published almost twenty years ago, but, to be honest, not a lot has changed, especially in the more mature age group. Younger couples may profess different views outwardly, but once communication between them is examined carefully, it is all very similar. How much of this is culturally acquired and how much genetically determined I leave the reader to decide. Therapists must perforce work with what actually happens in the consulting room, not what they think *should* happen.

It is one thing to argue these points about gender difference at a dinner party, quite another to have to deal with them face to face twenty-four hours a day, seven days a week, with a new partner who until now has seemed to hang on your every word. It has to be said that, whether or not there are other problems, *the communication process itself* gives rise to huge and avoidable misunderstandings in the early years. A spot of refereeing and re-training by a third party, without the need for depth work, can work wonders.

It is important then that couples learn to accept "natural" difference in the sexes, just as they must come to terms with their partners *as they are*. Take the time-worn example of the woman who opines, "You never bring me flowers. If you really loved me you would bring me flowers!" Hubbie scratches his head. "I put your shelves up, don't I? I live here, don't I? What do you want flowers for?" *"Because that is what I would do* to show I loved a spouse". In other words, "If you loved me you would be the same as me".

People are imprinted with values and attitudes by their family that they take as universal truths: "Fair dos for all", "Respect your elders," "Protect children and animals", "Keep your head down and your nose clean". Then there is the work ethic that dominates one family, the entrepreneurial spirit that drives another. Live and let live in one—messy rooms and eat when you are hungry; in another, fear of anarchy that leaves the household rule-bound and spotless. While courting, lovers tend to blur their prejudices and principles, which seem unimportant, for they are to build something quite new where such things do not matter. But, once living together, it becomes shockingly clear sometimes just how different, unalterable, and frequently objectionable are the partner's values.

The man who put shelves up, but never verbalized his love, may see himself as Romeo incarnate for all his wife knows. For her only flowers will do it. She has two choices. She can go on hurting and sulking at his seeming lack of love, and nag him into resentfully doing her will. Or she can sigh at the absence of flowers, but judge his behaviour *by his own lights* and be grateful. First, though, she must know what they are. That means having a look, not wasting her time trying to turn him into a carbon copy of herself. She must learn the painful lesson that people can only give love the way they know how. It does not come specially designed and gift wrapped.

Strange though it seems, in the early years of the couple's cohabiting, they have to get to really know one another. They believe they are of one mind, but actually they are relative strangers. They need to find out what Norms the other has subscribed to over their lives, and respect them. Once respected, it becomes easier for each of them to modify those Norms, and even develop a few shared values and attitudes that neither had before. This is the process of becoming not just two people under the same roof, but a marriage, "the third element".

Norms in a partner cannot be discovered by issuing them with a questionnaire. They are found when there are ruptures in the ordinarily smooth exchanges of day to day couple life, such as the flower conversation above. Bumping against a foreign Norm, being adversely affected by it, can teach much if the affected party is not too offended to be healthily curious towards their partner's "strange" behaviour.

The first big joint Norm needing a firm-up is *commitment*. Surely, if they are moving in together the pair must be committed already? Not necessarily so, I am afraid. There is very often a qualified commitment: "I am committed to you so long as you treat me properly". This could be a lov*ee* (see Chapter Three) looking after their own interests, but it could also indicate a wounded person engaging in self-protection. What if mum and dad fought constantly, the same sex parent seeming always to get the worst of it? This partial commitment does not reflect lack of love so much as a fear of repeating history. The point is that the other partner senses the cautious attitude and misinterprets it. Often the cautious one is unaware that their commitment is conditional, as well as being unaware of the reason for it. If this is eventually pointed out to them by an observant partner or therapist, perhaps genuine reassurance can be brought to bear.

Incomplete commitment has many causes. Unfortunately, some people know deep down that this relationship is not right, but they are lonely, feeling rather battered by life, and long for comfort. It could be the familiar rebound story. They tell themselves they will make it come right in time, or it may be the best they can hope for, or "it will do for now—let's wait and see."

There are many complicated Oedipal reasons for lack of commitment, as discussed in Chapters Four and Five.

Incomplete commitment is often the fundamental issue when couples still in the early years of the relationship are referred for therapy. Commitment cannot be faked indefinitely, though some couples do conspire to pretend that everything is all right in the commitment department when it is not. The faker foolishly believes that pretending it will make it come true. The more committed one is permanently anxious, wondering if they are imagining things. They often become very controlling, trying to extract proof of commitment. This behaviour would cease once true commitment arrived, but, alas, until then the suspicious and worried controller will be blamed for the couple's problems.

If either partner senses a lack of full commitment in the other, then what should be ordinary domestic quarrels are felt as immensely dangerous, harbingers of marital doom. A clean, or even occasional dirty fight becomes a serious threat to the continuation of the marriage. If a couple never feels safe enough to fight, (followed by a delicious making up!), real communication will wither and die. It is vital that couples truly feel they are in this relationship for better and for worse; that bad patches will be followed by good; that in the lean, ugly, miserable times the other will still be there for them. In quarrels, each must learn how far they can safely go with the other. This can only be done by trial and error. But how can they experiment if they fear the other will pull out?

Norming occurs over time as the pair settle down to their new identity as an "item", a married unit. Apart from all the celebration and happiness, there is much work to be done. Ways must be found to live together in harmony despite differences in temperament, taste, and habits. The need to decide on housework, shopping, feeding the cats, etc., is self-evident and usually does not take long. But what of money, privacy, frequency of sex, method for solving disputes? These often touch on quite deep personal issues that the pair have probably never thought about, let alone discussed. They can be quite frightening.

Lillie and Leo

Lillie and Leo had lived together for one month before deciding they needed professional advice.

After a whirlwind love affair both felt sure they had met the right person for life. Leo's great-aunt died and left him her bungalow, so they wasted no time and moved in together. The house was old-fashioned and needed repair, but they looked forward to doing it up together on their tiny salaries.

Keen walkers, both had been overjoyed to discover one another's passion for the countryside, conservation, and log fires. Their most romantic evenings had been spent round various pub fires after one of their hikes. The great-aunt's bungalow had a real fire, which they took as a good omen.

The first time they lit the fire, everything went wrong. First they argued playfully over who was to light the First Fire of their life together. Somewhat reluctantly, Lillie gave in. Half way through building it the phone rang and Leo went to answer it. Trying to finish off the fire, Lillie reorganized all the wood to make a ledge on which the coal could be safely placed. Leo returned and was furious. "Leave it alone!"

He apologized, and then irritably explained that he knew all about fires; he had done a Tibet trail and lit fires for ten others every night. He had spent his life lighting fires. He squatted on his heels and began rearranging the sticks.

"I lit the family fires in our damp holiday cottage in Exmoor till I was fifteen!" protested Lillie. "No one else could get them to go, so it was always left to me." She squatted beside Leo and proceeded to move a piece of wood "to get some air in".

Leo slapped the hand that held the wood and reiterated, "Leave it alone I say."

Astounded, Lillie thumped him in the arm and told him to bugger off.

Suddenly they found themselves glaring at each other, red in the face.

Embarrassed, they both laughed, but were very scared by the intensity and suddenness of the primitive emotion stirred up in each other by so small a matter.

After that, everything about doing up the house became a trial. He wanted dark wallpaper and traditional furniture. She wanted Ikea, lots of light, and pale lilacs and green fabrics. Both saw the need for compromise—they were reasonable people—but somehow could find none.

What was happening here? *Norming* is about finding ways (Norms) of operating together that avoid undue conflict on the one hand, but allow for difference and even disagreement on the other. The Norm established is then automatically used to save argy-bargy over every couple decision. This involves practical matters such as who should light the fires, but also more important, potentially tricky ones such as whose will should prevail when both cannot have their own way.

If they are going to spend the rest of their lives together without fighting over every decision, power issues need to be settled early on. Understandably, neither wishes to surrender power, however much they love each other. But neither wants to bully the other into surrendering either, precisely *because* they love each other. The first months, and very often years, are spent negotiating this delicate area until both are content.

They could just take turns in lighting the fire (they did, subsequently); but this was not any old fire. It had very special connotations. Both had endured positions in their original family where they were rarely appreciated or allowed to shine. They shared doubts (so far not confided) about their ability to contribute to family life in any way that would be applauded or even noticed. Accordingly, both badly wanted the credit for making this ritual fire precious and memorable. Unconsciously, both had vowed that in this new relationship they would *insist* on being noticed. We begin to see now why the first lighting was a fiery business indeed!

We see also that Lillie and Leo both had a healthy interest in maintaining their individual power base. To give it all up and allow oneself to be enslaved is as problematic for future marital relations as refusing to give way at all.

A note on the importance of hate

This snippet from an early relationship shows how soon hatred can be stirred up just by trying to live together harmoniously. Love by itself is not enough, whatever the romantics say. Lillie was horrified by the bruise that came up on Leo's arm that night, "But for a split second I really hated him." Hate in these kinds of circumstances arises from disappointment in the idealized beloved. It reawakens immature rage felt by the infant when forced to realize that the world does not revolve around them. How dare the other person, appointed king or queen of my heart, so badly let me down? How dare they not understand my needs when I have accorded them such great honour, laid my own love at their feet? They must slowly and painfully learn that the beloved has needs, too.

Hate flares where frustrated love abides. Indifference is the opposite of love, and its enemy, not hate. Hate is hot and can be dangerous, but like any fierce heat it can also be forged into something clean and new. Where indifference is concerned, neither therapy nor the other spouse can do anything. So, if you hate each other you could still be in business!

In the end, Lillie and Leo's rather naïve mutual adoration was transformed through many episodes of hatred into a more mature, more respectful love. Difference was openly fought over and some power on each side honestly yielded. Instead of romantically believing the other would lie down and die for them if required, they started to allow one another to have their own rights, preferences, and *separate* needs.

When a couple first come together, they cannot exist *à deux* in a vacuum. Old, separate boundaries are redundant. In practical terms this is evidenced by the need, say, to work out the bank accounts: joint, or some joint and some separate? Are the separate ones private? What if he dislikes her shopping habits and she his drinking? Who pays for what when they go out together? He is a saver and she a spender. He likes to stay home; she loves holidays. So what is going to happen about a deposit on a flat?

Norming, then, might be defined as the generating of a couple boundary, all those shared "givens" within which the couple will conduct their emotional as well as practical dealings with each other. These givens may be tweaked, nudged, and refined as the years pass, but often remain basically the same until the couple unit reaches its Storming period. Or even its mid-life crossroads. But that is for Chapter Ten, on "the later years".

Distance versus closeness

Another massive Norm to be worked out in the early years concerns levels of intimacy. Some people need closeness approaching fusion in order to feel secure in their relationship, while others find such a proposition intrusive and even frightening. Generally speaking, everyone needs to be dependent on, and close to, others, but they also need to feel independent and separate at other times. Many couples experience serious and chronic misunderstandings, with subsequent misery, as a result of never having sorted out this issue early on.

Paul and Polly

Paul went to sea at sixteen. His mother had genuinely loved him, but fussed over him as if he were an invalid, over-feeding him, dressing him up "in short pants and frills—at eleven!", drilling him to show perfect manners and never "show her up" in public. Once a sailor, he broke every rule he could think of: drinking, womanizing, a bit of drug-running.

Eventually he settled down with Polly and found a nine to five shore job. Polly was very busy with her hand-knitting business, travelling a good deal and working late into the night on her fashion designs. A born organizer, she made sure there was always food in the fridge, the bills paid, the house clean. But she never found time to watch TV or relax at home. Paul was happy with what he called his "ships in the night" type of relationship.

Although he was unaware of it, his contentment arose from having all the nurturing aspects of mothering without any of the nagging, or the possessiveness and cloying affection that so embarrassed him as a boy. He was a happy man.

After seven years, Polly became pregnant. Her whole personality seemed to change. She became dreamy, careless about the state of the house. She took a year off, handing over the running of the business to her deputy. Worst of all, Paul complained, "She needs looking after like a baby herself!" He was both hurt and outraged.

Paul wanted his tough wife back so he could pretend he was an independent guy again—a real "new man" who could look after himself as he did at sea, while allowing his wife to earn the big bucks without being threatened by her success. This picture of himself was now smashed. Her neediness, as he saw it, made him feel sick, but until therapy he had not dared to tell her. It took him a long time to accept his own need to be close to his wife, *but in secret*. In their happy years an outsider would have wrongly thought them a distant, if friendly pair.

For her part, Polly said that becoming a mother herself had made her realize just how far she had deliberately stayed away from Paul, trying to be the opposite of her mother and sister, both of whom had clung to their husbands and then been deserted by them.

Early in the pregnancy, before she withdrew into her preoccupied state, Polly had longed to compensate Paul for all she thought she had deprived him of, and gain the attention from him which she had for so long avoided, fearing ensnarement. "Cold grub in the fridge is not like hot food on the table," she would say, only to feel puzzled and hurt when he started coming home late from work, letting her meals go cold and then eating alone. She feared she had neglected him too long, so intensified her efforts, which distanced him even more.

Polly wanted more closeness and Paul could not bear it. The Norm established several years ago had been disrupted by the pregnancy. They were now well into the Storming phase. Renegotiation was urgently required. First, though, both needed to understand the part their separate histories had played in their marriage; how and why their respective complementary distances had been set up.

Clearly, different people at different times want different distances from each other, or to get very much closer to one another, and there cannot always be a convenient "fit". She may want intimate relating just at the time he craves a bit of space for himself, or vice versa. This is life, this is marriage, and tolerance, not panic, is required. There will be better times when the "fit" is good, or when one noble soul understands the needs of the other and forgoes their own, trusting the favour will be returned on some future occasion.

In *Schopenhauer's Porcupines* (2002), the American therapist Deborah Luepnitz retells the fable recounted by Schopenhauer, of which Freud was also fond, concerning the problem of human intimacy. A tribe of porcupines mills about on a cold winter day. To get warm they huddle together, but soon their quills poke one another, causing sharp pain. So they move away from each other to stop the pain, but then lose body heat. This makes them huddle together again, but perhaps at a safer distance. All day long this negotiating of distance and closeness goes on. There is no ideal distance/closeness. Pain may be borne for the sake of the warmth gained. Distance will then be demanded when the cold is easier to endure than the pain.

Luepnitz gives an example of her own:

> ... a young woman applicant to a cloistered religious order was sent to me for psychological evaluation. She seemed genuinely ascetic and contemplative, and I said so in my report. Her spiritual advisor was not as cheered by this as I expected. These young women, she said, will spend the rest of their lives relating only to each other, and thus require exceptional social skills. A Carmelite cloister, I learned, is no place for a loner. [Luepnitz, 2002, p. 4]

In Appendix II (p. 235) I have quoted Kahlil Gibran, the Lebanese poet writing in the 1920s. His advice to couples in *The Prophet* is sometimes read out at weddings and addresses this very issue. Unless the pair have already lived together for some time, I fear the message is lost on besotted newly weds who may not yet have realized the importance of separateness as well as togetherness.

Clingers and Avoiders

It must be said that couples do exist where there is "a resolute refusal to engage with the reality of the other" at all (Colman, 2005, p. 58). The pair may seem locked together, but are actually dedicated to *avoiding* relating. If you try to coerce your partner into being what you just *know* they ought to be, in order to make your dream of marriage come true, then you are in a world of illusion and delusion, a world of one—yourself. You cannot bring the other person under your magical control, but many marriages split up because one partner goes on trying, growing more embittered with each attempt. Such a person will have had rather more disappointment in parental figures than the average, and the coercion is a desperate, but futile, bid to put all that right.

If magically controlling the other really worked, and you made them perfectly attuned to you, responsive to your every thought and need, they would not be a genuine *other* at all, would they? They would be an extension of you, a fulfilment, an embodiment of all your hopes and longings. This fantasy person does not, *cannot*, exist. You cannot turn a pack of salves for lacks and losses inside the self into a living breathing person. Partners are not pills and balm, but have wounds of their own to deal with. If you want your couple to work, this fantasy must be given up. Trying to metamorphose your partner into a Prince or Princess Charming only means you are blind to the real person to whom you have committed. You, of all people, know how it feels to never be really seen!

The "Clinger", then, fails to connect at all with the real partner, who is starved of mature love. The Clinger is imprisoned within a relationship to their own self.

The opposite of the Clinger (who seeks to control the partner) is the withdrawn, isolated, "Avoider". Often such persons appear "deep and spiritual" to new acquaintances, not least because they are often very learned or have arcane interests. They prefer to relate to abstract concepts and theories rather than to people and emotions, or cultivate intellectual stances towards the impersonal, so safe world of "politics" or "the arts". They may be excellent at communicating *information*, but nothing personal and warm is really shared for fear they may be intruded upon, *raided*, by another person wanting to come closer.

Such people may seem very interested and involved in the world, but in fact are averse to true intimacy. In fact, they more or less live in a world of their own, sometimes using partners as a sort of guard dog to protect them from the world of relationships. The non-avoider is the one who does the socializing at parties, who does the relationship work for the two of them. Meanwhile the Avoider may hold forth on a pet subject, or stay all evening with someone of similar disposition where talk happens, but there is little personal input or exchange of feeling. They may lurk in a corner trying to be invisible, not out of shyness or a wish to be rescued, but to be safe from intimacy.

When their partner complains of neglect and/or loneliness the complaint is ignored. Often the complainant doubts whether they really did verbalize their hurt or just thought it, so convincing is the Avoider's capacity to shut out unpleasant aspects of reality. Pressed, the Avoider may respond with withering sarcasm, or "insolent" silences that so wind up the other party they are afraid to try again. (This is the object of the exercise.) Occasionally, when pushed or "nagged" (as the Avoider sees it) beyond endurance, they will fly into an uncharacteristic rage and can be violent.

Some readers may worry that this description applies to them or their partners, but once again the existence of grey areas must be highlighted. We are not talking here about the wide and perfectly ordinary range of introverts/extraverts, intellectuals/artists, doers/thinkers. Many people will veer towards the avoiding end of the spectrum and others towards the clinging end without being especially unusual. For the true Avoider, the preservation of an unassailed interior life where they reside in solitary safety is absolutely essential. The Avoider cannot stand involvement with, or even sometimes recognition of, the partner's painful feelings. This is not because he or she *wishes* to be nasty and hurtful. They simply treat the other person's separate and independent world as the spider-phobic treats spiders. They *stay away*.

Should you fear you have committed either to a Clinger or an Avoider, do remind yourself that there are degrees of avoidance and degrees of clinging. In therapy, both parties can be enabled to see and take responsibility for their own tendencies. With the help, rather than the criticism, of their partners, it is also possible at least to broaden their mode of relating, just as it is possible for the suffering partner (the clung to, or the avoided one) to develop more tolerance of the other's tendencies.

Where there is a refusal to accept any responsibility, and/or a refusal to collaborate, you put up with it or leave. There is no denying that leaving can sometimes be the healthiest option. Sadly, some people cannot change. Some are too proud or too fearful to try.

The terms "Clinger" and "Avoider" are clumsy, especially as at various times we all need to cling or avoid. However, the rather extreme personalities to which I refer above have been described by several authors, although the descriptions do vary in the detail. For example, one of the famous early pioneers of marital therapy was Dr Michael Balint (1968), whose term for a Clinger was "Ocno-phile", and for the Avoider, "Philobat". I admire his work enor-mously, but find that I cannot deploy terms that seem to me to be pompous and inelegant. I trust that should you come across them, though, you will now have some idea of what they mean.

Because we are all a bit narcissistic, some degree of antipathy to the reality of *otherness* (not-me-ness) lies secreted in every marriage at the start. Where Norming proceeds satisfactorily, each partner comes gradually to cope with the inevitable disappointment at the other's shortcomings. By this is meant their inability—which at first feels like refusal—to become whatever it is we require of them (to be ever close at one end of the spectrum, or to leave our private inner world alone at the other). This acceptance of disillusion, the agreement to live and let live, if you like, is probably the most important Norm of all. If the partner cannot be loved "warts and all", *one's own impossible demands withdrawn*, the marriage will be torture for both, if it lasts at all.

Doing deals

At the Forming stage people consciously select a partner on the basis of what is in Robin Skynner's "shop window" (1983), but they also peek at what is in "the back room" (see Chapter Two). Whatever is hidden there becomes part of an unconscious "deal" that becomes more and more cemented as the Norming phase progresses. The deal itself becomes a Norm, its conditions and obligations assiduously observed without the parties ever being aware of it.

Edward and Lavinia in The Cocktail Party

I read T. S. Eliot's 1950s verse play of spiritual awakening when I was a young idealist in my twenties. I identified then with Celia, who, at the end of the play, attains sainthood. I read it again recently, and this time it was the less than saintly married couple who riveted my attention.

Among the people at Lavinia and Edward's cocktail party is the "Unidentified Guest", who delivers a spot of timely couple therapy, resulting in a dawning of self-knowledge in the pair. Their collapsing marriage (Lavinia had abandoned Edward just before the play opens, leaving him to cope alone with their guests) can now restart. Their childhood hurts cannot be undone, but the best can be made of a bad job.

The Unidentified Guest understands, long before they do, that Edward is a man who cannot love. Lavinia is a woman who believes no man can love her. They are a perfect match. As light begins to dawn, Lavinia says:

> "It seems to me that what we have in common
> Might be just enough to make us loathe one another" [Eliot, 1950, p. 123, Act II, ll. 382–383]

Reilly (the erstwhile Unidentified Guest) replies:

> "See it rather as the bond which holds you together.
> While still in a state of unenlightenment,
> *You* could always say: 'he could not love any woman;'
> *You* could always say: 'no man could love her.'
> You could accuse each other of your own faults,
> And so could avoid understanding each other.
> Now, you have only to reverse the propositions
> And put them together." [*ibid.*, ll. 384–391]

The longstanding Norm for this couple had been: "We will accuse each other of our own faults so as to feel blameless and badly treated ourselves."

Storming starts when Norms are challenged. Will Lavinia and Edward now learn to own their individual psychological make-up instead of attributing it to the other? Or will they loathe each other all the more now they have both been exposed? Will she stop asserting that "he cannot love" and begin to consider "maybe I am unlovable?" Will Edward cease to accuse his wife of coldness and commence an enquiry into his own inability to love? What has cemented this deal is their shared isolation. Will they learn to bear the distress of their isolation rather than blaming the other for it?

(Literary minded readers may like to know that James Fisher discusses this play and other T. S. Eliot works in his book *The Uninvited Guest* (1999). Several Shakespeare plays are also placed beneath his microscope, including *Othello* and *The Winter's Tale*. I especially liked *Much Ado About Nothing*, where he shows the drama's relevance to the internal parental couple.)

Hal and Heather

This couple came to therapy after Heather had hit Hal several times. They were struggling, but failing, to maintain their early Norms, which had been laid down too prematurely, almost as an emergency measure. Resilient Norms cannot be imposed, but need the time to organically develop.

Heather had been married twice before. Both times she had been verbally and physically abused. She had two much-loved children in their early teens. She was most anxious to protect them. She had sought on the internet a gentle, comfortably-off, cultured man, interviewed several, and married Hal after a three-month courtship.

Hal was an art expert who supplied stately homes and conferences with pictures. He relied on his genteel, public-school background and his golfing friends to provide him with work, admitting he was useless at "putting himself about". He shuddered at the words "marketing" or "networking". Accounting was not his forte, either; he employed others to keep the books. He had managed to earn a reasonable living in this way for years. He had been engaged twice, but the fiancées had pulled out at the last minute.

Heather ran her own Life Coaching agency. On marriage to Hal, she set about improving his business too, by improving him. He felt a bit ashamed, but was glad of the help, as his business affairs were really in rather a muddle. She drummed up much more trade for him, hosted elegant parties, and computerized all his records and financial dealings.

All went well for the first few months. Hal cherished Heather, was grateful for all she did. Heather, and her son and daughter, all thrived on Hal's kindness, appreciative of his gentleness after their former family experiences.

Then Hal's much-loved sister was diagnosed with terminal cancer. His best friend died in the same year. He carried on working and socializing, but at home was morose and withdrawn for months on end.

At first Heather stepped up her part in his business, on top of her own full-time job. After a while she grew irritable, restless, and critical of him. He seemed so wrapped up in himself, leaving more and more of the work to her. He would promise to visit a prospective client and forget. He would turn up late or cancel important meetings that cost him thousands of pounds a time. Heather took him to a psychiatrist, who said he was depressed and prescribed drugs that had no effect. She begged him to try another drug, and another, until he found one that suited, but eventually he stopped taking them at all. Finally, he refused all further treatment.

Heather was exasperated, Hal apathetic. The one-sided rows started. Heather raged at Hal to stop feeling sorry for himself, get off his behind, and rescue his business. He adopted a *mea culpa* attitude that only made Heather's fury worse. He dragged himself to work, tried to do better, but repeatedly failed to attain even the standard achieved before he met Heather.

Heather now ran everything: shopping, cooking, the two businesses. She resented it mightily and continued to rant at Hal, who looked sheepish and contrite but never actually managed to *do* much. Heather had secretly hoped they could earn a lot in a short time and then retire to live in comfort for their remaining lives. Hal had let her down badly, destroyed her dream.

Hal started to drink wine at his club, and came home late and dopey, which incensed Heather even more. She was working all hours while he got drunk. At this point she began to physically strike him "in an attempt to get through to the blockhead". He stood like a statue, leaving her to get on with it, until she wore herself out and dissolved into tears.

The original deal, as far as Heather was concerned, was that Hal would rescue her from her abusive past, heal the wounds of her previous marriages, and so avoid any need for mourning and self-examination. In exchange she would "train" Hal to get his life in order, "make a man of him". Finding that this might be a life-long endeavour, and his much-idealized gentleness also went with weakness and lack of resolve, her bitterness knew no bounds. She had been betrayed again.

Hal had required of Heather that she organize and tidy up his life, providing the excitement, colour, and risk-taking he dare not seek for himself. But, along with her energy and talents, came her need to dominate and control, to have everything done her way and in her time (like the aunt who had brought him up, and the strict school he had attended).

Hal's resentment was never allowed into consciousness; indeed, he seemed eager to accept all the blame. His depression was real enough, but there was gain for him in prolonging it. He hid his angry refusal to cooperate with his wife behind illness. His almost total inertia so infuriated her that she was rendered unable to sympathize with the genuine grief. This increased his loneliness and made the grief over his dead sister harder to recover from. But it also served the purpose of enraging and rejecting Heather without his having to even raise his voice.

The deal had broken down. Both were terribly aggrieved and disappointed.

To her dismay and horror, Heather felt that now she was proved no better than her former abusers.

In fact, she was expressing Hal's denied rage at *her*. At the same time, Hal carried all *her* denied sadness and grief about her two ghastly earlier attempts at marriage in *his* depression. *This was the real deal beneath the apparent deal: each would bear something intolerable for the other.*

Some limited understanding was reached after many months, but in the end Hal could no longer bear his misery, nor Heather her uncontrollable violence (which she never felt anywhere else but with Hal). They divorced soon after.

The Norm eventually established, of giving to each other what they themselves could not countenance (Hal his violence, Heather her depression), was an unconscious attempt at healing wounds in the self through the other. But the cure, as is sadly sometimes the case, proved worse than the disease.

CHAPTER NINE

The couple's life cycle. The early years: Storming and Performing

Storming is to couple development what adolescence is to an individual's development. It is a time following a fairly quiet period, when all seems to be thrown into the melting pot again. The couple, like the teenage individual, struggle to redefine their shared identity out of all that has gone before, and struggle with the new opportunities surrounding them now. It is a time for rebellion and asserting one's rights within the marriage, but also a time when past joint difficulties and lost chances can be put right or made up for. It is a time of much turbulence, be this expressed in loud disagreement, quiet rebellion, or vague statements of dissatisfaction.

There may be attempts by one to modify, or even drastically alter, the Norms by now taken for granted, while the other resists any change. Where there is a flexible couple boundary that can accommodate newly emerging needs, the pair may constructively fight for fresh or adjusted Norms, giving the marriage a much-needed boost.

Once the couple has Formed, then Normed (however satisfactorily or incompletely), it is as if energy runs out and the couple need a bit of a rest before the next spurt of growth—"the calm before the Storm"? All this work has taken months, more often years, and sometimes never got established at all. In such cases, the couple system lacked the resources for the work from the beginning. The pair either break up, or they just drift along in a parallel but scarcely intimate existence. The system stagnates.

If clinical experience is anything to go by, I would suggest that usually Norms are more or less settled after five or six years. This will be sooner in the case of two well-balanced persons with little personal "baggage". You will no doubt make up your own mind whether pronounced Storming in marriage, with the deepening of bonds afterwards, is preferable to a stable union, where the occasional squall is all there is to worry about. As with financial investment, high risk can mean high rewards or bankruptcy. Low risk guarantees protection from that, but the return is hardly exciting.

Meanwhile, children may have come along, careers been established, disasters—personal, financial, medical—weathered. In-laws, ex-partners, and step-children have been absorbed into the system.

Different couples react differently to this calm, pre-storming period. Some feel a deep peace, and wish it to go on forever, whereas others soon become restless and seek change. The request for therapy often arises when one partner has begun to "Storm" and the other remains content with stability. The happy partner cannot understand what all the fuss is about. When it becomes evident all is not well, they either panic or retreat into incomprehension, blaming the other for spoiling things. Inevitably, rows or sulks ensue.

Although only one partner may actually express disquiet, they frequently speak for the couple as a whole. In most marriages one partner is more tuned in to latent processes between the pair than the other. Sensing a slow widening of distance, this partner may become lonely and eventually depressed. The disharmony (the non-depressed one claiming "you're just no fun any more") is then blamed on the illness, rather than the inability or unwillingness of the "well" one to "hear" the sad one's plea for a review of things.

A wife who feels angry and rejected may attempt to have it out with her husband, who sees only criticizing and controlling behaviour. He disappears to the pub, making her feel even more rejected. In fact, his incapacity to meet his wife's needs may have much to do with health or work worries that he cannot, or dare not, discuss with her. But why dare he not talk to her? He ought to be able to, if the marriage has been satisfactory for some time. It appears, then, that both are growing restive. One reacts to this by "nagging", the other by avoiding conflict through absenting himself. Storming itself is a perfectly ordinary developmental stage in every marriage, but to work it out there has to be communication, communication, communication. This couple are not communicating.

When discontent is more than a passing mood, or sign of temporary personal stress, it needs to be aired properly, early on. Many, especially, but not exclusively, men, find it hard to "whinge", leave it far too late, and defensiveness, even bitterness, can set in for the other party.

Sensing a gulf opening between them, one spouse at first enquires as to the reason. Unfortunately, they are brushed aside, confirming their fears about loss of closeness. The partner who cannot speak often then *enacts* their unhappiness instead of putting it into words. Alcohol abuse, overworking, affairs, anxiety, and short tempers can be symptomatic of marital discord that could have been avoided, or at least reduced and better managed, if tackled earlier. Yet so many couples still subscribe to the absurd view that if you ignore problems they will go away, or so they hope. Others ignore them for fear that naming them would expose all manner of other "worms in the woodwork", or that, if named, the unwanted problem will have to be faced. Too right!

Often both parties become gradually aware of a gnawing discontent rather than a particular problem or complaint about the other. This can be traced to boredom and disappointment. The marriage has become predictable, repetitive, lacking novelty or even the time for novelty. Routine and responsibility—kids, mortgage, promotion, the car, the school, the garage conversion, fills every hour. It is easy to be stressed and bored at the same time. Bed is now for sleeping rather than sex and pillow talk.

An affair is common at this time (it used to be called "the seven-year itch"), or one partner may take up something very new in the way of hobbies or studies. Commencing a dancing class, going to the gym, or building a racing car may be commendable attempts to brighten up one's life, but if it is the *marriage* rather than one individual that is becoming dull, these activities may indicate that the restless partner, whether they realize it or not, is moving away from the marriage, not trying to improve it.

Why was it not possible to bring the matter into the open, and with good humour to *jointly* set about enlivening the marriage? The same activities may then be taken up, but from a different viewpoint. The couple may agree that they do not have enough separate hobbies to make them interesting to each other, or they may choose to pursue a new activity together. It does not matter. It's not *what* you do, but *why* you are doing it that counts, and also how conscious or otherwise both partners are of the underlying currents between them.

The first indication that Storming has begun may be when someone repeatedly asks themselves: "Is this all there is?" They have married, maybe even reproduced, bought the car. They are on the housing ladder and prospects for promotion or business success are good. They should be feeling great. But they feel lost: they've done everything by the time they are twenty-nine!

Others of the same age may feel burdened by duties and responsibilities for their families, which they are managing perfectly well. But again they ask, "What is all this *for*? A treadmill of bills, going to the office, carting the kids to ballet and football. Fifty more years of *this* to live through?" It feels like purgatory, yet they know it was once all they longed for. They have done well, accomplished all they set out to do, and yet their life stretches ahead, full of more and more of the same. Trapped. They feel they must rebel, or disappear.

The Peter Pan syndrome is almost the opposite of this. A couple have enjoyed a heady few years together, full of parties, travel, and joint projects. In short, they have more or less done as they pleased. One starts to get broody, despite having truthfully claimed in the Norming phase that children were not on the agenda. The same one begins to feel the need for roots, a proper home, committed friendships. Peter Pan is growing up. The other one isn't. If a split is to be averted, one needs edging forward, the other holding back. Can they work this out between them? Or will Peter Pan be shamed and shouted at for being immature, while the other one is accused of welching on agreements, changing their mind. How dare they grow up? It was never part of the deal.

Again, the critical issue here is self-awareness versus deadly blame. As people mature their aspirations can change. No one is right or wrong. If the dissatisfied person can be honest with *them-selves* about their wish to revolt, take full responsibility for it, then discussion with the other party becomes possible. Sadly, many refuse to acknowledge how low they feel, or how guilty about "rocking the boat". This is particularly so when, on the face of it, they have nothing to complain about. They may convince themselves that it is the other partner who is lagging behind, or is at fault. Once mutual blame sets in, rows follow. The discontented person may be the sort who does not wish to grow up, or the kind who is fed up with already being old and bored. In both cases, the danger lies in denying to themselves that they really are suffering these bad feelings. Avoidance renders them susceptible to all manner of distractions, many potentially injurious to the couple system.

If the problem is shared with a partner who can see these doubts are not personal criticisms of them, then steps can be taken. Even if the current domestic, financial, or professional situation prevents big changes, small ones can be made, and bigger ones planned for in the future. *Being understood* by the spouse itself eases the trap, for the secret is out, but it has not produced the feared catastrophe of blame, humiliation, abandonment, or revenge. Attitudes can soften on both sides once there is a shared formulation of what is really "up".

Another common feature is *stormy* Storming, more and more frequent quarrels without any real trigger, and without any satisfactory resolution or making up. This is disturbing and painful when the Norm so far has been to talk out disagreements and negotiate compromises. Something has obviously changed; it never used to be like this.

But what has changed? Is one or both less *committed*? Has the accepted *power balance* shifted? Is one party struggling for more or less *distance* even though that old chestnut was supposed to have been dealt with years ago? Or has the *deal* hinted at during the Forming stage and struck properly, if unconsciously, at the Norming stage, become redundant? If any one of these has altered, then all the others will be affected to some degree. When Norms are destabilized no one can be sure of anything. The goalposts have moved. This accounts for the non-resolution of the quarrels. Nothing is what it used to be, so old, automatic strategies and procedures no longer work.

Natasha and Norman

Natasha was pretty in a pale, fragile sort of way. Norman was built like a rugby player with dark eyes full of mischief. They had been legally married for six and a half years and had two children under five whom they both adored. Natasha ran an animal sanctuary and Norman was a successful IT salesman.

Norman insisted on "seeing somebody" when Natasha began her "three-day crying jags" every time there was a quarrel. He felt obliged to shut up as soon as the hankie came out. Eventually he sought to refrain from bringing up contentious issues at all, but this resulted in their scarcely speaking to each other for weeks. His main complaint was her increasing coldness toward him, for which there seemed no rational explanation, though he kept begging for one. Her riposte was always "not in front of the children" and by bedtime she was too tired to talk and certainly not interested in sex. But they still shared a bed.

The neutral territory of the consulting room allowed Natasha to put her side forward. He was only being nice to her now because she was thinking about leaving: he knew she was only currently staying for the sake of the children. There was no point in this therapy. As soon as she capitulated he would be back to his old tricks, which seemed to consist of taking her for granted and ignoring her at social occasions.

Natasha's word "capitulation" made clear there was a big battle for *power* here. In terms of *distance* Natasha had certainly moved away from Norman. She was adamant about sticking to her new position, though she was clearly as miserable as he was desperate. The Norm of her giving in to him for the sake of domestic peace (her parents rowed bitterly and then divorced) had vanished. She had started literally to walk away from quarrels, then dab her moist eyes for the rest of the day and weep again in bed. This regime successfully evaded any need for surrender, while leaving her husband powerless. If she then refused closeness when he tried to make up, he could be brought to the edge of panic. Holding all the cards for a change gave her no joy, though. His public behaviour improved, but to maintain this progress she had to keep him so frightened by her aloofness he would do anything to please. In getting rid of his bullying, at home and in public, she had also lost his company and loving attention—the good bits of their relationship.

Under his tough exterior, Norman was very insecure. He became exasperated, angry, and confused, as well as scared. He hated the new status of beggar, yet he would do anything to win her back. Natasha dare not remember her former love for her husband for fear of yielding to his promises to reform and then being taken for granted again.

So what about their *deal*? Natasha married Norman because she needed and wanted protection. She longed for children and a united happy family of her own, totally opposite to the one in which she grew up. Norman was the youngest of eleven boys. After him, his parents gave up trying for a girl. It is easy to see that he was bound to grow up unhappy with his maleness, feeling unwanted and superfluous. Norman longed for a beautiful, *female* baby doll (a gift to his parents who would then *have* to love him?). He would cherish and protect her; but also control, possess, and bully her.

The *deal*, as far as Norman was concerned, went like this: "I will protect you, which will make me feel big, strong, wanted. But I am also vulnerable and scared: you must let me in, reassure me with constant closeness". Natasha's offer (see Chapter Three, "Partner-seeking as job application") was: "Yes, I will make you feel big, very big. Because that really suits me. You will protect me from having to grow up and fight my own way through life".

The underside of this deal, though, was that Natasha had to put up with being dominated and undermined. She could not bear conflict, would feel physically sick as soon as the decibel level went up. She feared terribly for the children in case she foisted on them what she'd had to endure at their age. So she never complained when bossed about or embarrassed in public. Norman had no idea he was a bully and thought his social persona was just being "the life and soul of the party". Until the weeping fits, he had been blissfully happy with his marriage.

Natasha arrived in the marriage disempowered and remained disempowered. The need for therapeutic help came about because she had gradually realized that very fact. She'd had enough (even though she had asked for it). But she had no idea how to retaliate without incurring the conflict situation so reminiscent of her parents. Her solution was to freeze her feelings as she froze out her husband, whom she saw as the cause of all her problems.

The deal was off. Natasha would no longer make Norman feel big by allowing him to treat her as small.

Norman and Natasha were both lovees (see Chapter Three), believing the ideal partner to be one who would love them in exactly the way they wanted to be loved. It never occurred to either that every deal has a shadow deal. The shadow of Norman's genuinely protective love was his bossiness and humiliating public rudeness. Beneath Natasha's delicate appearance and submissive behaviour was a woman of sterner stuff. Once her lovee requirements were met, she'd hoped she would find peace. But her husband's unwitting bullying dragged to the surface the buried accumulated outrage at her parents' bullying. Having realized she could manage on her own if she had to, her double dose of anger overcame her fear of independence and she rebelled.

Natasha had all the power now, but did not know what to do with it. Despite her rebellion she still loved Norman, though for the moment she dare not let herself know or feel this. I am glad to say that in time (quite a long time) both learned to be less of a lovee and more of a lover.

In the following case, it was the withdrawing of *commitment* that appeared to be the cause of couple breakdown. In fact the commitment was withdrawn only because the original *deal* was no longer working for the other partner, who, like Natasha, had the temerity to try to change things.

Vera and Virginia

Vera and Virginia met at a charity conference. They had lived together happily for some eight years before tensions and arguments took over their normally peaceable lives.

Virginia was well known on the charity scene, a formidable and tireless campaigner, always giving lectures, writing pamphlets, and talking on the radio. Vera was her amanuensis, indispensable, loyal to a fault, honoured and grateful to be of service, both to the charity and to Virginia. She did all the secretarial work, and wrote the speeches. Both women worked long hours, unflinchingly supporting one another in their different roles.

Vera was adopted. She had no idea why she had been abandoned in the first place. Then her adoptive mother gave up on her or was ill—she was never quite sure which. She was put into foster care at three, and again at six. She could remember hardly any of her childhood except the terrible loneliness. However, she excelled at school. Her reading was voracious and her skill with several languages quite remarkable. She gave up a good but boring job to become Virginia's full-time but unpaid assistant.

Towards the end of the seventh year, Vera started having dreams, rather pleasant dreams, in fact. Before, she never remembered any dreams at all. She dreamt now of elegant parties, becoming famous, exotic travels, not as Virginia's companion but in her own right. When the dreams stopped, her mood lowered and she found herself growing irritable.

She tentatively suggested they go out more, meet people other than charity folk, have a bit of fun before it was too late. Each time the subject was raised Virginia changed it to something work related, or would look annoyed and say, "Later, later."

Meanwhile, Virginia's work expanded. She had to take on extra clerical help. Naturally, she chose a beneficiary of one of her charities, who soon became as dedicated to her as Vera had.

Vera started to show signs of jealousy, which she felt forced to suppress so as to avoid Virginia's scorn. Instead, she planned surprises—days out, special meals, flowers. Always Virginia reacted with coolness, but Vera hoped she was secretly pleased.

Eventually she began to realize that Virginia hated having to receive gifts of any kind. Virginia could only give, not take. She thrived on gratitude, even worship. But Vera loved her still, it made no difference. She devoted all her efforts to pleasing Virginia, but the more she tried the more she failed. If she dared to ask for more time with Virginia or to do something together outside of work, she would again be dismissed with the excuse that there was no time. Increasingly she would come to her workstation, where they normally had an early morning cuppa together, to find the clerk ensconced with Virginia, taking dictation. Soon Vera was taking her tea alone.

One day Virginia told Vera that it was time she went her own way. She, Virginia, would not hold her back. What Vera needed was to be more independent, meet new people, have a life of her own. Virginia was proud that she had paved the way for Vera's liberation and she would keep a keen eye on her progress. Virginia was sure that with her resourcefulness, Vera could find a nice place to live within a month.

Virginia did not know how to grow. Her partners were all subject to the same *deal*; that they should live out the role of a charity case so she could feel secure in her own person, *a person who tirelessly gave*. From the moment Vera could no longer oblige, and wanted a more reciprocal adult to adult relationship, rather than a mother–child one, she became redundant.

Vera wanted to renegotiate their old deal (many marriages do this successfully many times) but Virginia could never agree. As far as she was concerned, the problems were all Vera's. She was selfish, moody, and possessive. She had lost her ideals.

I am sure that I seem as unsympathetic to Virginia as I felt at the time. For I never met her; Vera came to see me after a suicide bid. All the same, I am certain that if we knew more about Virginia's background, her seemingly cruel behaviour and self-delusion would make sense.

What about the Storming stage with a Clinger and an Avoider (see Chapter Eight). Greta and Gavin (below) illustrate this, though Gavin was able to slowly progress in the end.

Greta and Gavin

This couple had been cohabiting for nearly five years when they came to therapy. Greta wanted Gavin to propose marriage now they had been together a longish time, but he wavered. Greta feared he lacked commitment. Gavin had left his wife for Greta, though there were problems before she arrived on the scene. He was reluctant to face another possible break-up. Both their stances seemed understandable.

Greta's other complaint was Gavin's addiction to pornography on the internet. She had never refused him sexually, so why should he do this? She had even tried watching it with him, so as to please and excite him, but she felt he never really wanted her there. He never actually refused her admittance to his study, but then, he was a wonderful, understanding, gentle man, who never raised his voice or engineered ugly rows. That was why she loved him so.

After the initial joint consultation it is my custom to see each partner separately as part of the assessment process. Gavin came first. He painted a picture of Greta as a very insecure, controlling woman who covered this with all-consuming maternal concern. Despite her full time PA job, Greta spent hours ironing his shirts (that she had chosen) and preparing special food even when she knew he was dining with clients at lunchtime and would need only a snack. She told him about her day in endless detail when he came home, before running his bath. During the working day she would text, e-mail or phone several times. "I am never allowed to escape, not for a minute."

When I asked what the attraction was, he blushed and said sex. He had never had much confidence in that department, and she was as conscientious about sex as she was about ironing his shirts. She taught him all she knew. She always offered so he did not have to risk rejection. She wore expensive underwear, garters and such, and laid before him all the sexual variations she could think of.

Did he love her? After five years he still did not know, hence his inability to propose. He knew he could not leave her though.

As to the pornography, he regretted having to do this, but it was the only thing that soothed him when he'd had a bad day (He sold insurance packages to large firms and could make or lose a lot of money in one day.) True, it was useless when Greta tried to join in, but he had never been able to face conflict situations so he just went along with her.

Gavin, an only child, had loved his folks; but his mother smothered him with love, as possessive in her way as Greta. As a result, he spent much time in his room or in the garden shed, or hiding down at his gran's. His father suffered from serious asthma and was permanently off sick, the household organized around his medication, his attacks, and his need for a dust-free zone. Gavin felt he could never relax, must always be "on duty" for his parents, and certainly never cause a domestic disturbance!

Greta came from a large family—indeed, had never really left them. At Christmas and on family visits they treated Gavin perfectly politely, but he felt left out. He called them the Mafia. He felt Greta used him as a substitute for her brothers and her beloved father when they were not available. He said this thought was ridiculous, but I believe he was absolutely right.

In many respects Greta was the perfect candidate to meet the requirements of an Avoider like Gavin. Gavin could not own his penis for fear it would bring to him unwanted intimacy and intrusion; in other words, a demand for relationship. Yet he loved the soothing and releasing experience of orgasm, as well as the rare feeling of personal power when he had a woman under or on top of him who would do anything he asked.

So he gave his organ to Greta, and let her take all the responsibility for orchestrating the when and how of their lovemaking (if it could be called such!). She was skilled enough to make him feel he had been the dominant partner, a real man. She knew that such a gift would bind him to her tightly. He could never manage sex on his own with an "ordinary" woman: he would always need her, Greta. She had bargained without competition from the internet, however, and this really alarmed her.

When they had sex Gavin never fantasized. He left even that to her. She would enact sexy little stories, naughty chambermaids with feather dusters and such, and tell him what to do. Gavin's need for pornography was a need to have fantasy provided for him where he could manufacture none of his own. I wondered if, as a child, his mother was so invasive that he feared she could read his mind, and accordingly banished all sexual fantasy for good.

Neither Greta nor Gavin were engaged in intimate relating. They were utterly dependent on each other, addicted to the safety each provided for the other. Yet each lived in a world of their own. Both were relating *narcissistically*. In borrowing his penis and doing his man's job for him, she "left him alone", sparing him from emotional involvement with an *other* that he would have experienced as engulfment. In servicing his needs this way, she also ensured his unswerving loyalty. What other woman could or would do this for him? He would be there for her forever, like her family. Like ivy, Greta the Clinger could feed from and off him indefinitely. She would never have to be a separate person.

Their *deal* would have worked had Greta's over-solicitousness not driven Gavin nearly mad with fear. His terror was that she would not only take over his penis, but, like his mother, she would take him over body and soul, eat him alive, as he feared his mother had swallowed up his father. (Merely taking over his penis suited him, for she always gave it back, pretending she had never taken it in the first place.)

The arrangement was not working for Greta because Gavin was so averse to being controlled, that she feared he might one day find the courage to abandon her. After five years he was beginning to switch off his mobile phone; he even "lost" it once. And once it was allegedly stolen. Now he was spending more and more time "on the computer", locking the door "to keep the dogs out". Keep her out, more like!

No, their deal was not operating smoothly enough. In its quiet way (for they never shouted at each other) Storming had arrived.

Just a footnote: Greta went on insisting that marriage would solve their problems. Gavin went into individual therapy with someone I recommended. He stayed with Greta a further five years, during which time he became more able to verbalize his concerns with her rather than resorting to his study and his pornorgraphy habit. In therapy he came to terms with the kind of empty person he had always been. He started trying to make proper relationships for the first time. In their tenth year he left Greta. From the outset Greta declined the offer of separate help for herself.

Comments on the couple stories

You will have noted from these three examples that Virginia and Vera's couple system was the container–contained variety. The only way Virginia could herself feel contained (emotionally safe) was by containing others. When Vera disturbed this balance by asking for new conditions, Virginia's commitment withered.

Gavin and Greta were a cricket ball couple. For ten years they went to parties together, hosted Christmas for both their families, did their duty by nephews and nieces, to all intents and purposes a long-wedded couple. They had regular sex, decorated their home, and bought the latest DVDs. Greta ensured there was always something to talk about, and to do. They stuck it out for ten full, busy years, but with very little real communication or intimate union. What glued the walls of the cricket ball together was Greta's need to cling plus her preparedness to supply Gavin with his "drug", and Gavin's need to avoid while depending on her for his supply of orgasmic relief.

Natasha and Norman went through a very distressing time indeed while sorting out their Storming phase. They almost split up several times. But they shared a flexible system that was elastic enough to withstand all manner of pushing and pulling as they learned to fight through their respective agendas. Finally, they stood together with their children at the centre of their refreshed family system that now looked as smooth and spherical as a healthy balloon (see Figure 12).

Performing

Most people who are unhappy with their own marriages imagine all others to be "performing" well, all the time. Nothing could be further from the truth. Attaining the stage of true Performing deserves a marital Oscar. The hard work, angst, negotiating, fighting, and *waiting* that goes into achieving it is incredible.

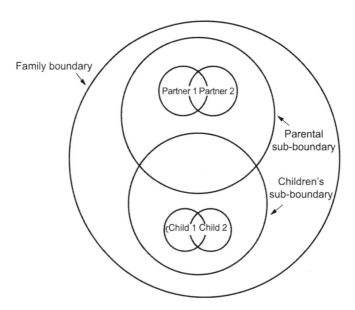

Figure 12. Stable family system.

Performing is that happy and fulfilled time in a marriage where the system and the components (partners) within it are operating at their maximum potential. Distance is comfortable, power distributed amicably and ungrudgingly. Norms are automatically relied on rather than questioned. Boundaries are firm, but able to yield appropriately to internal and external day-to-day stresses. The two partners have separate lives, interests, and characters, but their joint personality grows stronger each day, as does their love and regard for one another.

This is the kind of marriage all right-thinking people would like to offer their children, but it is a counsel of perfection. Aim for it by all means. Should you achieve it intermittently you have done very well. But for heaven's sake accept that you are no saint. The perfect parents and the perfect marriage have yet to be invented. You can only do your best, and struggle on. If they love you and you them, the children (and your partner!) will in the end forgive. As one day their children will have to forgive them.

During the Performing stage, the happy realization that there is no need to "work at things" leaves time and energy to take pleasure and pride in the children, the holidays, the social occasions, the job, the hobbies, the keeping fit—all those matters than can so easily become tiresome chores, or resented obligations, in a marriage that is stuck in some earlier phase. For once the system looks after itself. There is no need for "deep talk".

CHAPTER TEN

The couple's life cycle. The later period: middle years and beyond

Middle years

The couple as joint personality (or shared living system, if you prefer) goes through a mid-life crisis just like any individual. "Crisis" derives from the Greek *krisis*, meaning decision. It has come to be associated with wars, emergencies, or illness. I prefer to see it in the couple context as a crossroads, a time of decision-making that will influence the rest of the marriage's life span. It does not *necessarily* result from a major problem or sudden drama; rather that the couple have travelled a long, long road together, but now have reached a junction. As a unit they must decide, explicitly or implicitly, whether to go forward into new territory, back to familiar ground, or branch off, jointly or separately, in some new direction. Or they might decide to stop, pitch a tent, and, for the time that remains, pleasurably watch the world go by. Letting fate take this decision is extremely risky.

Even if things are ticking over comfortably and there are no external pressures on the couple, there is a growing sensation inside and/or between them, spoken or not, of either stagnation or restlessness. They have long since achieved marital maturity (done their Forming, Norming, Storming and Performing). They have possibly finished child rearing and gone as far as is possible in their separate or shared careers. What is left for the couple to do now? "Out to grass?" (Depressing.) Change everything now we are free? (Scary.) Consolidate the security we have built, or spend all, living to the hilt while there is still time? Focus our attention on the community? On our spiritual life? Take a course of study? These are big questions. The biggest is whether subsequent plans are to include both partners or not. If they have differing designs for the future, can they still survive as a couple while pursuing different paths?

No wonder many pairs try to ignore this stage. It is so much easier to drift.

They will adopt their time-honoured methods of coping with relationship issues—putting their joint head firmly in the sand, perhaps; talking it out hopefully; *enacting* the discontent by drinking, say, or having an affair. Or they will convert unacknowledged mid-life anxiety into physical symptoms—depression, panic attacks, fatigue syndrome, hypochondriasis. In therapy it is not usually the crisis *per se* that requires intervention, but the couple's way of handling (or avoiding) it. The mid-life crisis comes to all couples in one form or another. It is not in itself worrying. It is merely a stage of development, a bit perturbing maybe, but also an opportunity for review and forward planning, the commencement of a new life chapter. What matters is whether the joint crisis beneath each other's behaviour at this time is recognized by both for what it is, and whether they can collaboratively discuss their future.

It is important to remember that we are not talking here about two separate middle-aged persons, but the living organism that is the marriage arriving at the crossroads of its life. If a couple set up home in their twenties, their relationship is in its "middle age" in their forties. If we are referring to a second or third marriage, which began in the couple's fifties, the couple's mid-life period will not arrive until they are in their seventies. And what about couples where one partner is twenty years older or younger than the other?

Selena and Sandy

Sandy is a sixty-year-old solicitor's clerk. His wife Selena is forty-two, a cancer nurse. The couple have brought up two daughters now in their mid teens. They have been legally married for twenty years. Their fairly uneventful, seemingly contented marriage has now reached its middle years.

To understand their relationship's mid-life crisis, we will look a little closer at the couple's backgrounds. Selena's father died in a motorway crash when she was thirteen. Her mother became withdrawn and moody, never really functioning properly after her adored husband's demise. Selena took over the role of mum to her several brothers and sisters. In effect, she kept the family together, both practically and emotionally.

Until the couple's mid-life crisis erupted, Selena continued to operate like the pre-adolescent she had been when she lost her father. From a developmental point of view, Selena had not been able to afford *progression* to adolescence proper. Fighting for her independence, experimenting with her own values, defining her own identity in the face of disapproval, had not been options. She bypassed the adolescent phase altogether. As we shall see, this stuckness dovetailed nicely with Sandy's requirements, so at first they were a comfortable fit.

Sandy was the much loved, protected only child of a war widow. He had never had a girlfriend before Selena, whom he met at church. Their courtship was gentle, protracted, and conventional. Only when his mother became terminally ill did it occur to Sandy to propose. He had never properly separated from his mother. The deal must have been that Selena, perfectly groomed for the job by her own family, should carry on where mother left off.

If Selena was still operating as a pre-adolescent, Sandy could be described as a toddler still. This in no way implies criticism. We are merely attempting to clarify how people get stuck at various stages of natural development while the rest of their personality continues to grow. Both these adults were, on the face of it, well-balanced, well-educated, decent folk. All the same, neither of them had reached anywhere near mid-life *individual* development. Neither had even approached adolescence. But, chronologically, the *marriage* had entered its middle years, with all the associated "big questions" begging for answer.

Unlike their mum, Selena's two daughters had no trouble at all in claiming their adolescent rights. Weird music, even weirder clothes, loads of boyfriends, rebellion galore, became the norm in this erstwhile quiet, respectable household. Sandy was horrified, retired to his study with the newspaper and his briefcase. Selena, to her astonishment, grew more and more curious about, then envious of, the girls' fun, and even their tears. At least they were really living, she felt. She started to dress fashionably and listen to their music. All the longings that had had to be suppressed when she was thirteen had returned with a vengeance. Her restlessness knew no bounds.

Eventually, the couple came for a brief period of therapy, after which Selena was referred to her own therapist. Sandy was unwilling to continue with "all this navel gazing" and withdrew. In that short time, Selena tried to help Sandy liven up a bit, but he still wanted the original deal and was angry about her need for change. They divorced three years later.

Selena's individual therapy helped her understand and accept responsibility for her choice of partner, rather than blaming him later for being boring. Her original *unconscious* demand had been that he should replace the father she lost, while supporting her identity as carer–mum, the only job in which she felt confident. Sandy's demand was that Selena cosset him, as did his mother, without him having to face the world on his own. In marriage e*ach would protect the other from having to progress to the next developmental stage.* He was stuck at two or three years old, unable to let go of mother. She was stuck at puberty, unable to move into adolescence proper.

By the time the marriage came to its mid-life period, Selena was seeing in her daughters all she missed out on in her own youth. Until now it had never occurred to her that she had been deprived of anything. She felt desperate to make up for lost time. She also recognized that Sandy's impending retirement and dependence on her really threatened any growth on her part. She came to couple therapy feeling panicky, trapped, and guilty about hating her husband.

Sandy was bewildered and very, very angry with what felt like a betrayal. (From the perspective of their unconscious pact, it was indeed a betrayal.) Sandy had not the faintest idea how to recognize anger in himself, let alone express it: mum had made sure there was no reason for him to ever rage at her. He coped with disowned rage by claiming his wife had inexplicably gone batty. He wanted me to make her revert to her former self, to "see sense". Impossible, since Selena craved change while Sandy wanted protection from it. Sandy could only stay if Selena stopped changing. Selena could only stay if Sandy tried to change, but he had no wish to. No one's fault. Just an everyday tragedy.

The couple's mid-life period is different to the Storming phase, even though both represent a chance to rework the basic emotional conditions on which the relationship is based. Storming feels like a second chance; mid-life feels like the last chance. The stakes are higher, for, as we have seen with Sandy and Selena, the choice *has* to be taken at the crossroads, even if it results in heartbreak or divorce.

Between the couples who come for therapy at this stage, there is almost always a painful tension between one individual's needs for fulfilment or self-expression and the demands and pressures of the marriage, or marital partner, which prohibit this. This goes much, much deeper than a selfish desire to do what one wants irrespective of the other's needs. Over the years, the human personality seems biologically programmed to go on developing indefinitely. While marriage serves the purpose of perpetuating the species, for a time it also slows or diverts this natural tendency to fulfil *individual* potential. As child-rearing responsibilities disappear, the drive towards separate self-determination returns stronger than before. This is especially so if the person has rushed, or been pushed into, serious commitment/family raising before having fully established themselves as a single adult.

Perhaps the man or woman yearns for the early romantic years, before the stresses and strains of child rearing and/or career put paid to wine and roses. At last they can try to recapture them. But what if the other one longs to go trekking on their own in the Himalayas, before that old rugger/hockey injury ensures that the knees give out?

Such ambitions are more than mere pleasure seeking or time fillers. They represent a longing to rediscover, explore further, one's personal and separate identity, without the drain or dilution of other identities, roles, and obligations—parent, consort, breadwinner, professional, *partner*. Time is short and bodies wear out, so there is much now-or-never motivation to get unfulfilled ambitions satisfied. This is more than greed or sensation-hunger. It is what

Jung (1934) called "individuation", a striving toward all that is possible in oneself, achieving one's full potential. It is a process of "becoming", which, if blocked or ignored, makes the subject feel only half alive.

The marriage, too, can grow lifeless long before it has accomplished everything of which it is capable should the partners—through laziness or fear—conspire to disregard this phase of their relationship.

On reaching middle age, many people are drawn to spiritual matters. They find themselves investigating philosophical or mystical ideas. Those who are already religious may set out to uncover the true nature of their God, who till now had been the God of their childhood, exactly as their parents and church had described them. Some change religion, feeling other faiths have a better understanding of the world. Others take a different journey to find a meaning to their lives—through art, landscape, or literature. "Meaning", to some, only has value in a social or political context. They offer their services to the community or to charity. Dedication to such projects often results in jealousy or feelings of neglect in the partner.

All these methods of individuation are healthy, wholesome developments in the human life cycle, but when one partner's mid-life agenda for the marriage conflicts with the other's it can prove very inconvenient! The deserted wife or husband finds it very hard to view the Himalayan trek as more than an escape, a spree, or a self-centred attempt at proving something. Can it really be an odyssey into the most private self, an exploration through Nature of one's very soul? Is it truly a long deferred attempt at communion with, and a wish to give thanks for, the planet that has sustained the partner? Is this trek psychologically necessary to him or her?

The answer is yes. Melancholia in mid-life is extremely common, and is almost always bound up with frustrated hopes and a sense of wasted time and opportunity. We all need to make sense of our lives, find meaning in it, if we are to stay psychologically well.

You can love someone all your adult life and not fully know them until they start getting restless or withdrawn in mid-life, and in the mid-life of your marriage to them. They are unable to tell you what is wrong because very often *they do not know themselves*. Couple living does require a certain amount of hiding away one's true (or least developed) self for the sake of peace. A reclaiming process occurs in more mature years, as various superfluous identities can now be cast off. The last, till now embryonic, identity clamours to manifest itself.

If the partners are themselves in mid-life, and the marriage too is in mid-life, then this sense of needing to grab last chances before it is too late is intensified, leading often to dramatic clashes. An illness, redundancy, retirement, death of a parent constitutes a wake-up call to one partner, while the other one, who may have a different mid-life agenda, finds themselves suddenly confronted by a stranger.

Estelle and Ed

Ed was a typical "East End working class kid made good". He ran a successful chain of "security firms" in Thailand—I never did manage to work out exactly what this meant. It involved his travelling to the Far East three or four times a year, for weeks at a time. Over the past five years—he was now fifty-four—his businesses had enjoyed fast expansion. He was now considering buying property in Thailand and living on two continents indefinitely.

The children were now independent, so he could see no reason not to do this. Estelle, on the other hand, had hoped they would buy a Cotswold property with a thatched roof and a huge kitchen garden. They would settle into a comfortable old age, with him home by the fireside at last.

Estelle had suffered for years with slight agoraphobia and fatigue syndrome, but nothing so serious as to stop her working from home as a self-employed accountant. She was rather isolated, living for her husband's periods at home, using his time away to plan special meals, or redecoration, or the garden, for his eventual return.

Shortly after his announcement that they were to have two homes (he would occupy the one in Thailand), he went away on business once more. Estelle was ironing his shirts one night, and suddenly stopped mid-sleeve. "Like an automaton, unable to think, only knowing I must *do* this, I walked into his study and switched on his computer." (Normally she never went near his computer as she had her own, for her work.) She guessed his passwords for various accounts; he had been very careless.

She found e-mails and accounts that shocked her to the core. For years her husband had been visiting high-class prostitutes in London, and bar girls in Thailand. He had spent a fortune on them—holidays, parties, and clothes. Latterly, one bar girl had become a regular mistress.

She could not believe her eyes. He had always been kind and respectful to her and the children. They had enjoyed lovely holidays abroad and he had bought her a pony, even though he loathed animals. He had been a model husband. What on earth was happening?

Ed agreed to come and see me. He came across as a "lovable rogue", full of charm and fun, clearly fond of his wife and grown-up children. Could this be the same man?

Ed told me he was "the runt of the litter", the youngest and most laughed at. He'd vowed to be rich one day and show them all!

At twenty, he was pressed to marry by his own parents and by Estelle's rather large, conservative Jewish family. They were worried that the courtship did not seem to be leading anywhere. Ed resisted, proposed, broke it off, then re-proposed when both families came down on him like a ton of bricks.

Truth to tell, Estelle had been an excellent, but unexciting wife, said Ed. Marvellous with the kids, great cook, OK but predictable in bed. He had *done his duty* by her and would go on doing so until he died—marriage was marriage. But a business proposition had come up in Thailand that was impossible to refuse and it involved living there.

Eventually he admitted that yes, he had fallen in love with a nightclub girl twenty years younger than him and he wanted to set her up in the spare house. Or at least in a flat, which would keep the new house "clean" in case Estelle suddenly decided to visit. But with her agoraphobia this was unlikely.

It was clear that Ed wanted to have his cake and eat it, but his motives, though immature, were not entirely self-interested. He told me the story of how he forgot his school lunchbox one day, so stole another boy's. He never got found out, but afterwards his face came out in terrible sores that itched and bled for weeks. In the end he told the headmaster about the theft, and his face cleared up within two days.

This was a man with so much conscience and dread of disapproval that he dared not tell his family or his prospective wife that he had no wish to marry; that he wanted more than anything to travel, earn a lot of money, have a great time with lots and lots of women before he dreamt of settling down.

Having tied himself to Estelle, his true nature would not leave him in peace. He began a double life, slowly and occasionally at first, until this second life began to take over, especially after the children left. Had Estelle not stopped her ironing when she did, jolted at last out of her (self-imposed?) blindness, Ed may have got away with it. I cannot help wondering though, whether the carelessness with the passwords on his computer was Ed's way of tentatively confessing to the "headmaster"!

Estelle's part in this whole mess was far from "innocent". Wronged she may have been, but surely she could have read the signs earlier? Ed never called her in the evening (Far East time). And she could never contact him in the evening (Far East time). She never asked about finances, yet sensed outgoings were hugely beyond what they jointly spent—she was an accountant, after all. And when he came home he seemed exhausted and uninterested in sex for some while. She asked him to bring home brochures about temples, gardens, and such, in which she was very interested, but he never managed to. She never questioned this. In fact she drew a veil over anything that might disturb the *status quo*.

The point of this vignette is to highlight the strong drive in humans to find and follow their true nature (and this can be naughty as well as nice!). Ed may not strike us as a very spiritual sort of chap, but his character could not stand the straitjacket in which it found itself. Had he been able to confront his parents at twenty, the disaster would have been averted. He did "the right thing", so winning the approval of his family at last, then spent the next ten or fifteen years kidding himself he was happy and acting the ideal husband. In mid-life, though, and in the middle to late period of his thirty-four-year-old marriage, he could no longer suppress his true self.

For all her collusion over the years, Estelle, too, was finally prompted by some hidden part of her self to face up to the falseness of her life. Her divorce was a nightmare for her, as more and more lurid details of Ed's life in Thailand were exposed. But she now knows herself much better, has become a person in her own right rather than a man's appendage, and stands a very good chance of making a new and healthier relationship, should she so choose.

I have known several couples where the man has led a double life for years. Anita Shreve's novel *The Pilot's Wife* (1999) illuminates this syndrome very well. Sometimes there are two lots of children, or the "legitimate" wife takes in children from the other family if the "non-legitimate" relationship ends or the second woman dies. I have never experienced the man to be in any way evil. On the contrary, they usually swear commitment to both women, and are very good fathers to both sets of children. What is also common to these cases is that the "legitimate" wife in some way aids the process by "ignoring" what has been happening for years, under her very nose. This in no way minimizes the trauma when she finds out, or the husband confesses.

I am still amazed by the number of perfectly kind, loving, apparently well-adjusted people who are able to put different parts of their lives in separate "boxes". One box is never allowed contact with another, and when inhabiting one box, the others cease to exist. Therefore, no guilt is felt and no one gets hurt—for a time. This *dissociation*, as it is called, accounts for the ease with which people of integrity can conduct secret lives they would usually describe as reprehensible. It also accounts for the ability of many partners to go on believing in the fidelity, financial honesty, or whatever of the other partner, who is patently "breaking the rules". When both partners wear blinkers, as did Estelle and Ed, it may be decades before the truth comes out. But when it does, terrible bitterness and recrimination is inevitable.

Collaborative dissociation is based on lies and is anti-growth. It also wastes many years, during which the partners may have mended their relationship, or been honest enough to part and make a better one.

The late period

What about the late period of marriage, supposing that the vicissitudes of mid-life have not parted the pair? Most major issues have been ironed out by now. When people say, "Look at those two old fogeys over there, never speaking a word—that's marriage for you", I often think, yes, it could be boring. But oh, imagine not *needing* to speak because the attunement is so good. Imagine companionship deeper than words. It happens.

Ageing can be a gloomy subject, so it is important we keep a balanced view by considering all those happy marriages which have come through years of trials and tribulation to their last peaceful phase, and which have no need of therapy.

When an elderly couple do seek help, their "problem" usually has to do with "putting the books in order". After forty or fifty years of marriage there is much the couple can congratulate themselves on (lasting so long as a pair, for a start). But often there are regrets or resentments that have never been spoken of, or fully addressed, and need now to be aired.

For example, a child may have been born with Down's Syndrome, or mentally ill. Although it is all history now, angry or disappointed feelings can still lurk about how the other partner handled the situation at the time. Moderate depression in very mature marriages is common, and often relates to traumas way back in the past that can, none the less, be processed successfully by the pair, and laid to rest.

Childbirth is another very common unresolved issue. Where were you when I was in labour, alone and scared? What did you do when I had post natal depression and no one in those days knew what it was? (Usually the complaint is that the husband quit the field, unable to face the pain.) On the male side there are often accusations of wives holding back their job prospects, or not "letting" them do things, especially if it took them away from home, or involved physical risk. Underlying all these complaints are the ancient voices from childhood and infancy, the old, unavoidable letdowns. "Where were you when I needed you?" "Stop controlling me." "Come closer." "Leave me alone." "I will do anything if you will love me." "Don't bribe/blackmail me." "Let me lean." "Set me free."

As we grow older, we see our parents and our friends die or become frail. We cleave even more to our partners if they have been a source of nurture for us over the years. We become more able to forgive and forget if we are first able to air that which still wounds, or has never really healed.

Sadly, some partners decide it is all "water under the bridge", believing the best thing is to "forget" (by which they really mean suppress, avoid, deny, cover up). What can be done about the situation after all these years, they say. Much. Very much, I answer, after having witnessed healing and renewed mutual blessing between elderly couples.

If the issue is still raw for one party, they have been silently carrying hurt for *years*. That can only limit the quality of love they can offer in the last precious years. Talking it out can bring about an understanding by the offending party of which they were not capable before, when perhaps they just did not know what to do or say. They are older and wiser now. Saying sorry can rejuvenate the marriage dramatically. When, inevitably, death parts the pair, the regrets and "sorrys" have already been said. This will ease the grieving process.

At this late stage in the couple cycle, there is always the ever present, but usually warded off, fear of the other one's demise, of being left alone. Such abandonment reawakens long repressed fears experienced as a babe in arms, that one day, long before the infant is equipped for it, those arms will no longer be there, to hold, soothe, and make safe. How to live without the long-loved partner, the now dead mother for whom he or she stands, *and* face the prospect of one's own death, all at the same time? It is a lot to ask of an elderly person.

Jake and Janice

Janice was going to be seventy this year. Jake was seventy-two. Next year was to be their golden wedding. They were a lively couple, sprucely dressed, well informed, much travelled.

Jake was on Viagra. Janice used a hormone cream for vaginal dryness. They made love about once a month. They had always enjoyed sex. The problem they presented in the first meeting was whether or not they should stop using these aids, which would, in effect, mean the cessation of a sex life.

Their marriage had been long and happy on the whole, but they had not had an easy time. One daughter was autistic and died of pneumonia at twenty-three. There had been another daughter later who was very aggressive and insisted her parents never wanted her (not true). She had emigrated to Canada and never spoke to them again. It had taken decades to come to terms with this, and even now they hoped she might contact them at some point.

There had been a time, when in the navy, that Jake nearly drowned in a submarine. For a long time afterwards he suffered from post traumatic stress syndrome. The accompanying depression made him irritable and difficult to live with, but they stuck it out. Then there was the nursing of both sets of dying parents, another drawn-out business.

It seemed odd that a couple who had weathered all this without help should seek assistance over such an apparently small decision.

Yet the decision was far from small. Both partners had come from families with chronically ill parents and no brothers or sisters. They had been bereaved of two daughters. Jake had almost lost his life in that submarine. All they had now was each other—and their sex life.

Good sex is more than mutual pleasure, more than a loving communication, more than a means of procreation. It builds bonds of steel that come to be relied on in the troubled times, in times when words fail, or other comforts lose their power to console. It is also an affirmation of shared life, a mutual reassurance that neither is ever alone. When their first, autistic daughter died, Jake and Janice could not share their mixture of relief, guilt, and terrible sorrow, but they still had sex. It was their only real point of connection for a year or more. After the submarine near-disaster Jake could not talk about it, but he could curl up in bed for a cuddle, which would lead to gentle, tender sex. (He insisted this helped him more than the antidepressants.) When their second daughter emigrated, breaking both their hearts, they took a long cruise "to get over it" and enjoyed a second honeymoon.

And so sexual relations had become a deep unspoken language between them, in the good times and the bad. They feared that giving up their language would mean they would cease to communicate and their relationship would evaporate.

Second, there was an assumption that stopping sex meant facing that you and your partner really were old, and could die. Here was the central anxiety.

Before approaching that anxiety, they needed to revisit the loss of the two daughters. Their mourning had never been completed. At the time, sex had been a comfort, but also an aid to denial. The magical belief was that sex could defeat death and rejection. They had avoided much of their grief, defied it, because really letting it in would have been unbearable. After the passage of so much time, they could begin to bear it and share it now.

This is what I mean by "putting the books straight". Most elderly couples have unfinished business between them. When it causes great worry by relocating itself in some other significant area of the relationship (in this case, sex), addressing it is of the utmost importance.

Janice and Jake were getting to the stage where the sex act was a bit of an effort. A cuddle seemed to suffice just as well, but they were scared to stop in case all they had built together over the years fell apart. Sex had been their standard defence and consolation in all crises. They were really frightened.

Life without the other was unimaginable. As they had grown older, both had been trying to fend off any anxiety about illness and death by having more, not less sex. In daring to face and speak of these anxieties at last, even though they probably had another twenty years ahead of them, the reliance on a talismanic sexual solution lessened. They came to appreciate that whatever aids they used, they were mortal.

This led them to see that, despite their evident health and strength now, perhaps it was just as well to plan for life alone, should that come to pass. Horrified at first by such callous thoughts, they began to own up to themselves, and then each other, just how afraid they were of being left by the other. Gradually they were able to help each other develop skills, knowledge, and hobbies that would enable them to carry on alone. Janice learned to drive and read maps. Jake learned to do the garden and organize a drinks evening with canapés. As they tutored one another, they made many a macabre joke about one or other of them "falling off their perch", and referred to myself as the "grim reaper". But at last they were facing reality. There was less talk about sex (but I am sure the cuddles continued!).

The learning of new skills was useful in its own right, but the primary object of the exercise was to unglue this very fused couple.

The joint personality had so taken over that each would find it especially difficult to manage should one die. They needed to regain their sense of being a separate person, disinvest some of their individual capital from the marital bank, so to speak.

Loss of a loved one is a terrible thing, but when most of one's personality is also invested in them, the bereaved partner feels dead and empty too. It is as if they have both gone on ahead into death, and whatever may or may not lie beyond, together, leaving behind just a husk. Such people usually lack the will to go through the grieving process and die too, soon after, when there may have been many happy years left for them.

Fortunately, Jake and Janice came to understand the value of mourning and how astute they had been at circumventing it. They were able to be healthily sad about the loss of their sexual prowess rather than frantically trying to prolong it in order to pacify other anxieties. Both missed the thrill badly, yet could scarcely recall what it felt like. In accepting the end of sexual intercourse they were able to face also the possibility of death or infirmity. There were no more spooks left in the cupboard to fend off. They would settle for cuddles and love from now on. It was more than lots of people their age had.

Different couples have different "currencies", without which the relationship is unsustainable. For Jake and Janice it was sex. For others it may be property, or money, or career status, or the children's and grandchildren's doings.

I have seen what seemed like a rock-solid marriage of forty years crash when the retirement villa in Spain fell through, due to lack of funds. Each blamed the other. This was not about money, but a shared preoccupation with self-reliance. Both parties could only function in harmony when the houses they bought, redecorated,and sold were doing good business. The triumphant couple proved over and over, with every purchase, that their alliance was invincible. Together they could manage their lives and the world. (Who needs parents? Unsurprisingly, both had been badly let down by theirs.)

They put up with all manner of imperfections in each other over the years, an affair on either side included, but neither could bear the other making an error over property. This was seen as the worst betrayal in the world. Needless to say, such a currency was developed by them as a result both of their family backgrounds and the deal struck between them at the Norming stage.

An identification of long established "currencies" in the older couple makes it possible, even at this late stage, to substitute a new and more helpful one.

In the later years of marriage, emotional and physical dependency on the partner increases. ("Have you seen my glasses, my dear?" "Did you put out my pills this morning, love?") One's life has come full circle. The partner is becoming more and more like the very first care-giver. In some there is enormous dread of this, for their first encounter was a difficult and unsafe time. As a result they have all their life avoided dependency and cultivated self-reliance. For them, growing old is a nightmare. They fervently hope they will depart this world without having to lean on anyone else, least of all their partners. Many elderly people grow seriously depressed, and even contemplate suicide rather than face physical or mental incapacity that would bring back the emotional agony of having to depend on an unreliable other.

At the other extreme, some partners wholeheartedly welcome another chance for that dependent bliss they once knew at mother's breast, being bathed, powdered, wrapped in fluffy towels, cooed at, and then deliciously, drowsily fed. Life has dictated they must give all this up, but now age returns to them the right to be unconditionally loved, whether or not this includes physical and practical care. Yet there is no magic potion to keep their elected carer alive and well enough to dispense this bliss. Life, it has to be said, can be bloody unfair.

Should good fortune prevail, however, the lucky recipient will be doubly blessed. The first powerful partner made and housed him, without his consent or participation. And all the time she belonged to someone else. All the time separation loomed. Weaning and walking beckoned—a gain and a loss. The last partner, though, has been actively chosen in a spirit of collaboration and equality. In old age the delights of being cared for may feel the same, but this is no second childhood, no retreat to the past. Coming to the end of life's journey with a *chosen* partner who still loves you reunites you with all you had thought lost in infancy, but without any of the power complications. Neither are there painful partings and third parties to contend with. Surely this must be the highest form of couple self-realization.

CHAPTER ELEVEN

Major psychological forces affecting every couple

D onald Winnicott was a pioneer child psychiatrist and psychoanalyst whose specialism was the relationship between infants and their mothers. Back in the 1960s he gave us the concept of a *transitional space* between the pair (Winnicott, 1971). This was an abstract, creative area that was neither mother nor child, but a space between, where both could mentally *play*, and where *the boundaries separating them could be temporarily dissolved*. An area where rules, obligations, order, and acting sensibly is banished can produce astonishing new ways of going about things. Ask any management team engaged in brainstorming. Ask any abstract artist. Ask anyone who has enjoyed the perfect orgasm.

In the same way, well-established couples also have a place where things can "transit", literally "go across", in both directions. What was once two distinct personalities now intertwine inside that shared force-field, bits of one person blending, exchanging with, challenging or borrowing from, bits of the other. This intimate play produces different combinations of personal characteristics in each spouse at different times. Some of this play is ultimately healing; sometimes it balances dangerous currents between the pair. Sometimes it can be deadly.

Facing trainee therapists puzzled by this idea, I ask them to think of the married pair in their sitting room with a bucket between their armchairs, into which they can throw thoughts, moods, ideas, feelings, grumbles, any bits of themselves they want to dump, at least for the time being. Each person can stir or shake the bucket as they feel the need, or just leave it to sit there and "stew". Due to alchemical processes in the bucket, some new products belonging to neither spouse, yet now available to both, will float to the surface or sink to the bottom. Some items will remain unaltered, but are left there for the other partner to take up if needed.

Both parties plunge into the bucket's contents from time to time. Items may be borrowed or swapped. Often they are claimed as their own and not the partner's at all! These swaps and borrowings will come to colour the couple's dealings with each other in a characteristic way. Sometimes these "playful" experiments in melding result in permanent changes in each couple member; permanent, that is, so long as they share the same bucket (remain a couple).

Much of couple therapy involves three people (the couple and the therapist) peering into that bucket. After studying the contents, items may be added, removed, modified by the couple, sent back to their original owners, or simply understood and accepted as necessary exchanges that help the marital system run smoothly. Couple therapists call these processes *mutual projective identifications*. I find the bucket analogy easier, if less grand. I shall provide some examples shortly.

Projective mechanisms occur under the rubric of *transference*, so let us deal with that first.

General transference

That which each partner consigns to, and retrieves from, the metaphorical bucket depends on their respective developmental history and current aspirations. They cannot put in what they do not psychologically possess. Yet, without a sense of lack, and hence need, there would be no motivation to take anything out. The bucket, then, is both a shared receptacle for unwanted aspects of the two selves, but also a kind of bran tub into which each can dip in the hope of fetching up something that will heal, mend, or protect their sense of self.

I see some readers shaking their heads. "All this developmental history stuff. Am I really supposed to go along with the idea that just because I was weaned too early I have inevitably grown into a pathetic heap of dependency? Or that my potty training turned me into a Scrooge?" Of course not. The way you are now is a multi-factorial business that involves genes, child-rearing practices, culture, schooling, religion (where applicable), effects of travelling, collision with other minds that have profoundly shaped your self precepts. We are certainly not talking here about a single cause producing a specific effect.

Let us look a bit deeper at the first instance, the prematurely weaned infant. An experience of such sudden and, to you as a babe, inexplicable abandonment by the breast will have had a strong effect on your organism's sense of safety. (I say "organism" because primitive sensations such as fear of extinction are experienced as much in the body as the developing mind.) Let us suppose this sense of discontinuity or rupture is reinforced by struggles to keep down the unwelcome solids: you feel you are about to choke and die. The more you cough the filthy food out, the more the carers shove it in. It is a gross physical assault, oral rape.

Then mum goes into hospital for an operation. Dad is off to work, absent. Your mum returns, still poorly and unable to cuddle and play with you. Already your feeling that the world, and your place in it, is pretty insecure is being powerfully reinforced. You will have to make mental arrangements (build defences) to insulate yourself from future repetitions of this terrifying privation.

It is these defence mechanisms, maybe long dormant, that are unavoidably challenged in the enclosed, intimate world of marriage. As with infancy, there is nowhere to hide. If you are lucky, your other half may help you strengthen these defences, especially if they share the same fears as yourself. Alternatively, you may find you have chosen someone who can loan you their sense of safety, or allow you to shelter under it, so you need not worry about tightening up your defences. Phew! It is even possible that your mate can facilitate the growth of your own, new sense of safety in the world, so that old defences become redundant. They can be dismantled.

As explained in Chapter Two ("Finding a mate"), we all protect ourselves, along with our treasured image of ourselves, in new situations that could threaten us. We do this by *transferring* former experience to the present time, trying to make a match. Where we see similarities in the new circumstances, we hang on to them, thus reinforcing our pre-existing view of the world. Any strange experience that does not fit our pattern—so long as it is not *too* strange— we try to absorb into an expanding database. New events, now dwelling alongside the old, take on some of their emotional colour and so are rendered less intimidating.

Our continued existence shows we have survived by this method before, if only by the skin of our teeth. If coming through it was a near thing, then how much more dangerous could *totally* new situations prove, those events where nothing fits our old theories about the world? Better to stick to what we know.

This means that if we cannot squeeze some parts of the new experience into the old, even by amending or broadening the base of the old world assumptions, then the ultra new is *rejected* as dangerous to the psyche. In future, any elements of experience similar to these rejected components will also be banished from our awareness. By the time we show sexual interest in the other (or the same) gender, we have consistently narrowed our perceptions and bolstered our interpretations of reality so that we now possess a complete model of the interpersonal world, which we assume not to be a model at all, but to be actually real!

When courtship begins, shocks and disillusion are in store if the loved one's version of reality is very different. It may not have occurred to us before that all realities are subjective.

Through the learning process described above, already patterned by experience, children actively seek out familiar situations to confirm their evolving pictures of reality. To an onlooker, such situations may sometimes seem unwholesome, but, from the child's point of view, at least the situation is *known*. They have accrued strategies to cope with, circumvent, or endure such situations.

Thus, we find at school, and later in life, that victims locate bullies with unerring accuracy; visionaries find acolytes; prophets find a cause and even martyrdom. Followers find leaders (be they people or ideologies). The king or pope of the playground rules still, in the family or the workplace. The scapegoat still has his or her head metaphorically pushed down the toilet, in the boardroom or the armed forces. *History is repeating itself.*

Particular transference

No matter how much genuine love exists in any marriage, this whole business of having been drawn by the past to someone very special, someone who, on the face of it, satisfied a table of requirements, will permeate the relationship. This is a *general* transference of the past to the present. In day-to-day living, each party also moves in and out of *particular* transference to their other half. Often their two particular transferences interlock. This may be for good or ill.

Arlene and Abe

Arlene's mother was diagnosed with post natal depression which lasted for a year after Arlene was born. She was plagued by recurrent breast abscesses, so the baby had to be bottle fed. Arlene then developed an allergy to the various milks that were tried, requiring emergency hospitalizations. Eventually, she was returned to mother's recovering, but still sore, breasts to prevent her starving to death. Mother could hardly bear to touch the infant for fear of further pain, and out of revulsion for the whole business of childbirth. According to reports from other family members later on, her father seemed equally averse to the infant, hiring nurses to care for her.

After this early struggle to survive, Arlene progressed to nursery school, where further allergies dogged her. She was thin and pale. At first other children tried to bully her. Fortunately, she was endowed with a lot of courage and anger, which she used to stick up for herself. She learned that if she was to get by in life she must fight hard, never give in, never trust anyone else, or even her own body, which had let her down so often.

She chose Abe for her husband. He was a GP—surely no accident. A kindly soul with gentle manners, a love of home, and devotion to dogs, he provided all the security Arlene craved, while leaving her to the academic pursuits at which she so excelled. She wrote book after book, confident there was no competition to worry about. She had to be "out front" to feel safe, but all the same longed for the maternal care that had been so absent. By having it served up on a plate by Abe, she had no need to admit to herself or anyone else that she was hungry for it. Invincible, independent, "top dog" she would always be. This was her canine-loving husband's nickname for her—"my top dog".

Abe had been brought up in the country. Such spare time as he could afford away from his patients was spent bird watching and walking his several collies. He pronounced himself "surprised by love" when Arlene descended on him during his last year at medical school. (Arlene was a young lecturer at the same university.) He had never had a girlfriend before.

His mother had died after giving birth to him. His father was a remote and rather feared famous surgeon. Abe coped with the absence of warmth in his childhood by retreating into nature and animals rather than people. He had not expected that he would ever marry. He was delighted and flattered to have been wooed by so eminent a scholar, who so clearly needed him. No one had ever needed him as a child. At first he worshipped her.

We can see now how each transferred past experiences to the present in a general way. What about specific transference though?

After some years, Arlene's reputation waned as new researchers in her field competed for publishing honours. Abe retired early, and became more monkish than ever. He read more and more mystic literature, became preoccupied and uncommunicative.

The formerly successful marriage began to come apart at the seams. Arlene hated Abe's emotional distance, *so like her father's* (particular transference). Earlier, she had enjoyed his being a foil for her own ambitious nature, his disinterest in any form of competition. Now she projected into him her own fear of failure: she saw him as a cowardly loser.

In turn, motherless Abe had regressed to the defensive solitude that had so comforted him in his youth. He confessed that the marriage had been harder work than he had ever imagined. He had hoped Arlene might remain the substitute for the mother he'd never known, but in truth he had found her bossy and demanding of his energies, especially as her career waned. In these later years, Arlene had become *the dark, disappointing side of his idealized mother* (particular transference). In the earliest years, she had been the embodiment of his fantasy of a perfect mother. He had never met the real Arlene at all.

Transference always has a grain of truth in it. Arlene was indeed feisty and opinionated, but not a bully. Abe was increasingly withdrawn and cool, but more out of sadness and fatigue than a wish to hurt or reject. Getting these very distorted perceptions into proper proportion often marks the start of a successful therapeutic enterprise.

Ambivalence

Many of the stories in this book demonstrate how easy it can be to hate the person you love most in the world. Partners are often shocked and horrified by the degree of fury that overwhelms them when their old wounds are prodded. As they do not realize what is *unconsciously* occurring, they become frightened, thinking that underneath they must be an evil and destructive person. They vow never to "lose it" again. If they succeed in the pretence that hatred does not exist, then conflict cannot be sorted out. It is driven underground. A spurious peace prevails, but the joint personality starves.

Ambivalence is hating and loving the same person, often at the same time. It is most distressing. Children deal with this by splitting mummy into two. There is the witch mummy that won't let him watch late TV—how he detests her, could kill her. Then there is the fairy mummy who cuddles and kisses him goodnight. He adores her. If he keeps them separate in his mind, two people, the one cannot spoil or contaminate the other. He can keep the good one safe from harm. Couples do this, too.

Cath and Charlie

Charlie had always put his lovely wife on a pedestal. She was cleverer, more witty, and sociable; more popular than he could ever be. What he did not appreciate was that he also hated her for making him feel correspondingly small, invisible. He was merely her sidekick. Everybody knew it, but were too polite to say so.

Occasionally, he played the field, dismissing his peccadilloes as just little diversions. Cath never found out. His philosophy was: "What the eye doesn't see the heart need not grieve over." At first his affairs were all with women whose lives were a complete mess. He helped them out with advice, money, introductions, a bit of pampering. They thought him wonderful, a godsend. *Who was on the pedestal now?*

His last two affairs, though, were with "expensive and clean" prostitutes. A friend at work had "dragged" him along to have some "special treatment". To his great alarm (and excitement) he found he enjoyed cruel and humiliating games. It came to him in a flash on the way home the second time, that his "victim" had been his beloved wife. He decided to get some help.

Like many apparently confident, assertive women, Cath depended on Charlie to admire her, reassure her of her worth, and bolster her self-esteem. Sex was vital to her. If a few days went by without it, she would become panicky and feel old and unattractive. She would douse herself in perfume, buy new lingerie, light candles.

During his short-lived but plentiful affairs, Charlie lost interest in marital sex. When Cath's seductions failed she felt degraded and hated him. It never crossed her mind that he might be cheating on her. She assumed him to be either useless, "past it", or she was no longer desirable. She taunted him, cursed him for his lack of manliness, and sneered at his excuses. Then she would turn her hate on herself and sink into depression. At this juncture Charlie came to her rescue: they made up again, the affair forgotten—until the next time!

Both parties hated and loved each other in equal measure. Both had an ideal spouse in their waking mind, but an opposite loathed partner hidden away in their "sleeping" one. Only when the affairs came to light and the shouting died down was there a chance to bring the split together, releasing the hate and envy from both sides. After that the hunt for the origin of the ambivalence could begin.

Projective mechanisms

Back to that bucket!

However healthy and well functioning we are, all of us have incompletely resolved issues from the past about which we may be able to do little on our own. Why bother, as they rarely intrude so much into our daily lives that we cannot carry on? Anyway, we have amassed lots of defence mechanisms over the years to help us cope, so we experience little need to find out where those defences came from, or why they are still necessary.

Once we are cohabiting, though, these "little" sore points and sensitivities have a habit of looming large. It is relatively easy to disguise them at work under our professional roles, or in a social group whose mix changes regularly. At home, however, enforced intimacy exposes them.

One of the most positive aspects of living together is the hope that the other half of the couple may be used to heal, compensate, re-enact, or take the blame for all the emotional burdens we have carried for years. Meanwhile, the other party is aiming for the same thing. There is nothing conscious or calculated about this desire. It is simply what happens between intimate pairs. Knowing about and identifying it, though, can change lives and save marriages ("can", not "will!").

Unwanted, disapproved of parts of the self can be attributed to the spouse, affording great relief, of a sort.

Josh and Janine

"She's such a nag and fusser, whereas I'm laid back, cool." (She's bad and I am good.)

In fact, this man is quite unable to motivate himself within his domestic environment. He relies on his partner to take all the decisions, then blames her for nagging. This way, it is all her fault and he never has to face up to his inertia and its causes. (No one has told him the definition of nagging is "the repetition of unpalatable truths".)

At work, Josh is the nagger. He badgers his employees for poor performance, pursues and criticizes them, yet gives them no guidance or example. He covers up profit loss by blaming the inferior work force and is forever "fussing" over new training programmes or regulations that never materialize.

Janine, his professional wife, occasionally longs to be "laid back and cool" like him. She has been so, in the past, when her former consort did his share. *She* feels nagged by this, her second husband, who regularly harangues her for goading him, for making his life a misery.

To some extent, he has a point about the nagging. His busy wife yearns to switch off, be lazy, be pampered for a bit. Seeing her partner take these luxuries as of right makes her blood boil. The lazier he gets, the worse the house looks and the more she will have to clean up after him. Secretly, she so *disapproves* of relaxing, she only feels entitled to do it when the house is spotless. The husband therefore *fulfils the role of her conscience* in preventing her from having the wicked relaxation she really wants. She attributes her own wish to be lazy to him, then verbally punishes him for it.

Who is setting up whom?

Another example: "He's so aggressive. He tells me I am such a drip. But I love him, so I nobly put up with it."

This virtuous, long-suffering lady (or so she presents herself) may well have a partner who finds it easier to speak his mind than she does. But by provoking him into explosions of anger she can ventilate her own, by proxy. Depending on the woman concerned (people are different), she may be sexually aroused as well as frightened by this display of power. Another woman may feel confirmed in her "chosen" identity of victim. Yet another is relieved to have someone else express what she so fears expressing herself, lest she lose total control perhaps, or incur others' dislike and rejection.

In both these couples, the voluble, active one is used to make the other feel not only more comfortable, but above reproach. At the same time each partner reinforces their spouse's behaviour while roundly condemning it.

Reggie and Rhoda

Over the years of their long marriage, Reggie and Rhoda had separated many times. The apparent cause was usually a physical fight, money, or an affair on Reggie's part.

Both parties had filed and "unfiled" for divorce on numerous occasions. They treated each other abominably, yet seemed unable to break up for good.

On the face of it, Reggie dominated and controlled his wife, handing out pocket money, checking all her receipts, rifling through her handbag. If she objected, she risked being hit. He came and went without informing her, staying away for days at a time. When she had had enough she would take out an injunction and he had to leave the house.

At this point Reggie became weepy and helpless as a baby. He neglected his café business, scrounged beds off his many pals, weeping on their shoulder until they got fed up and passed him on to someone else. He took far too many tranquillizers and drank too much beer. Every day he called Rhoda and begged her to take him back.

The once oppressed and obedient Rhoda then took charge. He was to bed down in the café's little staff room and not see his boozy friends at all. He must stop the pills, see a counsellor, and make no phone calls to anyone except her. And she wanted her own bank account. If he could manage all that for a month or so, she might consider letting him return "a step at a time".

Reggie and Rhoda both had dreadful childhoods, which will not be examined here. The point being made is the way in which control and dependency were passed between them. Each break-up followed an identical pattern. Once reconciled, Reggie returned to his old habits and Rhoda to hers. A few months or years later the whole drama repeated itself.

Both took turns at playing the tyrant and victim. Disowning and projecting her victim self into Reggie allowed Rhoda to "get even" with him (and some childhood perpetrator?). Reggie permitted this, so long as he could return the favour later by projecting *his* "victim" side into her, and enjoy being the tyrant. Had they stayed in the one role, the marriage would never have lasted, because each needed to defend against the spectre of helplessness and abandonment by controlling their partner (and some earlier figure who abandoned them?). But each had to have someone extreme to control, in order to obtain the heady sense of safety that omnipotence brings. They had unconsciously arranged their relationship so that each got what they so desired, at least half the time.

Both saw themselves as the mature, competent one in the relationship. Both accused the other of being a controlling bully. Both claimed the other needed treatment. This projective fiction ensured they maintained self-esteem.

Therapy was not a success. Their games were too precious to be given up.

A more cheerful version of these mechanisms is the scenario I call the Merry Widow. A rather rigid, self-controlled, gloomy old man dies after fifty years of marriage. Everyone feels sorry for his mousy, frail widow, all alone and unprotected. She surprises everyone by spending the life insurance on a Caribbean cruise and a new wardrobe of fashionable clothes. Why had she allowed her husband to dictate how she lived? Why had she not rebelled? Who had really been protecting whom?

It is quite common for a spouse to surrender their autonomy to their partner, in exchange for being shielded from life's vicissitudes. Perfectly capable people will pay such a price if it means that at last, *at long bloody last*, they will have someone to call their own, someone reliable, someone who never goes away.

Early in the marriage, the Merry Widow's independence and capability went into the marital bucket. Out of it she pulled her husband's fear of life, his need to cling. He drew out her denied strength and autonomy. With such a delicate mouse to care for, he can feel and seem big and manly. He needs to feel this way so badly he would never desert the woman who made it possible.

The husband has lodged his dependency in his wife, so feels genuinely strong and protective: this is no pretence. His wife has *absorbed* (introjected) this dependent quality, while he has taken in her care-giving, organizing and decision-making attributes. His pride benefits from these mutual projections. She gets the secure, predictable attachment for which she has yearned.

Indeed, we may guess that the fifty years' arrangement has worked so well that the wife's long-term deprivation has been "corrected". Now she is widowed, she can withdraw her projections, re-own her capabilities and fully take up her place in the world.

Mirroring

From the outside, a marital pair may seem to have very different personalities. But, as demonstrated in the above cases, there is usually a mutual preoccupation with the same issue. There is also a paradox built in, so that the parties take up one side or the other. Both may be deeply concerned about success, and fear failure terribly. But which one is to carry the fear or failure, and which the actual success?

Other mirrored motifs are dependency versus control; dominance versus submission; intimacy versus distance; aggression versus passivity; neediness versus need provision; extraversion versus reclusiveness; and intellectuality versus emotionality.

Love at first sight may well be due to people immediately recognizing their mirror image in the other person. Both are passionately involved with the same inner dilemma, but are coming at it from opposite directions. The more irresistible the attraction, the more deeply etched in their psyches is the inadequately resolved issue the partner is required to heal. Love at first sight can only last if one of the partners "agrees" to carry one side of the paradox for life, or they "agree" to trade from time to time. Refusal "to play ball" where there is long-stored, strong emotion to be shared out will create enormous battles that will drain both people, turning love to hate.

Where joint personal/historical issues are not so deeply ingrained, other aspects of the relationship can compensate for, or retrieve marital energy from, the to-ing and fro-ing of this powerful dynamic. Much exhaustion is caused in both parties when the projected qualities are not accepted by the intended recipient, resulting in an unconscious tug of war to ascertain who is going to carry what for whom.

The mind and body are the same organism. What affects one is often expressed by the other. Many fatigue symptoms presented to GPs are due to the constant strenuous effort of one or both partners trying to project something into the other by mental force, or wearing themselves out by trying to resist or throw back projections aimed at them.

Regulating

Over time, couples work out a method for stopping tensions spiralling out of control. They establish a regulatory code of which neither is aware, but which proves effective all the same. The more potentially explosive the relationship, the more such a code is needed.

Jim and Jo Anne

Jim was a fellow of an Oxford College, an expert on American literature. Jo Anne was American. They had met while she studied for her doctorate, her subject to do with land conservation.

Jo Anne's family were high flyers academically, but all she ever wanted as a child were her horses and the outdoor life. She worked hard at school to satisfy her parents, then found a college where she could pursue her own interests as well as study. Her mother had always been unstable, so Jo Anne found it hard to rebel. Shortly after she entered the (non famous) US college, about which her parents complained bitterly, her mother committed suicide. Her father became very depressed and drank heavily. She tried to help him, but he pushed her aside. She started living with other students, but hated the partying life they led, especially the uncontrolled drinking, which reminded her of her father. She found herself a deserted building on the edge of town and moved in. No one seemed to notice or care.

One night her father staggered into her "camp", as she called it, weeping one minute and railing at her for having let her parents down the next. They quarrelled, and Jo Anne made him leave. A truck ran into him some twenty minutes later. He was killed outright.

In her mid twenties Jo Anne made a vow. She would earn her doctorate at a famous university, so as to appease her parents. Then she would make a clean break, buy a small ranch with the considerable sum of money left her by her parents, return to the USA and live life her own way. Falling in love with Jim had put a stop to all that. They had been married ten years now.

Jim came from a large, working-class family in Liverpool, the first and only son in living memory to go to university. He was constantly teased for being an egghead. "That's one up from a poufter," he explained. He always had his head stuck in a book, hated all sports, and felt happiest on his own. Only his mother reached out to him fondly, but even she shook her head and called him "my little changeling". Jim supposed he must love her, but, to be quite honest, they had no shared interests at all. He was ashamed of her being so "common". He was also deeply ashamed of being ashamed.

This pair undoubtedly loved each other, but tormented one another, too. Jo Anne felt she had already sacrificed half her life to her parents and now it was slipping away again. She loathed the cold and damp of England, the confined spaces compared with America. A staunch Democrat, she hated the dinners, ceremonies, manners, and attitudes that still pervaded Oxford. She found a few horsey friends in whom Jim had little interest. Increasingly, their lives became more separate.

During the fifth to ninth years of their marriage they separated three times, for a trial period of three months, after which both wanted reconciliation, having sorely missed the other. During this period Jo Anne took Jim to the USA for long holidays. Both were wretched. She was not free to indulge her passion for the wide-open spaces and he hated the non-intellectual atmosphere of small town America.

They considered living half the time in the USA and half in England, but Jim's tightly scheduled academic year would not permit this. Jo Anne would settle into Oxford for a while, but eventually started "to climb the walls" again. Jim felt guilty and blamed, which made him depressed, withdrawn, and irritable. Feeling neglected, Jo Anne was doubly angry at having given away her life to others and now to her husband, who seemed not to care. The rows sometimes came to physical blows, which both deeply regretted afterwards.

Jo Anne and Jim were both nailed down by enormous guilt. Jo Anne felt responsible for her mother's suicide and her father's death. Jim felt he had betrayed and rejected *his* mother, who had at least tried to reach him. She now suffered from dementia. It was too late to make amends.

Both had dealt with their guilt by marrying a loved, but impossible partner. Jo Anne had married an academic like her father, but one who prevented her from having her ranch life just as he had. Jim had married a woman he *had* to make it up with, this time. He must put everything right for her, and never, never leave her.

They did have some interests in common (American literature for one). Whenever they had a good phase together, it was so good that neither of their consciences could stand it. Too much happiness could not be permitted. The fights started again, over who was ruining whose life and wouldn't it be better for them both if they parted for ever? Jim so wished to make Jo Anne happy, but could not leave Oxford. Jo Anne could return to America, but would have to give up Jim. There was no compromise because their very choice of partner had ensured neither could ever be satisfied. This ongoing suffering appeased their guilt to some degree.

This couple *regulated* happiness. They rationed it carefully so they each had some, but not all, of the life they wanted, just as in childhood. One might argue that they should have married someone else, but how then would they have managed to steal a bit of joy while simultaneously paying off their debts to their respective families? The preoccupation with family guilt bound them tightly together.

After further clarification of this formulation of their problem, each went into individual therapy to work on their family issues.

Other regulators may be the particular way a couple handle money, sex, power, or the in-laws. As ever, with unconscious psychological mechanisms, there is nothing intrinsically good or bad about them; they are just mental tools we all use. They can contribute to consolidating a relationship; they can wreck it. In this case, regulation of happiness was used to keep the marriage in unhappy stasis. They could neither part nor properly unite. This was the only way they could keep their consciences clean. Needless to add, there was much ambivalence and projection in there, too!

Relocating

The very real problem presented to the therapist often turns out to be a smokescreen covering an underlying problem, which the couple feel is too unsafe to tackle. The relocating of a problem has its uses, but only for a time. Eventually the smoke screen can cause more trouble than the problem it is hiding.

Hugh and Harriet

Hugh is a software engineer, Harriet an educational psychologist. Harriet phoned for an appointment, saying I must promise not to laugh, because they were on the edge of killing each other. It was no joke.

In the first session, Harriet explained that Hugh's snoring was driving her crazy. In their seven years together he had always snored a bit, on and off—the sort of thing you can cope with. "But this year it has really, seriously escalated," Harriet said, while Hugh studied the cracks in my ceiling as if the answer to the meaning of the universe resided there. He was weary, embarrassed, and angry, but determined not to show any of this. "We are talking herd of elephants here, actual *trumpeting*, not a spot of heavy breathing," a flushed Harriet continued.

Harriet had tried every remedy she knew, starting with earplugs (totally useless), then gently rolling him over—but his body went rigid, refused to budge. She tried dipping his head, chin to chest, but he snapped it back up again. She then shook him, but he just growled ferociously before gathering up the whole duvet and pulling it over his head, leaving her exposed and cold. Then she tried putting up with it, in the hope he would stop once deep sleep was established. "Not a hope in hell." By the third week of this nightly ritual she was in tears of despair. "Even sobbing would not wake the brute."

Civilized people, they attempted to discuss it over dinner one night. Hugh kept shaking his head disbelievingly, insisting he did not snore, at least not in the ghastly honking way she demonstrated for him. He refused to look at his weight, beer consumption, or wear a clothes peg to keep the septum open. Laser surgery was out of the question. Harriet accused him of not taking her needs seriously.

Harriet then suggested he sleep in the spare room for a bit. Hugh was furious. He threw down his knife and fork. "Fuck that!" he said, before marching out.

Harriet tried again later, this time expressing her willingness to take turns in sleeping in the spare room. "After all, it isn't bloody expulsion from Eden," she quipped (she spoke truer than she knew!). Sulkily, he agreed, but then the next time he trumpeted and was asked politely to go, he feigned sleep and refused to hear. Harriet's shouting her request did nothing to help the situation, for he rose bolt upright in the bed, bellowed "Fuck off!", and promptly fell asleep again. Next morning, he swore he remembered nothing of all this. He accused her of making it all up, or at least exaggerating.

Week four found a desperate Harriet creeping into their bedroom to plant an ancient tape recorder she had found in their desk beneath the bed, on his side. She would prove once and for all that he made a great noise. As the snoring reached crescendo, she clicked the "on" button. He woke up. She tried several times; the same thing occurred. "He doesn't wake when I shout my lungs out, but he wakes at the soft click of a button. What the hell is he playing at?" Hugh was enraged at being recorded. "Who the hell do you think you are? You have no right!", etc.

Refusing to sleep in the spare room herself, if he would not, and after six weeks with barely any sleep, she trickled cold water down his neck. He swung round, knocked the cup from her hand and thumped her in the chest before collapsing into instant sleep again.

Next day, both of them appalled by the bruise, they agreed they should visit a therapist.

Hugh was not a talkative type, whereas Harriet was easily able to articulate her feelings. I believed Hugh (well, almost), when he said he never remembered these night-time incidents. My hunch was that we were seeing great denial and passive aggression here, which was winding up Harriet more than the snoring. His total disregard for her requests to stop, while in the daytime acting as polite and friendly as ever, drove her into confusion as well as rage. Could she be imagining things after all? How could he be so cruel? Did he no longer care? Was she going mad? Was Hugh mad, to be so able to live comfortably in two worlds, like Jekyll and Hyde?

I believed Harriet's accounts, too. She really had tried everything before resorting to draconian methods. She certainly looked exhausted as well! The joint refusal to use the spare room suggested a big power conflict, but the rest puzzled me, until I saw them both separately. I asked each to tell me more about their life together, *apart* from the snoring.

Their little girl had just started school. Harriet was planning to return to work shortly. She had had a troublesome pregnancy, so was forced to stop work early on. For nearly six years now she had badly missed her colleagues at the clinic, and the social life that emanated from that. She feared she was no longer attractive, having put on weight. She was bored and lonely. Because she understood the reasons, though, and was about to put it all right, she kept these doubts to herself.

Hugh's firm was being taken over by a multi-national. There was fierce competition for new posts, which he feared he might not win. He knew he was good, but not that good. He would need sophisticated management skills, too, that he doubted he possessed. He knew Harriet was low, didn't want to burden her with more worry, and so said nothing. He was working late to impress the new employers and trying to catch up with the latest technological developments in his field. He felt responsible for much of his wife's low state and vowed to do better in future, though, to be honest he felt worn out. If she would be a bit nicer to him it might help, but she seemed so, well, silently angry these days, hard to approach.

Sexual relations had all but ceased in recent months. Both were low in spirits so could not help the other. Both were playing a waiting game, trusting things would get better, when all the time they were getting worse.

When these underlying issues came into the open and were thoroughly aired, the snoring lessened (or Harriet found it more tolerable). On bad nights they did indeed take turns to sleep in the spare room, creeping back into their shared bed in the early hours for a cuddle.

The undeclared suspicion that the other no longer cared was what had for weeks kept one deeply asleep, the other wide awake. When reassured, the nights became easier. The "tests" of affection and regard were no longer necessary: "If you loved me, you wouldn't mind my snoring", and "If *you* loved *me,* you would stop snoring and apologise." "If you loved me you would go to the spare room and let me sleep," and "If *you* loved *me*, you would not send me there."

This couple were too proud to admit their fears openly, too afraid to show their bitter anger at the loss of sex, for which each blamed the other. The problem had to be relocated to more manageable territory, in the hope that a downsizing of it would be easier to handle. Sometimes times this ruse works, but not for Harriet and Hugh!

Re-enacting

Partners are sometimes selected because the chooser intuits that here is a person who will re-enact an old family drama with them.

This will give them another chance. Perhaps they can make it come right this time.

Peter and Portia

Peter had always enjoyed a close, hearty relationship with his father, both being keen on sports and hiking. He remembers his mother as a shadowy figure at the sink. In his mind she is bland, always there, like the wallpaper. He has no especial feeling for her, apart from gratitude for bringing him up.

Portia was brought up by a working, single mother, whom she felt she could never live up to. Mum was brave, independent, a fighter. She did not trust men, or the government, or anyone in authority. "She lived through gritted teeth," said Portia.

Mother looked after her in all practical ways. Portia always had the right toys and clothes, went to a good school, and was helped with her homework. For holidays she usually went to her gran's. Mother mysteriously disappeared in those times. Portia later learned she took painting lessons in France, living hand to mouth to pay for them. "She was passionate about pictures, but never mustered any passion for her daughter," complained Portia, over and over again.

From Portia's account, it seemed her mother had been badly hurt by her father (whom her mother refused to discuss). She appeared to have frozen all her feelings except for her art, presumably a better bet than men, in her eyes. Portia, too young to understand any of this, was greatly damaged by her mother's cool matter-of-factness. The child was never kissed or cuddled, never read bedtime stories, or played with, except in the most perfunctory way.

Portia found another emotionally cold mother in Peter (who also replicated an absent father!). Peter was amiable enough, but he really preferred the company of men. She was left at the sink (like his mother) while he played rugby or cricket, or took off for long walks with his now ageing father. Portia felt left out, ignored.

Portia was determined to be noticed, loved even, this time. At first, she played the little wife role for all she was worth, cooking special food, laying out Peter's clothes and polished shoes each day (just as his mother had, no doubt). He never noticed or thanked her. Next, she tried to be a *femme fatale*. The only response she ever got was, "You're not going out like that, are you? You look like a tart. Put something else on."

She tried going to rugby matches and the booze-ups afterwards. No one talked to her. The jokes were crude and sexist and she usually came home with a cold. Peter seemed relieved when she stopped attending.

Then she tried to become "interesting" by joining the National Trust as an active member. Peter never commented, except when she was late preparing his meal in the evening, or there were no dry shirts.

Friends told her she was a doormat, should get liberated, stand up for herself. Others said she ought to have a serious talk with him about how she felt neglected. Spell it out. She tried both. Peter frowned concernedly, suggesting she might be a bit bored. Perhaps she should find herself a little job.

Finally, after four years, she begged him to go with her to Relate, for counselling. He was amazed she should think anything was wrong. He was perfectly happy. She was a great wife, all a man could ask for.

She went to Relate alone. Here at last, someone attended to her properly. She came to see how all her partners had been "Peters", in one form or another. She had to face that her mother had been unable to love her in the normal way. No amount of "men-pleasing" could alter that, or make it better. Never mind what they, the men, wanted her to be. What did *she* want for herself? She left Peter, and began individual therapy with me in order to find out.

Summary

All these processes interact. I have used the stories above to show just one process at a time, but this does not mean that other forces are absent. However, one process usually predominates at any given time.

Some concepts—transference for example—I have mentioned elsewhere, but usually in relation to a mature phase in the couple life cycle, or to the earlier Forming, Norming, Storming and Performing period (see Chapters Eight and Nine). In this chapter I have concentrated on those phenomena that occur between all couples at some time, in some couples all the time, and which bubble up to the surface occasionally, however old or young the relationship may be. These processes are universal, but are illuminated and enlarged by the microscope of cohabitation. As well then, to become familiar with them, rather than have them sprung on you!

CHAPTER TWELVE

Unconscious communication in domestic life

I n the next chapter we will look at who needs therapy and why. For the moment, let us examine the "ordinary couple". They have their ups and down, but are basically managing their marital relations well, without giving the matter much thought. Life is far too busy. Yet, without being aware of it, a private language has grown between them, including a language without words. We all recognize the scenario of a couple attending a rather tedious party, but not wanting to be rude by leaving too early. They can signal one another across a crowded room with a mere lift of an eyebrow, the tongue run round the top teeth, a subtle, querying lift of one corner of the mouth. "Leave Now? Five Minutes? Half past the hour?" "Ready to go?" Instantly, the answer is returned in the same code.

Messaging

This I call *messaging*. (May as well be up with the times.) It happens in all areas of joint living, down to the most intimate.

"I know when he wants to make love, but daren't ask directly, for fear of rebuff. He chews my earlobe in a very particular way."

"Yeah. If she just smiles or pats my hand in reply, she's not interested. But she's got this shy little giggle that passes so swiftly you could easily miss it. This means 'yes'."

"Well, I'll be damned. I never knew that, about my giggle I mean! What I do know though, is that when you suck up to me like that, it usually means: 'Are we doing it tonight, or can I watch the football?'"

"Not true!" (From his face it clearly is, at least sometimes.)

"Does it not occur to you that I might prefer a long cosy chat about the previous week, as we have had so little time together? It shouldn't be just footy or sex. There are other options."

"Right, it could be footy *and* sex!"

"Very funny . . . But seriously, we could also do *no* footy and *no* sex, have something nice instead—put some music on, watch a DVD, perhaps?"

"Point taken, but you know I love my football. It isn't just the game, you know. It helps me unwind after a tough week."

"And what about my tough week? This is a dual career family in case you hadn't noticed. Had you not thought that even when I don't do that blasted giggle, I may still be persuadable?"

"Unghh?"

"Look, if you gave footy a miss now and then—I mean, not when it's your favourite team or anything—but now and then. Well, if we chatted or watched a movie, or went to bed with last week's Sunday papers that we never get chance to read . . ."

"Bed with the *papers* . . .?"

"Bed isn't just for sleep and sex, blockhead. Once I'm comfy, the cats are fed, the house all locked up safe and snug, and we've had a bit of a conversation, well, maybe I'll feel more in the mood . . ."

"Women! You want me to go a-wooing, don't you?"

"*Rather!*"

This couple are messaging very well. They use mock aggression ("you blockhead") to mute real crossness. They tease so as not to hurt, but all the same get their message across. (There is a very delicate line between teasing and hostile sarcasm.) As to the negotiating of sexual congress, they have evolved a system of signals that they do not deploy deliberately: "I think I will bite her ear to see if she is interested"; but which happen automatically. As this conversation shows, they only become aware of, and interested in, the messaging system after the event. They share a similar sense of humour, have learnt how to use it to soften conflict. Humour is one of the best tools in the marital kit, so long as it not abused. But humour can also be very sadistic.

Obsessing about latent communication, cleverly pinning it all down, is not conducive to marital harmony. All too often it turns into a point-scoring exercise, a nasty game of catch the other out. Sometimes too much self-examining by the couple drives partners to become self-conscious, or to alter their signals so as to confuse the opposition. (The woman above stopped her giggling, once she found out about it.)

On the other hand, this pair plainly demonstrate how a bit of discussion or review of the relationship from time to time can really improve things. This "watching football/making love/spending time together" tension would certainly have degenerated into an ugly ongoing fight had the couple insufficient love and trust for one another to have it out in the open early on.

There is a dark side to messaging, of course.

I once met socially a woman who collected porcelain figurines. Her much-loved mother had willed a cherished collection to her daughter, and over the years she had added to these. Now the daughter's house was packed with these ornaments, which her husband detested. He put up with them, as he knew how much they meant to her.

In later years, the marriage slowly but surely deteriorated. There were affairs on both sides, trial separations, even the start of divorce proceedings; but they always reunited, only to find it did not last.

Their final row culminated in the husband slowly walking across the fireplace, inspecting the mantelpiece carefully, choosing the order in which he was to destroy his wife's (and the inherited) choice pieces. In slow motion, he raised then dropped the "Spaniel", then the "Shepherdess", then the "Flute Playing Youth" on to the floor, saying "Oops" each time. The message was clear to both.

Other partners, legal action, living apart, had failed to split them up. Both sides were finding it impossible to break up, though each knew the marriage was over. Some shared symbol, such as the porcelain collection, was the only way to kill the relationship for good. The woman walked out, never to return.

This story is reminiscent of Edward Albee's famous early play, *Who's Afraid of Virginia Woolf?* (1962). The couple swear and hit each other, get violently drunk and expose one another's sexual short-comings to their friends, shame and ridicule one another without mercy. Yet we know they will always stick together despite their marital hell—until the husband does the one thing that lies way beyond their unconscious deal. They are, in fact childless, but have invented a child and talk tenderly about it as if it is real. Before their friends, he announces that the child has died. His wife cannot protest that he has broken the rules without exposing their joint lie. She has to watch her husband killing their child. Is he killing the marriage, too?

On a lesser scale, and allowing for genuine accidents, even burning the toast or leaving residues of excreta in the loo are messages. What does bad hygiene say to a partner? You are not important enough to look nice for? If you cared, you would love me if I looked like a tramp? You don't take trouble to smell nice for me, so why should I for you? I can't be bothered to change sheets/towels; you wouldn't notice anyway?

Linking

In most partnerships ritual behaviours and communications abound. They are seldom noticed, referred to or discussed, yet play a critical role in maintaining the stability of the relationship. When a couple have acute problems that seem out of their ordinary joint experience, they have the option to see a therapist or to sit it out. But both members of the couple will also bring "unfinished business" from the past that has no need of therapeutic intervention, because the partner deals with it through a set of behaviours or actions worked out together over the years. This working out is done unconsciously, although there may be some superficial awareness that the ritual, however irrational it may seem, must be obeyed.

These sets of agreed behaviour deepen a couple's intimacy with each other, especially when the link with the past is understood. In effect, the couple become willing therapists for each other, albeit in narrowly defined areas and not all the time.

Max and Megan

Max and Megan divided all household responsibilities and child care equally, but there was one job Megan refused to do. She was very happy to compensate by doing extra jobs elsewhere, but she stalwartly refused to make up their prized, specially designed log fire of an evening, a luxury they both enjoyed. Her excuse was that clearing it out was a dirty and dusty business. She could not stand the ashes blowing about, nor the soot lining the inglenook chimney before the fire was lit. It made her cough, and looked like old treacle. She detested the draught that whooshed down that chimney, and the splinters that came off the logs. It was all so distasteful.

Max knew this was all nonsense. Megan ran a chicken farm and kennels, and came home every day covered in unmentionable substances and reeking to heaven. She loved every filthy minute of it. Still, he was an easy-going sort of bloke, so willingly made up the fire, cleaning out the previous day's ashes.

One autumn, on the way to a holiday cottage on the Isle of Skye, Megan took Max and the children to her home town on the Clyde Estuary, where she had grown up on a tiny council estate. She had not revisited for thirty-five years, as all her family had moved away or died. The youngsters insisted on knocking on the door of her old home, to ask if they could see their mum's bedroom. The house was now much improved and enlarged, but the fire range was still there, all blacked and polished, but unused. Nowadays, with central heating, it clearly qualified as an "antique feature".

Afterwards, Megan fell virtually silent, all the way to Skye.

Later, weeks later, she was able to explain her withdrawn state to Max, who listened intently. Her parents had fought bitterly, night after night, when they thought the children were asleep. During the day, her mother often dabbed her eyes on her apron, saying she had a stye coming, but Megan knew she was suppressing tears. Her adored mother refused to admit anything was wrong. Megan felt helpless, impotent.

The worst times for Megan were watching her mother make the fire in the morning, while father ate his breakfast in the kitchen. Her mother would draw out the business so as not to have to be in the same room with him. Covered in soot, hair all over the place, she clattered about, banging shovels and pokers around to "prove" she was hard at work. She stayed on her reddened knees until her husband left for the shipyard without saying goodbye. Megan watched her mother get up, sighing heavily, and thought her own heart would break.

Megan had forgotten all about these scenes until she paid that visit to her old home. Her childhood had not been hell all the time; there were good family times too. Had she not grown up to make a good marriage herself?

Max held her hands while she wept and wept over her mother. She had had no idea she harboured such sorrow. Yet for years she had messaged Max to protect her from the fire that might arouse disturbing memories. He had "read" her message, but without at first comprehending its importance.

Since then, she has never again needed to cry over her mother. Max goes on building the fire, with a love and tenderness far greater than before.

There is a direct link here between the new fire and the old, which is easy to understand. Megan's weeping is evidence for the existence of that link. Other linkages are multiple, complex, and unprovable. They can still be useful, if thought about and shared responsibly.

Tess and Terry

Terry returned from a midday job interview at one in the morning. Tess was beside herself with worry, and had called the local Accident and Emergency department as well as the police. It turned out that Terry had failed to get the job, then spent all day and evening walking the streets or sitting in the park, quite unable to go home.

Tess's anger evaporated when she realized his state of mind. He sat at the kitchen table, head in hands, sighing, then smashing a fist down on the surface, before turning inwards again, resuming the sighing. Tess forced him to drink a hefty brandy (he never drank usually). This seemed to shock him into awareness of his surroundings.

"Now talk, love," ordered Tess gently. "And keep talking."

From the hints he gave, what Tess knew of his old family, plus what she intuited about his feeling towards his current family, she began linking one thing to another. When she experienced that comfortable "clunk-click" feeling of a seat belt settling into place, she knew she was on to something important. She mentally binned anything that did not "fit".

So what were her conclusions?

As a child, Terry adored his two years younger brother, Tim, who turned to heroin at fourteen. Tim was so naïve and gullible it was thought that he might have had neurological damage. Terry was unable to motivate Tim to come off the drug, so took to stalking him everywhere so as to catch the dealers in the act. He never did. Tim may not have been very bright, but he was certainly cunning.

At seventeen, Terry became infatuated with a girl at his college. One weekend her parents were away. Terry was invited to come over and consummate their relationship. This was the night Tim overdosed and died. Terry never forgave himself, though he hardly ever spoke about the death nowadays.

Terry's and Tim's mother developed a bipolar disorder after Tim's death. (This is a serious condition where a sufferer experiences mood swings from depression to elation, so extreme that they lose contact with reality.) About a year after the death, Terry did some voluntary work overseas. His motives, Tess surmised, must have been muddled. He was probably atoning for his neglect of Tim by doing good works, well away from sexy women, but also escaping his mother. Perhaps he could not face her intermittent madness, for which he felt responsible.

Then there was Tess and Terry's own boy, just eleven. Terry was an upright, responsible man, a staunch Quaker. But he rarely gave vent to feelings. He believed strongly that it was actions that count. For all Tess knew, he could have been brooding about their boy, without saying anything at all about it.

What about Tess herself? At forty, she had at last become pregnant, after years of trying. She had willingly given up her headmistress post to ensure a safe pregnancy. However, it had been Terry who very badly wanted a child (replacement for Tim?). She herself could have been perfectly content with her career, but wanted to make Terry happy. Could he be feeling bad about stopping what, in her professional circles, had been a meteoric rise?

Then there was Terry's own career. He was a very experienced social worker, and had risen effortlessly up the hierarchy. The job he was being interviewed for would have awarded him great policy-making powers. His especial interest was in outreach programmes for alienated youth. He wanted to write about it too, thus educating the public. This job was ideal; it was *made* for him. Was it too fanciful to think he might have come to believe it was his destiny? Well into middle age now, he may have been anxious to set a seal on his career by making a really big difference to society and squaring his conscience at the same time. Had he felt this job was the last chance?

As she mulled all this over, Tess became increasingly aware of what this post might really mean to her husband. In his mind he may feel he had failed his mother, brother, and wife. Perhaps he dreaded failing his son too. The job, so big, so influential—*his* job— had now turned out to be a pipe dream. There was to be no forgiveness, no paying for his failures by rescuing all those youngsters and writing inspirational books about it. He was a failure with a capital "F". That was all there was to it.

Once the links are spelt out, as above, it all seems very simple. What I have written here though, is the *distillation* of Tess's meandering thoughts and memories as she tried to reason out what could be happening to her husband. None of it seemed simple to her at the time. Still, she knew him well, as only a spouse can. And she possessed the munificent gift of making links.

In taking Terry through his own story over the next few weeks, Tess watched him gradually recover. He had previously made none of the links, and had on the contrary spent years trying to break them, so he could avoid facing his pain. Had he got the job, he would have done great work for the community, but would not have healed his own wounds. Perhaps the interview panel had been wise after all.

Reconstructing

Once links have been made between things that, on the face of it, are not connected at all, the linker can move on to the next stage, that of reconstructing the past, be this the recent or distant past.

Samantha and Sidney

This couple had been married nearly thirty years. They had two well-adjusted teenage children and a lovely apartment in a fashionable quarter of London. Sidney, a successful barrister, woke up one night dripping with sweat and hyperventilating. Frightened, Samantha switched on the bedside light, whereupon he announced he had to leave her, *"had to"*.

Samantha could only suppose he had undergone some sort of nightmare. She promised they would talk the next day. She tried to hold and comfort him, but he turned away with a loud cry of anguish, jumped from the bed, and slept the rest of the night in the guest room.

Samantha's picture of their long marriage was a rosy one. They had been happy until the last couple of years when they had become a bit distant. She presumed this distance was due to gynaecological problems that eventually resulted in her having a hysterectomy, alongside which Sidney had taken on new responsibilities at work. This had involved extra hours in chambers as well as toiling at home after dinner. (He had always been something of a workaholic.)

Over the years, the family had enjoyed many long trips abroad. Both sets of parents-in-law were great allies and friends. Samantha loved looking after her children and felt no need for a career. She was absolutely certain that Sidney had been as content as she was.

When Sidney was challenged after the night-time fright, all sorts of nonsense (to Samantha's mind) came tumbling out of his mouth. He had not been *un*happy really—more bored, sort of, in a rut, always the compliant, good little boy he'd been as a child. He was a good father, devoted husband, terrific breadwinner, had secured all the required status symbols—look at this damn, *damn* flat for instance: he loathed it, had dreams about smashing it all up with a hammer! And those ghastly holidays. He'd rather have grabbed a tent and a pushbike and swanned off to the Lake District alone.

Samantha thought he had gone mad. "You were, *are* happily married," she insisted. She brought out the photo albums of all their family holidays, day trips, every new car they had bought, the children's speech and sports days. Head in hands, Sidney refused to alter his position. He kept chanting, "I have to go, I just have to go."

Samantha began searching for explanations. Had he a mistress? Was he ill—this looked awfully like the mid-life crisis, though she wasn't exactly certain of its symptoms. He never really seemed to get over his mother's death three years ago. Could that be it? Was it something she herself had unwittingly done to make him this way? She simply could not absorb what he was telling her. He had to be mad.

Alas, Samantha was making all the wrong links, selecting only those that would support her existing hypothesis—Sidney was temporarily off his rocker. True linking is a careful, exploratory process, not a clutching at straws to avoid having to change one's view (though, let's face it, we all do it).

In fact, Sidney had just woken up to the truth about his life. He had always wanted to live in the country, but Samantha had always wanted the city life. He did not know what career was right for him, but it was certainly not the law. He had never had a mistress, not even another girlfriend before Samantha. He had never *lived*. Suddenly, he was overwhelmed by a rage to live.

Understandably shocked, Samantha scolded him. "You are selfish, a Peter Pan who never grew up. What about your responsibilities? You will wreck the children's lives running off this way. How can you do this to us?"

Sidney groaned. "That, *that*, the weight of all that! *That's* what I can't stand any more! I am sick with being so responsible."

These night-time rows went on for weeks, until Samantha approached her mother for help. A wise, sensitive woman, she enabled Samantha to slowly *reconstruct* her view of the marriage. Samantha had not been in error over the *facts* of their life together. What she had missed was Sidney's growing discontent in the latter years. She could hardly be blamed for this, as he was the type of man who never opened up about his hopes and fears—even to himself, according to his perceptive mother-in-law. Samantha's mum had watched his restlessness grow for years, but Samantha's vested interest in the marriage had blinded her. It was her mother who was able to observe and make all the links.

Reconstructing is largely educated guesswork, and often cannot be done by someone too close to the person who needs to rethink his or her situation. Samantha was powerless to help her husband reconstruct his past, as she needed to reconstruct her own as much as he!

Samantha's mum encouraged her to let Sidney take up his "mad idea" of renting a cottage in the country for a bit, arranging sick leave from work and "time out" from the marriage. Mum could see that continuing suffocation for Sidney would finish the marriage altogether.

Only when Samantha courageously faced that Sidney's break-down was a break*through* to his erstwhile hidden self was she able to let him go, release him from guilt-inducing arguments. His panic was due to his terror that, as always, she would get her way, force him to return to the marriage out of a sense of duty.

When she reluctantly agreed to a trial separation ("What choice do I have?"), he found himself a new job, with cottage attached, on the gardening team of the estate of a stately home. The children at first refused to have any contact.

Eighteen months later, the couple began meeting for weekends. Sidney was reconciled with the children. Samantha, meanwhile, had moved on. She had enrolled at university, made new friends, but still insisted on living in London, whether her husband returned or no. She seemed able to live without him now, if she had to.

Samantha just might have forced Sidney to stay. But Sidney's hunger for personal fulfilment, discarding his grey life (as he saw it), was stronger. Anyway, Samantha would have sensed his lack of commitment, while he would come to regard her as his jailor. They would have grown to hate each other.

Reconstructing is an interpretive art. Reconstructions are not certainties, but probabilities, possibilities, likelihoods. The person being "reconstructed" needs to participate in the process at some point, to firm up or discard hypotheses. The agreed historical facts need to be reconfigured also by the person(s) who wove a self-interested (self-protective) narrative about them; i.e., the person "nearest and dearest" to the subject. Through the linking process, new light (not absolute certainty) can be shed on questions that were unknowable or unverifiable at the time. A sensitive and genuinely neutral third party can often help in this process, for each party will have a vested interest in maintaining their own version of events.

Samantha had supposed her husband was happy, but never actually asked him. But then, he never complained that he was *un*happy. Poor Samantha had been living in a fool's paradise. How much of that paradise was of her own making? How much had Sidney colluded with her?

Karl and Kate

Karl, an Austrian sports instructor, spent his first three years in an Austrian orphanage. He was adopted at three by a resident British diplomat and his wife, and later educated at a British university, where he met Kate. He loved his new parents, enjoyed growing up bilingual, and was a natural sportsman He could recall only the happiest of memories.

About the orphanage, he is completely blank. He visited it as a young adult, accompanied by his adoptive family, wondering if it might jog his memory, but again, blank. All his new parents could tell him was that his original mother and father died in a plane crash that killed the pilot and his four passengers. There was a singular lack of any records concerning the crash. Old newspapers had not revealed anything useful.

At twenty-seven, after a long courtship, Karl married Kate. At first all went well. When their first son was born they were over-joyed. Kate looked forward to having another child.

Slowly, almost imperceptibly, Karl began to withdraw, stay out late, and avoid Kate's sexual overtures. At first she wondered if she were imagining things, but finally had to face that Karl really was pulling away from her. She wondered if he were jealous of their son, so tried to be extra attentive. This only made matters worse. When their son was almost three, Karl stayed out all night for the first time. Then it became a regular feature of their life.

Kate confronted him, angry and frightened. He admitted he felt miserable and lost, but did not know why. He just could not bear to look at his son. He was not aware of any jealous feelings, he said, only a sort of pity, and also—he hated to admit this—a sense of contempt for the child's vulnerability. He loved the boy. Of that he was sure, but at the same time he had no wish to associate with him, to be seen with him in public, to be responsible for him.

Kate was completing a part-time counselling course at this time. She asked for a special interview with one of the tutors. As they discussed the problem, Kate and her tutor began to *reconstruct* Karl's life to date, appreciating that they were hypothesizing, not inventing.

Why had he no memory of the orphanage? Does *anyone* remember incidents from such an early age? Did something awful happen, that he had to bury away from consciousness? There was nothing in his life after the orphanage that gave rise to problems. School, friends, relatives, all seemed perfectly ordinary. His health was always good. As a teenager he experimented with drink and drugs, but nothing very serious. University was uneventful, save for the odd love affair before Kate, which she had never really asked about in any depth. She did not know if the relationships had been sexually consummated.

Her own relations with Karl, apart from initial sexual shyness on his part, had always been relaxed and happy, until the birth of their son. The older the boy grew, the more Karl retreated from intimacy. It was tempting to think that some form of abuse had taken place around the age of three, and Karl was reacting to this. It would fit a lot of theories about abuse if he unconsciously saw his old self in his child. It might even be possible that he suspected he'd been abused, and was worried about carrying on the tradition with his own boy. He knew from Kate's reports of her counselling studies that the abused could become abusers themselves. He left the room when such topics came on television.

Another angle: Kate felt sure that the Karl's guilty "contempt" for the child's weakness grew out of a great fear that he would be unable to protect him. Rather like carrying a Ming vase about, terrified of dropping it. Could it be that he felt it was safer to avoid the vulnerable infant until he could fend for himself?

Was it possible that the plane crash was a fiction, to cover some more sinister story of abuse? Had they wanted to get the child to England out of the way, so he could not speak?

Why was Karl getting worse, not better? At three, he had been sent to a good home, so should he not be growing more hopeful as his son drew nearer that age?

Why had they waited until he was three before having him adopted? What made him a "difficult to place" child? Had he been disturbed or withdrawn without anyone knowing why? Perhaps the diplomat and his wife had taken pity on him, felt they could get him help in England?

They also considered the idea that no abuse occurred, and that the assumption that the diplomat's home was superior to the orphanage could be sheer prejudice. Karl could have been very attached to a particular worker who functioned as a surrogate mother. He may have been very happy there, and greatly traumatized by the enforced separation. This could account for why Karl's state deteriorated as his son approached the critical birthday.

It was possible that, having blanked out his own first three years, whatever the reason, Karl felt unable to rear his son until *he* had passed the three-year mark. Shame at not being able to father the boy could have made Karl shun intimate relations with his wife. His own life had become safe and happy enough to remember, from three on. Perhaps he felt that on attaining the same age, his son would be safe too.

Kate put these ideas to Karl *as possible scenarios, not inviolate truths.* At first he was shocked, then later said he felt relieved. Some kind of sense was being made of his mental state at last. He'd feared he was having some sort of crack-up, that his weird state of mind was meaningless. He had been especially worried, as he loved his wife very deeply and never wanted to lose her. This afforded huge relief to Kate.

Karl saw a therapist for a time, but in the therapy he never recovered any lost memories. He did come to terms with his feelings for his son, though. Once the boy had his third and then fourth birthdays, Karl's moodiness departed altogether and he ceased his night-time disappearances. The marriage bloomed. Eventually, Karl proved an excellent father.

This couple will probably never know what really happened to Karl, though the story is suggestive of some form of abuse. On recovery, Karl felt he had no need to unearth the details. He had a lovely wife and son. It was enough. Unless Kate had looked into the matter, though, and tried to reconstruct his life before he met her, he may have become very ill because of his inability to apportion any degree of meaning to his symptoms. The panics and self-reproach could have got worse and worse.

Quite often couples help to reconstruct one another's lives like this, without any need for external intervention. But there has to be enormous trust and frankness between them.

This type of reconstruction has caused much controversy in recent years. Most readers will be familiar with the publicity given to "recovered memory syndrome". It has been alleged that some therapists have put two and two together and made five. As a result, the patient was *implanted* with "memories", which were then "recovered". As a consequence, many people, parents in particular, stood wrongly accused of terrible crimes. I wish to stress, therefore, that the kind of reconstruction described here is *not* a rewriting of history. Nor is it a prescription by the therapist/reconstructor: *this is what really happened. Accept it as the truth.*

Mediating

Partners are often reluctant to ask "up front" for the type of caring gesture they desire at any given moment. They dread refusal, scorn, or disdain for their still wanting childish comforts that they should have grown out of years ago. In some couples, the unspoken dread is that the other one, far from satisfying the need, will recognize the vulnerability under the request and take advantage, empower themselves, and correspondingly disempower the petitioner.

The reverse of this is when a partner senses their own anger or destructiveness is not acceptable to their conscience. All the same, the need to *be* angry and destructive at that moment is irresistible. In both these cases, someone or something is brought in to mediate the exchange, to make it less risky, yet meet the requester's need to petition, or the angry person's need to get the uncomfortable feelings out.

Unconscious mediation techniques fashion a face saving compromise. Let us look at some examples.

A spouse shudders. "This room is so chilly today." To which the unwitting partner replies, "So bring an extra heater in. You're not helpless." The practical problem may be solved, but communication has failed. Without articulating the need consciously, the chilly partner is talking about his or her *internal* "temperature". They feel cold, unloved. Had there been no latent message in the comment on the cold room, the chilly one would have simply fetched a fire. Too fearful of rejection or shaming, this spouse could not say openly, "Please say something nice to me."

The worry here is that after repeated failure of such apparently small communications, the misunderstood one ceases to appeal to their other half. Either they smother their needs, becoming angry, resentful, or depressed, or they attempt to have their needs met in other relationships. To some extent this is healthy. It is unrealistic to expect one's partner to meet every need on demand. But if other relationships are too frequently resorted to, the risk of increasing couple estrangement, leading to an affair, is high. Lonely, neglected partners are not saints.

Is the onus here on the sender of the covert message to make their need more explicit, rather than have it mediated through the question of the cold room? Or should the non-receiver develop more sensitivity to this kind of hidden appeal? Dozens of these kinds of messages, wrapped in "innocent" conversation, are missed every day. Small misunderstandings like this may seem trivial in isolation, but think of the accumulated effect. Remember, too, that little miscommunications are models, rehearsals almost, for the big ones. Both sides need to get deciphering!

Couple members too scared or proud to attempt direct contact, unsure of the reception they may face, bring in a third party to convey sensitive communications. Dogs and cats are very common candidates. They are very, very important members of the family in this regard.

Candy and Cliff

This young couple had been living together for just six months and were still establishing their Norms (see Chapter Eight).

They were very much in love, but quibbled over how to manage money, what furniture and fabrics to have, where to eat out, or who to invite to dinner. They purchased two rescued mongrel puppies, with whom they were greatly enamoured. They found themselves squabbling over whose turn it was to feed the animals. Cliff complained that Candy did not give them fresh water often enough. Candy claimed he did not groom them frequently enough.

When the dogs were walked, Candy and Cliff took turns at holding the double lead, each consulting their watch regularly to see if they could take over yet.

Plainly, this competitiveness over the puppies was more than the simple affection each felt for them. From an onlooker's viewpoint, there was no sense of them using the dogs as substitutes for babies or companions, as is so often the case (and why ever not?). The dogs rather represented the couple themselves. Without being aware of it, each was showing the other how they wished to be treated: as special, first priority, love always to hand. At the same time, the non-stop playing and adoring of the yelping, nuzzling, frisky little creatures echoed the response each wanted from the other. Without ever verbalizing it, both Cliff and Candy were saying, "Look how they love me. *Look how lovable I must therefore be to you.*" In addition, there was a mutual challenge: "*I am better at loving than you.*" Underlying this was the fear in each that they might be found wanting in this new business of cohabiting.

Whenever Cliff was cross with Candy, the animals were fed late or there would be some other infringement of the pet care rules. Candy would complain bitterly of their neglect, while actually trying to communicate her own. Similarly, when fed up with Cliff, she would lie on the sofa cuddling one pup then another, or, if very angry, both at once. "*They adore me, even if you don't!*" This effectively excluded Cliff from their little family. He slunk off to play darts with his mates.

Gradually, they made up. This would be accomplished by Candy feeding one pup and leaving Cliff to do the other: "I am prepared to share." Out walking, Cliff might graciously offer, "You take them a bit further today, before I have them." One day, after their first really big quarrel the night before, Cliff said suddenly, "Hey, we could get the pups a lead each, instead of this joint thing. Then we could each have one, swap over at half time."

This relationship was still very new, the participants uncertain of one another. The dogs acted as go-between until they felt their relationship had firmed up sufficiently to tolerate frankness and proper negotiation, without going "over the top".

It should be repeated here that, as with other modes of unconscious communication, mediation rarely happens in strict isolation. Candy and Cliff *messaged* each other through the pups, but in order to do so had to employ *projection* (see pp. 154–158, Chapter Eleven). In other words, human needs, hopes and fears were attributed to (projected on) the animals. It might even be argued that using the dogs in this way constituted a *relocation* (see pp. 162–165, Chapter Eleven). However, this term is generally reserved for a specific and very thorny problem that is moved somewhere else to make it safer. Cliff and Candy were not having a "problem" so much as learning how to communicate with each other.

Sadly, much cruelty perpetrated on animals stems from violent impulses towards a spouse (or child, sibling, or other household resident). They are often the "fall-guys", the ones at the bottom of the pecking order who, because they are dumb, can be treated cruelly with impunity. It is all too tempting to take out frustrations with other family members on pets.

Also, many animals console, even heal (or point the way towards healing) terrible deprivation or loss, in adults and children alike. Their function in a home is never neutral. In his novel *Tomorrow*, Graham Swift (2007) has a central character, Otis, a cat who is the catalyst for major change in a couple's lives. (Incidentally, the novel also explores the effects of childlessness on an otherwise happy couple, the experiences of twinship between a brother and sister, and the way family dynamics pass down the generations.)

I once knew a couple who inherited a geriatric, mouldy parakeet from a relative. The husband spent whole days and months teaching it to say "Who's a good boy?" whenever he approached the birdcage. The wife spent equal time (when hubby was out of the way) training it to say "Silly bugger! Silly bugger!" The husband, a rather cantankerous, selfish character, was very pleased with himself every time the parakeet complimented him. One day, he noticed his wife had failed to do her usual morning clean-out of the cage, when she should have left out a fresh supply of food. Crossly, he approached the cage to do it himself, expecting the usual greeting. Instead he got "Silly bugger! Silly bugger! Silly bugger!"

The wife in this partnership told me this story. She had spent years trying to appease and calm this grumpy man. This bit of retaliation (her fury mediated by the bird) gave her immense pleasure, and the strength to carry on.

In-laws are often mediators. (Sometimes they "mediate" quite deliberately, acting as peace broker between the couple, but in this chapter we are looking at how one party can use an in-law, friend, or colleague to message their partner *unconsciously*.)

We all know men and women who, on marriage, seem to remain joined at the hip to their mothers (and sometimes, but less often, fathers).

Lydia and Lee

After two years of marriage, Lydia still shopped for clothes with her mum, borrowed recipes from mum, chose the flat's furniture with mum, watched the same TV programmes as—and reported back to—mum. She phoned mum every day. Lee had waited patiently for his new wife to "grow out of it", for she had not been so dependent on her mother before they were married, rather the contrary. By now though, he was becoming impatient, and felt the only role he was allowed was as breadwinner. He had no wish to be bossy or controlling, but was not prepared to be treated as a second-class citizen.

Lydia had always struggled to be free of her much-loved, but possessive mother, who had always made her feel a small, incompetent child. Now she was all grown up and married, she felt she had proved her adult status. She could now join the band of married women and do womanly things with them. Protected by her legal marital status, it had become safe to regress, go back and grab all the warm, attached, safe feelings she had denied herself as a teenager, when she'd felt she must at all costs throw off mother's influence.

At the same time, being a wife, and especially a mother, terrified her—this was the unspoken message she was trying to send to her husband. She wanted and needed Lee's support to make her feel more confident in her new role. She needed him to *not* just bring home the bacon, but actually educate her to be his wife. She was afraid to ask openly, because of her shame, and her fear, too, of his disappointment or even desertion. It felt safer to take her tuition from mum, grab all she had missed as a teenager, and provoke her husband into winning her back, at the same time. She was not aware of any of this, but someone else had put two and two together.

I am glad to say that Lydia's dad, who had willingly remained beneath the thumb of his wife for thirty years, finally took Lee aside, told him in no uncertain terms to stop being a wimp and take charge of his marriage. (This was overt, conscious mediation.)

Lydia's father and mother went for a long retirement cruise (engineered by Lydia's dad?). This afforded Lydia and Lee the time to share their fears about their still young marriage and start to put things right.

Lydia had used the situation with her mum to mediate her great fear of marital responsibility while sending out an appeal to her husband for rescue. Lee completely failed to read the message she was sending, until Lydia's father had a man-to-man talk.

Projective communications

As described in the previous chapter, human beings have a tendency and great capacity for dumping unwanted aspects of themselves into their partners, then attacking or admiring in their other half what they themselves have, as it were, given away. Therapists call this projection. It is a means of psychological evacuation. Projective *communication* is different to straightforward projection, in so far as there is a message to the other party embedded in the projected quality. Take Deirdre and Dick for instance.

Deirdre and Dick

Dick is a senior accountant in a big, successful corporation. At home, he cannot manage bills or his monthly bank statement. He does not know how to pay the plumber, organize theatre tickets, or make a weekly shopping list. This is all done willingly by Deirdre.

Despite his career achievements, Dick is still the lonely, bullied, orphaned little lad he was in the school playground, praised by teachers for his gifts in numeracy, but hated by all the other children, who excluded him. He does not ask Deirdre explicitly to make up for what he has missed. What would that do to his self-respect? But, because he attributes to her all the competency, organizational, and management ability he displays at work, she rises to the occasion, providing just what he needs. Because he has such a high profile career, Deirdre feels doubly proud at being so indispensable to her man.

Deirdre comes from an academic, but rather cold family. She never quite matched up to their standards, getting only a lower Second Class Honours degree in History, a "soft" and despised subject, according to their lights. By marrying, Deirdre has withdrawn from public competition, but loves being her partner's ideal consort. At home, she can deposit all the uselessness and inadequacy she formerly felt in herself into her darling, clever, but inept husband. Her projective message is: "Do not merely *carry* my shortcomings: *use* them to make me feel strong, capable and self-regarding!" Dick is saying: "Do not just *carry* my competencies. Use them to let me forgo my normal responsibilities, be true to the needy, deprived side of my nature."

If some of the above sounds familiar, you are right. Projective communications are what make up the "deal" made between all partners as they commit to one another (see Chapters One and Two). For the contract to work, these communications must be reciprocal and complementary, as in the case of Deirdre and Dick.

This is an example of *locked* projective communication, which is more or less permanent. The marriage will thrive so long as nothing and no one destabilizes the projective activity. Should Deirdre find herself a job that gives her self-regard and praises and rewards her gifts, she may find herself more reluctant to manage her husband's domestic affairs. What if a child comes along? Deirdre may want a full-time man, not a part-time child, to be the father.

On the other hand, if they are together long enough, each might slowly withdraw their projective requests as they no longer need these emotional favours from one another. They have "grown their own", as it were. The marriage has given Deirdre self-respect while compensating Dick for most of what he missed: he can manage now.

Temporary projective communications can be quite scary. It is as if the familiar partner has suddenly become someone else.

Nigel and Norma

Norma and Nigel are wading through their monthly bills, Norma wondering how they are ever going to make ends meet. She lays out her figures on the kitchen table, along with her credit cards. She asks for Nigel's cards and would he please let her have the latest bank statement?

Nigel refuses. She's making a fuss as usual. Things will work out. He is so cagey, she suspects he has overspent badly again, so tactfully confronts him.

"What is this, the third degree?" he scoffs. "On and on you go, penny here, penny there. As if any of it mattered. You're making a mountain out of a molehill. You're a pain in the butt, honest to God you are. I'm sick of it!"

Norma is shocked. This is not like Nigel. She sits, her mouth open, for the moment speechless.

Then he weighs into her, criticizing her household management, her spending hundreds on shoes (her admitted weakness) while trying to save a few pounds by searching out cheap restaurants, or buying second-hand books and DVDs. She's ridiculous. She doesn't plan properly, she's got her priorities all wrong . . .

She tries to fight back, but Nigel is in the grip of his passion now. His stream of put-downs seem never ending. Norma runs upstairs and throws herself, weeping, on to the bed.

Next day a penitent Nigel realizes he went too far and says he is sorry.

"I don't know what came over me. I just blew a gasket."

When Norma shows him exactly how he made her feel— ridiculed, sneered at, a waste of space, he groans.

"Dear God, *she* used to do that. My sister, I mean."

Norma knows that Nigel was brought up by a resentful elder sister after his mother left his father. Nigel was still very young, and missed his mum terribly. The sister foisted on to him responsibilities he was far too young to meet, which made him feel inadequate and stupid. When she raged at him, which was most of the time, he wanted to sink through the floor and just disappear.

Clearly Norma had inadvertently stirred up these memories through her perfectly reasonable behaviour toward him. Not understanding what was happening, so not able to frame the situation in words, *Nigel did to Norma what his sister had done to him*. He projected his own childhood experience into his bewildered partner, *to make her feel the way he had*. His message was, "Don't carry on provoking me about the bills. You are making me feel something I cannot bear. I will make you feel what I cannot bear, by doing to you what was done to me. Then you might understand."

Fortunately for Nigel, Norma did eventually understand. His apology was accepted.

Projective mechanisms are subtle and complex. I recommend to readers wanting to grapple further with these concepts Robert Hinshelwood's *A Dictionary of Kleinian Thought* (1991) and *Clinical Klein* (1994).

Summary

In bookshops up and down the country, the shelves groan with self-help manuals: "How to keep your man/woman"; "How to perk up your sex life"; "How to negotiate better/handle aggression better/get your needs met without asking". These manuals contain much that is sensible and useful. They do not feature much in my reading list, however, because my aim in writing this book is to enable readers to look at their own, unique couple (or ex-couple), in its individual context. I want you to see and understand how your couple operates *unconsciously*. Self-help books, however worthy, are rather short on this.

This book advocates a psychodynamic approach to understanding and helping couples. (Psychodynamic means "derived from, but far from the same as, psychoanalysis".) Should these ideas be new or alien to you, persevere. Once some degree of understanding is reached by both of you, what to actually *do* about things (or stop doing!), is more or less obvious. Change and mutual adjustment takes time; it cannot be accomplished overnight. Do not be too disappointed if either or both of you slip back into bad psychological habits occasionally. The fact that both of you are collaborating in this venture is what counts most.

A final, cheery comment for those wondering if "the other man/ woman" threatening the relationship is going to win out. Think about all the processes and mechanisms in this and the previous chapter. Consider how long, deep, and pervasive is this secret side of marriage that outsiders never see. Hard work over many years has been invested in building up this culture and language, accessible and comprehensible to only two. The third party has the devil of a job to speak that language, or negotiate the terrain so familiar and comfortable to the "straying" partner.

Only if the first marriage is really dead is the new pair likely to find the energy and motivation to start all over again, building an equally complex network of unconscious interactions to sustain and maintain the new relationship.

When do you know a marriage is dead? I believe it is when the pull and push of all these mechanisms and processes can no longer be felt. Two people living parallel lives under the same roof, but not knowing or wondering what the other is thinking or feeling (and not enquiring), hardly constitutes a live relationship.

Even if children, finances, holidays, and careers are smoothly managed, if there is no emotional connection, no *play space* (which includes fight space!), it is dead. It may fulfil the criteria for being an effective team, an alliance at best, but not a *marriage*. Peace may reign, but it is the peace of the churchyard. Far better the noise of the battlefield. For then survival, even victory, is possible.

CHAPTER THIRTEEN

Who needs therapy?

I n the first chapter of this book I said I would be writing about the "average couple" and their problems. By this penultimate chapter I find myself wondering what "average" could mean in this day and age. Thirty years ago, when I started couple work, a stereotype of the typical British couple still lingered in the public's mind. They were reasonably educated, white, legally and happily married, parents to a couple of well-behaved children perhaps, believed in fairness and decency, owned a car (washed each Sunday), and lived in a semi-detached home with a bit of a garden.

I suspect the stereotype was more myth or cover-up than fact, even then. For these couples were none the less deeply troubled or they would not have come to see me, especially in those days when psychotherapy was ill understood, and couple work (apart from the frontier busting "Marriage Guidance") still in its infancy. In fact, having therapy would have disqualified the pair from being the prototypical British couple. Even considering therapy at that time was more like proof of instability—to put it at its mildest.

Over the years, the clientele has widened unimaginably. What is average or typical now? I have worked with couples who have always managed a situation where one partner cross dresses; where the pair never have sex, but this not the problem they bring; where they can only have sex under very strange (to me, but not them) conditions, or are allowed sexual relations with others. Again, this is not the problem they bring. There are marriages where one partner is gay or bisexual; where the partners have separate homes and commute, have separate holidays and sometimes "sabbaticals"—a whole year off! Or where one partner's career is given precedence over the other's, who acts as housekeeper and main parent for an agreed period, before changing roles.

Granted, these examples are not run of the mill, but they are increasingly common. The arrangements described above function as a backdrop to the couple's problem; they do not directly cause the declared problem. These ways of living and partner choices may seem strange to some readers, and even to some of us therapists, but that is the couple's business, not for us to judge. Doubtless the choice of partner (see Chapters Two and Three) is relevant to an understanding of the pair's individual and joint personality make-up, but the very foundations on which their relationship has survived thus far are not the object of therapeutic change. The focus must be on the problems that brought them to seek help, which may not have much to do with the long-term context of their relationship.

We need to avoid normative thinking, trying to make everyone fit into what constitutes for ourselves the "right" or "best" marriage. Many a traditional "ordinary" couple with every social, financial, and educational advantage still hit grave difficulties at some time in their shared life. Others with "unusual" marital arrangements, such as those described above, may enjoy decades of contentment together before meeting a crisis.

Whether the couple fit the old stereotype or the emerging, more variable one, we need to take a developmental stance, study with them their personal stories concerning their key relationships from birth on, in order to help them make sense of their shared predicament. Therapy facilitates growth and insight; it should not convert, indoctrinate, or pass value judgements.

Alas, many couples pass judgement on themselves. Most of us are handed down a picture of what coupledom ought to be, from school, church, parents, magazines, and television soaps. Deeply rooted in our minds as well, whether we are aware of it or not, is a picture of how our parents actually seemed to us—which may not match up with the views they espoused! Then there are the TV pundits, the academic psychologists, and, indeed, the government, who tell us what is normal, healthy, and best for our children. All this shapes our contemporary view of what living as a couple should—and should not—mean. Accordingly, many people have been brainwashed into believing there is only one acceptable mould, and fear that they do not fit it.

Few can live up to the ideal set before us. Shame is extremely common in the couples who come to therapy. Indeed, needing help is itself seen as shameful, as if we should all be perfect. People who believe they failed to match up to parental expectations feel this especially keenly.

Lurking in the mind's more private area, there may be residual shame, too: about parents' desertion of each other; about their parents' or their own previous divorces; about children born out of wedlock—be these their own children from an earlier relationship, or their partner's, or any member of their original family. It may concern their being abused as a child. (Often in thirty years of marriage, shame has prevented abuse from being discussed or even mentioned!) There may be alcoholics, drug addicts or HIV in the family; episodic psychotic breakdown in self, parents, children or relatives. Violence may have been done to or by the person(s) coming for help. The list goes on. And on.

I wish to state clearly here that these matters are ubiquitous, inside my consulting room and outside, too. Money, social status, education, wisdom, and love galore is no protection against them. They are part and parcel of family life.

Incidentally, it is interesting how, when family trees are drawn up, the "unusual" feature very often passes down the generations in a characteristic way: e.g., it is always the first cousin once removed who runs off to Australia, squanders the family fortune, or whatever. This applies as much to accidental babies, elopers, and embezzlers as to more obvious, inherited conditions such as neurological, physical, and serious psychiatric disorders. However, the question of family "culture carriers" is a matter for future research. The salient point here is that the truly rare couple or family is the one with *none* of these situational factors to worry about!

In short, then, the answer to the question "Who should have therapy?" is "Anyone who feels the need". Were we to answer

"Anyone with a family skeleton in their cupboard", the nation's consulting rooms would be overflowing.

It follows that referring oneself, or being referred to a couple therapist, is not about being abnormal, sick, weak, or degenerate. In these politically correct days people tend not to use these words overtly, but I know from my work that these are the archaic (residues of childhood?) phrases that come to many people's minds at the thought of going for therapy. (Not for nothing am I often jokingly referred to as "the witchdoctor".)

Depending on experience with earlier authority figures, seeing a therapist can be a terrifying prospect, though some see therapy (equally erroneously) as a refuge where unhappiness can be conveniently dumped and nothing ugly will have to be faced. (Therapist as lovely mummy/daddy who sorts everything out.)

Seeing a therapist is not a medical matter. It is not the same as going to your GP with that 'flu that you cannot seem to shake off. Will the doctor refuse antibiotics? Are you not sick enough? Should you wait? Are you wasting the doctor's time, making a fuss? (Conversely: I am ill. I pay my taxes. The doctor *must* give me what I need.)

Couple tensions are not illnesses and therapists are not judges— or doctors. If you both feel you would welcome talking things over with a trained third party, make an appointment. You do not have to meet again if you feel there would be no benefit. You have not as yet made any promises; you are free agents.

Sometimes couples come just (just!) "to clear the air". They cannot fight at home without things getting out of hand. With a third party present, they feel heard by their partner at last because the other thinks twice before rudely butting in. Also, a third person's presence has the effect of muting emotionality and wild threats. The couple can converse more rationally, however heated they feel.

The therapist may be able to offer them a rough map by the end of the session. It is early days yet, so any map will be but informed guesswork. Still, it might enable the pair to go home and work *beneath the surface* of their communications with each other, each of them considering the *other* partner's sensitivities in the light of their family history, rather than going over the same old mutually blaming ground.

Occasionally, over time, this sketch map is filled in at home by the couple themselves. No more therapy is required. More often, the couple either continue in regular, usually weekly, therapy until they feel ready to leave, or they dip in and out of therapy for a few weeks or months at a time, only to return later when new difficulties arise. Couples are different and have different therapeutic needs. Therapy should be tailored to the couple, not the couple to the therapy.

What if one party wishes to attend and the other does not? Should the other push, persuade, nag, deliver an ultimatum, or wait? There are no right answers here, but it is very likely that the struggle over getting the second party to attend will mirror the dynamics causing the rifts in the partnership more generally. This in itself is worth thinking over, and may shed a little light. The reluctant party may (or may not) be prepared to discuss the findings.

One approach is to try to understand the underlying (as opposed to the professed) reason for the refusal to see a therapist. "They are all wankers" is just not sufficiently convincing, however sincerely such a view may be held. The spouse may feel bullied into "going before the headmistress". Or they may fear that they will be judged as wanting by the therapist, an inadequate husband/wife. Or maybe the therapist is bound to invade their privacy, "read their mind". The so far unmet therapist usually represents an authority figure. The reluctant partner will be reacting as they generally do to authority figures.

Some aversive parties fear that the partner who wants to see a therapist will be more articulate than them, and will win the therapist over. The consulting room is really a court of law and they are in the dock. Such a fearful partner might prefer to see the therapist alone at first, ensuring an unbiased hearing.

Some partners are impulsive by temperament and want things solved at once, whereas others, no less worried about their relationship, want to think it through and take a measured decision in their own time. Some people are very much in touch with their feelings and find it easy to put words to their pain. Others have to clamber through mists and fog to get to what they are really feeling. They genuinely need time. (However, they can procrastinate indefinitely on the grounds that they are just no good at this kind of thing.) Opening up your most intimate relationship to a complete stranger can be an extremely daunting prospect to some, whereas for others that very status is a huge relief, like pouring out your heart to the stranger on a train. If you are considering couple therapy, it is important that these temperamental differences are recognized and respected.

Motives for coming into therapy vary, and there is usually more than one. Curiously, it is very rare that one or both members of the pair explicitly request understanding from the therapist of what is happening between them, though from the therapist's point of view this is the object of the exercise.

If the therapist merely supplies what is requested and then stops, so that no understanding of the couple's unconscious dynamics (all the stuff in previous chapters) is reached by the pair, this has been a sticking plaster job only. The problems will return very soon.

Often the therapist is asked to take on the role of referee or judge: "Tell us who is at fault, him or me?" Or a translator: "I have explained till I am blue in the face, but my partner just will not or cannot comprehend my problem. Can *you* find the right words?" Similarly, some crave justification: "Surely all right-thinking folk would say, like me, that a good marriage should be a, b and c? Tell him/her I have got it right. *My partner just might believe you, a professional.*" Or an ally: "I have worked my socks off at this relationship for years and years, made it my number one priority. Surely I deserve better treatment than this from my partner? *You are on my side aren't you?*" Often a diagnosis is required: "Have we got it wrong where others have it right? What *is* our problem and what is the solution?" Or advice: "Tell us straight. Should we divorce and get it over with or battle on despite the misery?"

It is hard for desperate couples to hear "I do not know yet. Let's find the questions before we attempt the answers. Let's take our time and explore the terrain before we rush into makeshift solutions." Once over the shocking realization that the therapist is neither mind reader nor oracle, the couple can relax (relatively speaking) into a moratorium period. Agreeing that no irretrievable decisions will be made during the course of the early sessions takes the urgency and dread out of the situation, while we all try to make sense of what is really going on and why.

Sometimes a partner is "sent" under threat of desertion or divorce. Sometimes one party definitely wishes to leave the marriage, but out of guilt and a willingness to prove no stone has been left unturned, comes to the first meeting at least.

Sometimes the therapist is asked to tackle the other person's problem, the other person being allegedly depressed, or withdrawn, or never home, or half drunk most nights. The inference is, *there's nothing wrong with me*. Occasionally this is virtually true (I say virtually because no one is perfect). One party requires individual therapy or some other type of help to get them over it before couple work, if still needed, can commence. But usually this displacement on to the other partner marks the beginning of a challenge to the therapist. How to enable the couple to experience themselves as a "third element", "joint personality", "shared living system", not just antagonists battling out their differences while trying to force the other into the desired shape?

The rowing pair frequently stop in their tracks when shown the necessity for each of them to relate to the third element for a change, *to the marriage itself*. They have not yet appreciated that their marriage is rather like their child. However serious the hostilities may be, most parents aim to protect their offspring from the fall-out. Disagreements of themselves do not matter; they are inevitable. How the couple handles them matters greatly, though, both to the child *and* to the marriage as a joint personality. Both of these can only absorb so much trauma without ensuing damage. Realizing that their way of rowing (not what they are rowing about!) could wreck a longstanding and, until now, workable couple system, focuses the pair's attention on concerns beyond pure self-interest.

Jamiel and Jharna

Jamiel and Jharna, both in their thirties, had resided in central London for six months when they came to see me. Anglo-Indians from New Delhi, they were ten years married with two children, aged seven and nine. Jamiel had been promoted back home and then rapidly promoted again in order to come to Britain and head a new, specialized unit at the Commonwealth Office. He felt honoured, but rather nervous. He wanted very badly to do well.

Jharna looked forward to meeting new and rather grand people. She was eager to get clothes, food, entertainment, her home, etc., just right. She saw herself as very much "the diplomat's wife". The Foreign Office contributed to school fees. Both parents and children were delighted with the school recommended to them. For a while the whole family was busy, but very happy.

Trouble started around the third month. Jamiel's contract, hastily put together in Delhi, was being refined in London and taking an age to complete. Accordingly, his salary and promised perks were nothing like what he had expected. Jharna, meanwhile, bought carpets and expensive furniture for their rented flat, storing all the existing furnishings that were not to her taste. She gave lavish dinner parties, using bone china dinner services bought from London's most prestigious stores. Jamiel said nothing, hoping the contract would be sorted out soon.

The contribution to school fees turned out to represent but a tiny portion of the termly bill. Jamiel borrowed money and said nothing to Jharna.

Eventually Jamiel wrote home. His father helped him out with all the money he could afford. But this amount could never cover Jharna's spending. Father also recruited an Indian lawyer to contact his London counterpart in order to investigate the contract. The process dragged on for months. The legal fees were enormous.

By now Jamiel, normally teetotal, was secretly drinking. He was taciturn and solitary. He would not go out or join in plans to entertain. Jharna found wine bottles in the cellar and disused cupboards. Then she found the solicitor's bill. Jamiel had to confess everything.

Jharna was beside herself with fury. Why had she not been told, not trusted? Was she a child? Did he think she could not cope, could not help? She was aghast when she realized the extent of the debts. The children would have to leave the private school. They would have to move to a smaller flat in a less well-off neighbourhood. Had he any idea of the damage he had done? What would their new friends think?

Jharna phoned her mother in India every few days, relaying each new episode. Mother advised her to get Jamiel to see a psychiatrist. Meanwhile, she should transfer funds from their joint accounts to her own account. She should see a solicitor at once, about her rights in Britain should there be a divorce. Mother would talk informally to her own solicitor.

This situation would be distressing for any couple, but, on hearing the family backgrounds, the reasons for each partner's reactions became clear. Jharna came from an academic family where the women, through several generations, had prized independence. Many had held minor office in government or held university chairs. Jharna was not academically inclined, but hoped she could win approval and status in her family by being a high profile wife and society hostess. Many years ago her father had run off to Scotland with a visiting tourist, making no arrangements for the family he left behind. Jharna's mother financed the family for four years before he returned. In order to avoid further scandal—or so the story went—he was taken back into the household, but treated with contempt by the women.

Jamiel was the only son of two traditional Hindus, private people whose only ambition was to see their son publicly shine. They doted on and protected him, never quarrelled with him or he them. When they met his future wife they hid their disappointment at her lively and independent nature. They were not told of the Scotland affair. They set about trying to be good in-laws, but Jharna sensed their disapproval and kept them at arm's length.

Jharna's fury with her husband was understandable, but it took her some time to see he was also in receipt of her anger with her father for so letting down his family and her mother. It was doubly important to her that her own husband should be above reproach in all things. Then there would be no need to fully mourn her father's abandoning of her, for in effect Jamiel would have replaced him.

In his whole life, Jamiel had never failed at anything. He had no repertoire of coping strategies on which to fall back when finally he did fail. Confessing to his wife was *unthinkable*. After all, she represented his mother, who saw him as—implicitly *demanded* of him that he should be—perfect. How could he possibly disillusion her? He could not understand that his wife would have been perfectly able to cope and to tighten her belt had she been taken into his confidence. She came from a long line of highly competent women, after all.

Jharna's father, of course, had never consulted her over whether, when, and in what manner to leave home, so Jamiel's *secrecy* seemed to Jharna another major betrayal.

Eventually, both parties came to understand how their history was impinging on the present, over-determining their reactions to one another. Somewhat hesitantly they began to collaborate. They continued resorting to parents for advice and justification, however, which angered both. Jamiel was humiliated by Jharna's mother's interfering in their problems when he was trying to put it all right. He felt he was being treated like an irresponsible child. Jharna retorted that she could never, ever trust him again. She had to protect herself legally and financially, even if she was not yet ready to call it a day. She would give him one more chance, for the sake of the children.

She hated his taking money from his father, denouncing him as an inadequate breadwinner. His parents had never liked her; they were just offering money to assist him make a break with her. He wasn't a real man. (Her father wasn't either. Jamiel's real crime was that he had failed to make up for that!) Jamiel's shame at this was very great, but he was angry, too.

Both Jamiel and Jharna blamed the other's parents for the marital failure. Jamiel's mother had never taught him to stand on his own feet, and his father was no better, worshipping the ground he walked on. Jamiel threw back that Jharna's mother had always been a bossy troublemaker. No wonder her husband had left her.

Once the couple accepted responsibility for the fact that they *were* behaving like children, albeit for understandable reasons, given their histories, marital relations seemed to improve. They took on board the need to draw a boundary round their relationship, and to use each other for support rather than their original family. They had produced the problems and it was for them to sort them out. They began forging a joint personality, deciding together how to manage the in-laws, generating shared policies about what was and wasn't permissible to discuss with them. Until now each had clung to childhood, perceiving their first family system as safer than their marriage.

Just as things were looking up, Jharna revealed that she had been secretly continuing the calls to her mother and that together they had made a plan. Jharna would move out with the children, financed by her mother, but remain in London for the time being. Jamiel had three months. If he had not solved the money, the drink, and the depression by then, she was going back to India for good.

Normally, I never use teaching aids in therapy. On this occasion, however, I realized they had not really understood the need to squeeze the parents out of the picture at all. Their apparent cooperation with me was mainly politeness. In truth, both were offended at my "attacking" their much-loved families, claiming that I did not understand what family meant in India. British people just did not respect parents the way they did. True or not, this was a tough joint defence. I had to break through.

I drew them the couple system diagram shown in Figure 13.

At last, through a depersonalized drawing (no one needed defending, for no one was being criticized), they each saw how frail,

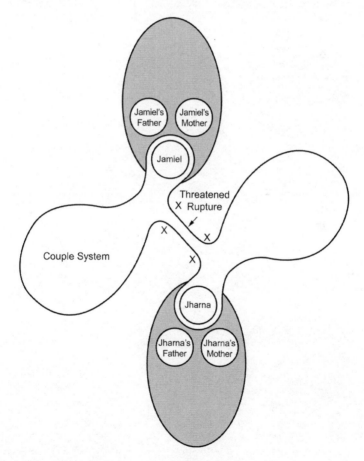

Figure 13. Dangerously tenuous couple boundary.

indeed, near to rupture, was their couple boundary. This diagram did not refer to just the present time, or to just this particular set of problems. If their future couple conflicts were approached in the same way, divorce would become inevitable. They and only they carried ultimate responsibility for the parlous state of their boundary.

Whether this diagram could drastically change to that illustrated in Figure 14 would determine their whole future. This finally convinced them of the danger they were in.

It was time to grow up, show the in-laws they were a team, an *indivisible* team, loyal to one another, with private areas in their relationship that no one else would be permitted to penetrate. They had to accept full responsibility for having recruited parents as

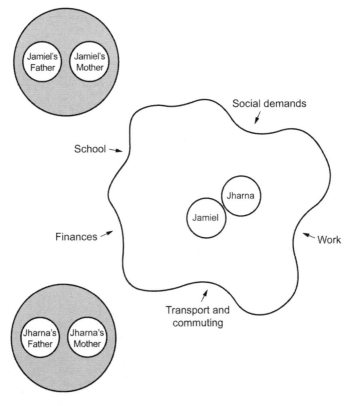

Figure 14.   Appropriate couple boundary.
Note: The in-laws are returned to their own couple systems and can only cross Jamiel and Jharna's couple boundary by invitation.

saboteurs of the couple system, so as to remove any guilty thoughts that they themselves might have made a mess of things. Blaming the other's parents would no longer do. From now on they had to fight their own battles, face to face with each other.

Much more work was needed, but this marked the turning point in the therapy.

Incidentally, it turned out that Jamiel had been having serious problems managing his new work force. This had contributed greatly to his depression. (Again he had been too ashamed to admit this to his rather fierce wife, so opposite to his gentle mother, accepting of all he did.) He used a variation of the diagram to teach himself where he was going wrong with his staff. He had been treating them the way his parents had treated him, and Jharna's parents had treated her—as dependent, helpless children. He thought he was being a good boss, checking all their work, offering endless suggestions, congratulating them on their work almost before they had produced anything. They felt patronized, infantilized, and resented him. Once he realized this, his management style altered. He allowed them to grow up. His working life, as well as his depression, improved enormously.

Throughout the course of a typical therapy the therapist fulfils many functions, all aimed ultimately at facilitating *understanding* by the couple of why and how they came to the position in which they now find themselves. This may involve greater or less exploration of childhood experiences, and may or may not involve one or both partners having separate therapy with another practitioner. All therapists develop their personal style over time, but, generally speaking, I like to see the couple together, then see them separately, then together again, so as to have a three-way discussion about the way forward, now we have (we hope) some clearer idea about the various undercurrents and their source.

Watching the couple from the sidelines during this assessment period, listening while they tell their story and argue with one another about their respective versions, helps me get a picture of life at home. I may need to ask about one or two things, but eventually I can start to offer ideas about what could be going on, which they can corroborate, modify, enlarge, or throw in the bin. This making of tentative formulations is my main activity, but not the only one.

Occasionally, I find to my surprise that I have been turned into a figure in the couple's drama. If I am to understand what is happening, I must let myself be that person temporarily (without, of course, losing my own personal identity and role as therapist).

Take Jamiel and Jharna, for instance. Many months into their therapy (soon after the desperate use of the diagram), I found the atmosphere between the frequent rows becoming very cosy. At first I thought, how odd! Then I began to see that I was being used as a sort of shared grandmother. To have me stand in for either of their mothers or fathers would have been too hot for them to handle, but while they were making the break from their respective families, joining forces with each other at last, they did need someone from whom to take comfort while going through this difficult transition.

We chatted about the children's doings, much as parents visiting Grandma would do in ordinary life. We looked at how Jamiel's job and contract was progressing, who was invited to dinner this week despite their reduced circumstances. We shared jokes and talked about world news.

Jamiel had never seen fighting between a pair before and Jharna had so hated her parents' rowing that she had sworn to marry a peaceable man. In ten years, until they came to England, they had never quarrelled. Now they had to learn how to constructively fight as well as to consult and support one another. As Grandma, I was quite often brought into their disagreements, not as a therapist who would poke about looking for "dark meanings", as they put it, but just as someone to appeal to, offload on to, get sympathy from, when the other partner was falling short.

Occasionally, "Grandma" banged their heads together, made them face things they would rather fume about than talk out. At other times I would take sides with one, then the other, acting as translator for each, like a loving Grandma wanting to reconcile them. I tried to take the sting out of accusations by reframing them in more acceptable terms. I am glad to say that in time Grandma became redundant. I returned to my more usual job of interpreting the latent processes between them (Figure 15).

Eventually, they grew confident in their marriage, as well as in themselves. They realized that they had scarcely known each other before coming to the UK.

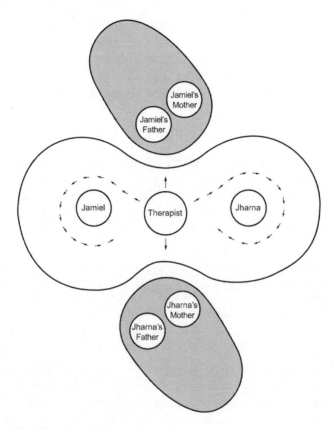

Figure 15. "Grandma" therapist at work.

Note: The arrows represent the therapeutic work. The therapist "Grandma" is pulling the couple pair together and pushing the couple boundary outwards against inward pressure from the in-laws.

In summer, they visited India for six weeks. Both families were faced with a united *adult* couple who could solve their own problems, but still wished for family connection. I suspect much of the former "wish to help" from both sets of parents had had to do with fear of losing a loved offspring to an undeserving marital partner.

Now and then, the therapist is unconsciously deployed as some now absent member of the couple's own family. For example, a couple may come to therapy following a son going off to university, or gap year travels. The son had operated as a go-between perhaps, a mediator, nipping quarrels in the bud. Or maybe he enjoyed a special relationship with each parent, which meant they must remain together if he were to be kept happy. Or maybe he was so troublesome they could both worry themselves sick about him, thus distracting themselves from the unspoken problems between the two of them. Perhaps they could both be angry and disappointed in him, so avoiding having to face their anger with and disappointment in one another. (Perhaps this is why he is leaving home; he is fed up with being got at!)

In order to perpetuate their back home situation, where the couple need not face their joint problems, the therapist is used by them in the same way they used their son. Until the therapist recognizes this, she cannot help them to tackle each other more directly.

Similarly, one of the couple's parents, dead or alive, can loom large in the therapy. Often the therapist is appealed to for an opinion, or attacked for no obvious reason, or comforted when she is not sad. The event only makes sense when it dawns on the therapist, or one of the couple, who the therapist is standing in for, who it is that is really being addressed.

However, these cases are the exception rather than the rule. Ordinarily, whatever qualities are disproportionately attributed to people, the attribution usually occurs between the couple. After all, that is part of why they chose each other. The therapist is better placed to witness and explore interpersonal distortions between the couple than they are, because she is less emotionally engaged. She is married to neither of them.

Many processes that occur *between* couples do so at a half-conscious or unconscious level. A perceptive therapist can observe, then sensitively and with careful timing relay this information to them. This widens their options to relate in a different manner, or aids them to understand the other's previously inexplicable behaviour or attitude, so that they no longer wish or need to deliver the usual hostile response. What the therapist cannot do is "change the leopard's spots", reconfigure the mind and behaviours of one partner to suit the other.

It should be noted, too, that no therapist can work blind. By that, I mean the two people who have consulted her need to be frank rather than selective about the things they tell. She can only work with what is offered. Limited contributions from the couple means limited feedback from the therapist. As with any relationship, though, time must first be allowed for trust to grow. A competent therapist can wait.

Naturally, all couples who come for help worry about future outcome. How often does therapy actually work, and can it make matters worse as well as better? How long will it take? I examine these questions in the final chapter.

What chance of success?

What about the question of therapeutic outcome? There are no absolutes here. We must forget the medical model of disease and cure. The couple is not diseased and therapy does not cure. Therapy tries to assist the couple system to grow and progress, rather than restoring it to some previous notion of healthy functioning. What would be the point of returning Jharna and Jamiel (see Chapter Thirteen) to the child marriage they had in India? As soon as fresh problems arose they would discover they were powerless to combat them.

Some couples will go further than others, depending on their openness to the therapeutic process, their histories, their preparedness to stick it out, and their personal capacities—which I shall discuss shortly. Some will go "far enough" (they decide, not the therapist), then choose to stop. Some will face defeat: the therapeutic focus then shifts toward dismantling the relationship with the least damage to all parties, including any children.

As to therapy making things worse, this is, in one sense, true. Couples who know in their hearts the marriage or partnership is over, but cannot face it, do arrive in therapy hoping for a miracle. Despite valiant efforts at resuscitation by all three, communication deteriorates. The death of love can no longer be denied. Therapy has *accelerated* the decline by bringing the sterility of the marriage into the open. At home, all manner of distractions has put off the day of reckoning. This could have gone on for years—"until the kids leave home"; "until mum dies"; "until my pension comes through". Their coming to therapy indicates that they are seeking someone who will be brave enough to switch off the life support machine and set them free, without either having to take the blame.

Many people find "digging about in the past" unpalatable. Granted, such explorations can be uncomfortable as well as relieving, but this does not mean the marriage will get worse, although it may have to get worse before it gets better. Such people fear losing control of their private inner world, which, with all its good and bad bits, has sustained them thus far. What if something ghastly appeared out of those interior shadows? Would there be shame, guilt, humiliation, pain? Unwelcome truths about oneself? Yes, all this is possible, as is *discovering potential one never knew was there*.

Often, as therapy gets under way, a spouse is dumbfounded to hear their other half expressing the pent-up love and admiration they have felt over the years, yet were too shy, or fearful of the response, to speak it. Something about the safe, neutral setting of the consulting room allows compliments to be paid on both practical and psychological talents that the complimented spouse never knew they possessed. It is amazing what wonderful things couples do *not* tell each other at home, because of the polluted atmosphere there. Therapy is not all bad news!

Many wounded people protect themselves from further hurt by turning deaf ears to proffered love, even rejecting it. The other partner eventually gives up trying. It is very painful for them to have to face the fact that their love is not wanted or is mistrusted. When the reasons for the rejector's inability to receive are understood, the offer can be made again. Some people genuinely believe themselves to be unworthy of love or happiness, or that they will be trapped or controlled if they allow themselves to become too attached. Some expect punishment should they dare to accept love. Once these unconscious assumptions, along with their historical determinates, are unearthed in the consulting room, there can be a new beginning. In this kind of relationship, matters can only worsen if they do *not* get help.

Rest assured, any worthwhile therapist will pace events so that individuals are not suddenly or unnecessarily exposed to undue stress. All the same, one has to be realistic. If a marriage is in deep trouble, then explosive forces are already at work. Can therapy be any worse than the strife at home?

Overly narcissistic people could not bear the wound to their pride that untoward revelations might produce, so are convinced therapy will only make things worse. Competitive and/or highly intellectual individuals, to whom the world of therapy is foreign, fear entering new territory where their particular prowess is not needed. They would feel horribly deskilled, so find some clever argument for not meeting a therapist. Some people believe therapy is the last resort of those pathetic creatures looking for an excuse for all their failures. They underestimate the bravery of—and the rewards for—those who *are* prepared to "dig". Some (only a few, I am happy to say) arrive for therapy defending against humiliation by aggressively asserting that all this stuff is hogwash; they are only coming because their doctor or partner or employer insists. They usually demand credentials, past "cure" rates, exact services covered by fees, etc. If there were not one small part of them that really wanted to come, they would not be here. We all need to save face.

None of these doubters can see what a therapist sees every day of her working life: immense courage, and a determination to pursue the truth about the self and the marriage, despite the absence of any guarantee. Desperation alone cannot account for this courage. It has something to do with the quality of the person(s), an openness to self-reflection that itself bodes well for the therapy. Having said that, many people who have never self-reflected in their lives can and do learn how. To witness such a person's dawning self-awareness, the pleasure and love on their partner's face as they realize it, too, is a special joy for the therapist. (You need some perks in this job!)

Those unable or unwilling to reflect on themselves, justify and rationalize their position by saying, "You can't put the clock back, mend hurts retrospectively." And, "What is the use in finding out *why*, when what is needed is *how*, how to make it better?"

The answer to the clock question is that if you do not revisit a hurt, accept fully and consciously *as an adult in the present* that it happened, it will always haunt you. If it was a small wound, you will probably deal with it whenever it is retriggered by current events, as you did then. You will find somewhere, someone or something to run to, away from the pain. Now you are all grown up, it may be alcohol, drugs, tobacco, food, shopping, or casual sex. Anything, *even if it kills you*, is preferable to facing the pain.

If it is a major wound, the child in you that still hurts will seek permanent comfort through a partner whose impossible job it is to put you right. (Meanwhile, of course, the chances are that the chosen one—be this a spouse or a series of "emergency" partners—is doing the same to you.) Revisiting the past cannot change that past, but its losses and sadnesses can be faced, mourned, and laid to rest. As a result, future relationships are no longer compromised, burdened by old ghosts. They stand a much better chance of surviving; not only because less impossible expectation is placed upon them, but also because the very choice of partner will have been beneficially affected by having dealt with past trauma.

The drip, drip effect of chronic trauma, say constant belittling by a parent, does not miraculously vanish once re-inspected in therapy. Certain situations will always prod the scar. But the *intensity* of pain will be less. Increasingly, that pain will feel as if it belongs in the past rather than a reliving in the present of what occurred long ago. Talking back to the ancients in therapy, with your partner listening and coming to *understand*, clears the way for the *joint* personality to grow. You no longer need to treat the spouse as if they *were* the perpetrator. Neither do you demand that they should heal your wounds.

As to the *how* rather than the *why*, my view is that we need both. But, unless the problems are very minor (in which case why has the couple come?), the *why* needs to be answered first.

If the marriage is well established, "bad habits" in communication will be pretty deeply rooted by now. Dirty fighting, veiled criticism, and manipulations of many kinds will abound. The alert partner will be wise to these and will have cultivated counter responses. Therefore, once the main "why" work is done, some restructuring of attitudes and retraining of communicational habits can be most helpful. The very act of renegotiating these brings the couple into more intimate and trusting relating. This part of therapy can also be great fun!

What qualities can the couple contribute?

What do the couple themselves need to bring to the sessions, in order to increase the likelihood of a positive outcome? More than anything, they need several capacities. I must stress here that I do not mean manifest ability, merely capacity. A willing couple and a good therapist can in time convert capacity to ability. Some conversions take longer than others. How long is a piece of string?

Alas, no one has so far devised a way of creating capacity where none exists. You might say no one has the right to judge another's capacity, as it is only a potential: it is invisible, not measurable. On the other hand, lack of capacity in certain areas needs to be recognized and accepted by a long-suffering partner praying for a miracle that is never going to happen. Enabling them to bear the truth can release them from a life of torment and guilt at failing to work that miracle. Therapy is not about maintaining marriage at all costs, but is to do with enhancing relationships that, however problematic, still have life and love in them (even though this may be displayed as hate at the time of referral).

To work successfully in couple therapy of the type espoused by this book, couples need the capacity to accept personal responsibility, the capacity to reflect on one's emotions and motives, the capacity to hate, the capacity to recognize one's anger, the capacity to mourn, and the capacity to tolerate not understanding anything. Last, but by no means least, is the capacity of each person to reflect on, and relate to, the joint personality (the third element, the couple system).

You do not need to be super intelligent or educated, though an agile mind that "cottons on" quickly is a huge asset. You do not need to know anything about psychology (sometimes this can even prove counter-productive). And you do not need to prepare anything—some people turn up with elaborate cases for the defence/prosecution, or a blow-by-blow essay on the latest row. All you need bring is whatever is bothering you *now*.

The capacity to accept personal responsibility

Let us suppose a certain partner has unconsciously selected the other to be her protégé. She is a "Rescuer", who just has to seek wounded birds and mend their wings. There will be many reasons for her having turned out this way, but couple therapy commences with her spouse complaining that she constantly criticizes him for being so helpless. He tries, but no efforts seem to satisfy her, especially now she has got the senior job she always wanted and cannot spend as much time at home.

Her complaint is that he never pulls his weight round the house. He cannot get the vacuum cleaner fixed, or challenge unfair bills, nor can he decide on the simplest menu without asking her advice. He is supposed to be a househusband, but is completely useless.

If we wanted to be spiteful about this, we could say she chose him to meet her rescuing needs and, when that became inconvenient, she blamed him for the very qualities she had married him for. Indeed, as many couples become more insightful about the hidden aspects of their union, such correct assertions are hurled about as weapons. This is an abuse of therapeutic insight, but it is often irresistible when a person is hurting. Revenge seems very sweet.

If both parties can disentangle here-and-now shortcomings (we all have them) from unconsciously solicited permanent ones, such as the above helplessness, then personal responsibility can be taken for partner choice, however inconvenient it has become. The demand that the partner now become someone totally different can be softened. Tension then subsides and serious negotiation can start.

Most readers will know very well the situation of one partner "setting up" the other, saying or doing the very things calculated to make the other behave in a specific (usually horrid) way, for which they can then be attacked. The attacker needs to accept responsibility for their part in writing this script, before the attacked one can let down defences and inspect their contribution to these nasty domestic dramas. When both parties are able to take responsibility for their respective roles, a new script can be jointly composed.

The capacity to self-reflect

For some this is as easy as falling off a log. Others, who spend most of their time focusing on the outside world of one-up-man-ship, decision-making, absorbing masses of data, rushing between meetings, and generally "Getting Things Done", find it a self-indulgent waste of time, or even embarrassing. This does not mean they lack the *capacity*, but they are unpractised, awkward. In therapy they usually feel uncomfortable in the early stages, fearing their more emotionally expressive partner has the advantage over them in this new and strange situation.

With patience and encouragement from their partner, rather than criticism, this art can be learnt. If they are unwilling to try, how can they ever be expected to take personal responsibility for their part in early marital choice, let alone subsequent upheavals?

The Avoider (see Chapter Eight) *cannot* self-reflect, let alone muse upon the joint personality, or any undercurrents between the pair. Mercifully, most people accused of being callous and cruel in the heat of marital rows are, in fact, some way along the avoidant continuum, but not at the extreme end. Many of these *fear* self-reflection rather than lack the capacity for it. They have learned other ways—withdrawal, winding up the partner, sarcasm, and put-downs—to protect themselves from what they see as psychological assault or humiliation. They turn away from invitations to self-reflect, or reflect on the marriage, because they have found an easier route to "winning".

This avoidant style of relating places the relationship in great danger. The other partner is given no option but to put up with emotional and communicational starvation, or to leave. Usually the one who will not self-reflect has found a partner loyal and accommodating, determined to make the marriage work. This partner makes heroic sacrifices and submits to barely tolerable loneliness for years. When this accommodating partner begins to reflect more deeply, their whitewashing of the non-communicating partner is revealed (for which the whitewasher needs to take responsibility). In therapy, when respective families are studied, the reasons for these two choosing one another will become clearer.

However difficult for the refuser, a commitment to self-reflection is essential if the marital dynamics are to change. If the other "loyal" party goes on making excuses for them, any nascent motivation to learn self-reflection in the avoidant one will wither. It is up to both of them to make this difficult shift. And yes, it could result in break up. Which is why the whitewasher has gone on whitewashing for years. If this partner can stand his or her ground, there could be massive improvement. It is a risk. The only other alternative is continuing the current misery that brought them to therapy in the first place.

The capacity to experience anger and hate

I am not suggesting for one second that good therapy involves reckless mobilization of hate and anger. What I am assuming is that recognizing hope and love inside oneself, and in one's dear ones, is pretty easy: it has to be, or the species would fall into chronic depression and die of it. On the other hand, a significant number of people have been schooled to believe that anger and hate is either wicked or dangerous, and, as a result, have learned to censor such emotions. But these "negative" feelings are just as important to survival, so long as they are known about and under control.

In therapy, people who have repressed hate and anger are often bewildered and frightened. They are bewildered because their hate and anger is not available to them, although they are full to the brim with it: this incongruence is disturbing. They are frightened because they sense, rightly, that a vital element to communication is missing, but if located it might have some catastrophic effect. They call the buried hate and anger something else—headaches or lethargy, perhaps. Or they attribute it to their partners—without the partner all would be peace and light again. But they do not wish the marriage to end. What a dreadful conflict to have to endure.

Very often, exploration of how both partner's families viewed and managed anger brings the subject into full awareness, but non-threateningly—at "one remove". Slowly, tentatively, the pair begin to talk about what arouses such feelings in their own marital dealings. The therapist is there as conciliator, watching the pace, making the talk safe. During this early time, such a conversation between the couple at home is impossible.

Sometimes there is so much hatred locked inside a person that they cannot access it for fear of being overwhelmed, going mad, or murdering someone. A skilled therapist can diagnose those people who need longer-term therapy on their own, to help the sufferer with serious issues only incidentally related to the marriage. Just because it is the couple who make the appointment, this does not mean that couple therapy is automatically indicated.

The capacity to mourn

As with anger and hate, I am not here promulgating the idea that misery is good for you and the more you grieve the better your marriage will be. However, the opposite of mourning—celebrating, being joyful—is not hard. We do not avoid it, whereas mourning is extremely painful and isolating. We tend to dodge it whenever we can. Why suffer if we do not have to?

This is an understandable, but short-sighted view. Mourning avoided is mourning delayed. A backlog builds up, and when one day the wall of the dam cracks, all the accumulated losses and griefs pour out under pressure. Far better to deal with them one at a time, as they happen.

The first mourning periods come when we are so young and undeveloped we do not even have the word—any word—in our vocabulary, let alone any idea of what mourning means. When we strain hungrily toward the nipple and it is not there, or warm milk fails to flow; when cold and wet we are left to endure it; when we howl in the night with nameless dread and no one comes, we experience loss. We are not, after all, the supplier of our own needs and we know not how to soothe ourselves. There is something out there that does it for us, and we are at its mercy.

If we are not able to conjure up the nipple simply through imagining it, the smell of skin and hair that tells us warmth is on the way, the reassuring sound of soft singing, then we are not omnipotent after all. We can create nothing. Therefore, the world is no longer safe. And if we have lost something now, then even if we find it again, we can lose it once more. The world may lose *us*, abandon us to chaos and the dark! Nothing can be relied on. This terror is stored in the nerves and sinews, the blood and bone, and never completely leaves us; but the modern brain enables us forget what we do not wish to remember—our first sorrows.

This is normal loss, through which every individual progresses. To escape its horrors and avoid the sadness involved, the infant seeks compensation in new distracting experiences, trying to sit up, playing with its toes, shaking its toy rabbit to see what happens to its ears. The youngster can grieve unto death or propel itself forward into the unknown, there to experiment and *learn*. Hobson's choice. This is how we grow, one foot on the brake of loss and disappointment, the other on the accelerator of blind hope.

When a third person enters our lives, traditionally dad, we experience another major loss. Having adjusted to the fact that mum is separate to us and has all the power, not ourselves, we now have to share her with someone else. It is outrageous. Here, too, is a source of hatred and anger (healthy and normal), if it is subsequently tempered with love and respect between all family members.

Chapters Four and Five, on "How your infancy and childhood affects your marriage", address these questions of emotional development through various stages, so I shall not repeat them here. Suffice to say that because life constitutes a series of losses, then if we are not to be always dogged by them we need a capacity to mourn as part of our survival toolbox. Mourning processes loss, frees us to "move on", but mourning is something we all wish to circumvent. I am sorry to say there is no true "moving on" without it. I am equally sorry to say that there are persons who refuse to mourn or admit the need for it. They are not easy to be married to!

I remember a couple many years ago who lost their sixteen-year-old daughter suddenly. She was killed on her boyfriend's motorbike, returning from a dance. Her parents were absolutely stunned; they lived like robots for weeks. Then the husband started to work all hours, frequently getting up at 3.00 a.m. "to check the accounts". His wife took to loitering in singles bars and picked up two or three men a week, going back to their cars for sex.

Neither of these partners knew how to mourn, let alone mourn together. Perhaps the pain was just so bad that only the anaesthesia of work could distract the girl's father from his loss, whereas the mother felt so anaesthetized already, as dead as her daughter, she had to have aggressive sex to force her to realize she was alive. (In the same way, traumatized soldiers in wartime often report the desperate need for sex, even if it means rape, after an "incident" where they have killed.)

Both husband and wife had considered suicide, but not spoken about it. Both histories revealed delayed or warded-off mournings, or mournings that had got stuck half way through. The therapy consisted in helping them assist each other catch up with this unfinished business.

For almost three years they could not take a holiday, dine out together, or allow themselves any shared pleasure. I am glad to say their daughter was eventually jointly mourned, and in the fourth year after her death, they commenced adoption proceedings for an Asian orphan.

Margaret Forster's novel *Over* (2007) poignantly illustrates the complexity of and radical differences between types of mourning. An otherwise happily married couple, who have lost a daughter in inconclusive circumstances, can only grieve in their own way. Will their inability to mourn jointly or to comprehend their partner's totally different way of coming to terms with it destroy their relationship forever?

The capacity to tolerate ignorance

This is what therapists are good at! We would be useless to those who consult us if we could not stand their confusion, distress, fury, tears, and mutual recriminations, along with our total ignorance of its meaning. Nothing makes sense to us at first, though we want to help. We must employ patience, let the story unfold, told in their particular way by the actors living it day by day. With the help of the couple's commentaries on our hypotheses, we begin to build a picture of this unique couple relationship, its especial way of going about things. The pair will confirm, disconfirm, modify our observations and hunches, until we all find ourselves precisely where we started, yet it looks different now. There is more light. Understanding has come to us like a stranger walking out of the mist, dimly perceived at first, then increasingly clearer.

Understanding is markedly different to *knowledge*. In therapy we cannot take a formulation and scientifically prove its correctness. No laboratory test will diagnose the couple's trouble, either. And no amount of instruction, advice, or sympathy will in itself be of much use to the couple. Understanding comes about through people in the room talking, talking, and talking about their shared concerns, before arriving at a new place, where the same facts, stories, and feelings now seem different, as if the mind's eye had changed lenses.

Often it is the couple who want things speeded up (fair enough; they may have been in pain a long time). But "not understanding" is part of the process and cannot be sidestepped. Many demand "tips", "exercises", or theories, or bring books along to show me, which claim to solve marital problems "in five easy steps". I am afraid none of these emergency measures is useful (although extreme situations do exist, where life-endangering crises demand speedy intervention by the therapist, GP, or even the police.)

I think the hardest thing couples are asked to do in therapy is *wait, while working*. Some try to short-cut this agony by asking for medication. Being miserable is not the same as being ill. Anti-depressants can be life saving for the right patient, but they are not panaceas or soothing lollipops. Unless you are so ill that for the moment you cannot carry out your daily routines, antidepressants and tranquillizers will not cut down the waiting time. They may even prolong it by reducing motivation to explore. When you take Paracetamol for a bad headache, and it stops, you also stop wondering why the headache came on at that moment. It ceases to matter. The distress in marital disharmony is a sign that something needs to be done. It acts as a spur to self-examination and keeps the mind alert.

However, a short spell of medication for *continuing* sleep disturbance, or tranquillizers for a *few days* in an acute crisis can be helpful.

In any case, individuals vary enormously in their response to medication, especially the newer antidepressants. When effective, they certainly raise mood and usually help with sleep (though some people say they are kept awake, minds spinning). A side effect with SSRIs[1] that is not often mentioned is a lowering or cessation of libido in both sexes (although I have had two husbands who reported the opposite). If there are already problems in this area, they can be made worse. These drugs are powerful and must be carefully monitored. They are not quick pick-me-ups. They will take weeks, not days, to have their full effect, and should never be taken "now and then" or withdrawn suddenly.

If you cannot get out of bed (*cannot*—not "prefer not to") in the mornings, have all but stopped eating, cannot do your job, never go out any more, and have lost interest in everything, then yes, see your doctor at once. Ditto if you are so crippled with anxiety that a trip to the shops or a meeting with the boss is a nightmare, or if you are having paralysing panic attacks every day. But if the best description of your state is that you are deeply unhappy and scared about your marriage, then we need all your brain power and concentration to be available, so as to sort out the problem. Fogging it with drugs and/or alcohol may be temporarily relieving, but it is no solution.

During early therapy sessions, tolerating ignorance (not knowing what the hell is happening in the room!) can be extremely upsetting. *Creating* ignorance by abusing substances that could blur thinking or block feeling in the wrong candidate is sheer foolhardiness. Do remember, too, that any symptoms of depression or increased anxiety *that are side effects of the couple's problem*, however bad those symptoms seem, will fade when (if) the therapy succeeds. Depression, whatever its cause, is always associated with the absence of hope. Hope is often instilled as the first improvement in couple relations is observed, long before the therapy is over. Let us not drug hope.

All the same, psychiatric symptoms independent of the marriage need assistance from your GP. Such an illness may exacerbate the couple's difficulties and, in these cases, judicious use of medication in combination with therapy is feasible. Sometimes, though, if one partner is ill, therapy should be deferred until a more propitious time. This is yet another reason for a thorough, unrushed assessment of the overall situation by the therapist. We need the right tools for the right job at the right time.

Relating to the joint personality

Each partner will have their own views on what is going wrong, and will apportion blame to themselves or to their spouse in varying degrees. Most couples seem to think things will get better once fault has been properly attributed (battle lines drawn in the sand!). It is sometimes very difficult to dislodge this view, help them to see that they also each contribute to a joint personality, which they can either succour through attending to it, or destroy by neglecting it.

The joint personality is in many respects an additional therapist in the room. We must take best advantage of it.

At other times, the reverse situation prevails. The couple talk endlessly and animatedly about "our marriage" as if it is a "thing"; a naughty child they are having great difficulty in controlling. The therapist is a child guidance expert who is supposed to fix this "child" without either of the partners having to change anything about themselves as individuals.

All three elements of the marriage, and their interrelationship, require patient study if the couple are to properly *understand* their union, rather than rushing to premature conclusions and remedies because they cannot bear the slowness and effort of talking truthfully with each other.

Summing up

Whatever trials and tribulations beset couples who seek help, there is always an underlying theme of Disappointment, a sense of hopes dashed, or an angry "This is *not* the way it was supposed to be!" A cursory perusal of human developmental psychology reveals why this is so. Disappointment and Hope are structured in tandem into the infant, as a means of stimulating its growth and learning. (If you are never disappointed, you will remain glued to the breast forever: if you have no hope, you will not seek compensation for loss in new experiences, and so will die.)

Hope, as they say, springs eternal, so poses little problem. Disappointment is different. Owing to staved off mourning over earlier disappointments, plus a determination to go on staving them off indefinitely, the mate in adulthood is expected—indeed selected—to provide all that was lacking. Simultaneously, they must resurrect all the happiness and peace that was lost, stolen or just dried up.

Both the compensation and the resurrection is an illusion!

> The Moving Finger writes; and having writ,
> Moves on: nor all thy Piety nor Wit
> Shall lure it back to cancel half a Line,
> Nor all thy Tears wash out a Word of it.
> [Lines from *The Rubáiyát of Omar Khayyám*, 1859,
> translated by Edward Fitzgerald]

When the partner *inevitably* fails the test, they *become* the arch Disappointer, and hate sets in. But successful mourning for that which can never now be repaired—letting go of the illusion— allows each partner to take back unrealizable demands made on the other, thus ending the cycle of repeated disappointments. An opportunity for a new way of relating appears, based on a true perception of the imperfect, but still loved, other. This other perceives the perceiver as less than perfect too, but still can love, warts and all.

> Here with a Loaf of Bread beneath the Bough,
> A Flask of Wine, a book of Verse—and Thou
> Beside me singing in the Wilderness—
> And Wilderness is Paradise enow. [*ibid.*]

A wilderness that is paradise enough. Now that is what I would call a very satisfactory therapeutic outcome for any couple!

Note

1. SSRIs (selective serotonin reuptake inhibitors) are the most often prescribed modern antidepressants.

AFTERWORD

I am frequently asked: "Do couple problems *always* have to stretch way back into childhood? Isn't that sometimes like taking a sledgehammer to crack a nut?"

The short answer to this is yes. There *are* easier and quicker ways to help, but only where appropriate. In this book I have tried to make psychodynamic concepts "user friendly". Of necessity therefore, the edited tales I have told all concern developmental matters and unconscious communications; the complex as opposed to the more straightforward.

Many couples find their own way to make good use of a therapist, who serves them best by *allowing* herself to be used (as opposed to *a*bused!) as needed. She should resist all temptation to entrap them into her preferred way of thinking, if that is not what will help.

One last story then.

Christine and Corin

This middle-aged couple were both married to someone else when they met. It was obvious that they were very much in love, but all the same wanted me to say if it was advisable or not for them to move in together "given the circumstances". They had agonized and agonized, but could not decide.

The background was as follows. Corin's wife had been ill with cancer for years and was dying in hospital. In another ward, Christine visited her husband who was in the last stages of emphysema. Scarcely able to breathe, he had croaked at her one night that when he was gone, she was to find someone else and be happy. She would have his blessing. Upset and tearful, she stumbled to the car park, only to find herself boxed in. It was the last straw.

Corin found her sobbing, and took her home in his own car. As they were both scheduled to visit the next day, he picked her up from her flat and drove her to the hospital where she could collect her car after visiting hours.

The following week they bumped into each other on the hospital escalator and stayed to have a cup of tea in the cafeteria. This became a habit. Eventually, Christine's husband died. Corin comforted her, knowing from his own experience what she had been through. They started seeing each other after that. Then, some weeks later, Corin's wife died, after making him promise not to ever leave her. *He musn't betray her memory by taking up with someone else.*

At this point in their account, both began to weep. It took them some time to get the words out. The night following his wife's death, Corin had felt desperate and called Christine, who came round at once. They ended up in bed together.

Since that time, several weeks ago, they had tried to stay away from each other, been chaste when they did meet. Both were lonely and wretched, and found themselves meeting regularly again. It became clear they had to decide what to do, once and for all. I was an expert. What did I think?

It began to dawn on me that this was not the consulting room; it was the confessional.

I asked them to let me try and summarize the situation to see if I had understood it correctly. I said life to them must seem very short and very precious at the moment. Having found a second love, which neither had believed possible before, it must surely be natural for two lonely people to want to be together. But—a big but!—each had also loved their spouses for years, even though the passion had faded long since. How then, to respect their spouses' memory without giving up what bit of happiness might be left for the two of them?

"That's right," they chimed in unison.

Did it have to be either/or, I wondered aloud. Could they consider honouring all four parties by allowing a little time for mourning while simultaneously looking after their own needs? They were, after all, two recently bereaved persons. They had needs and rights—for consolation, companionship, a shoulder to cry on, and so forth.

They were so busy being guilty they had never considered themselves as vulnerable individuals in crisis. What right had they, wicked lovers, to lay claim to *needs?*

Corin appreciated this point, seemed relieved, but was still haunted by a picture of his wife, heartbroken by the breaking of his promise, not to mention the indecent haste with which he broke it.

Corin had no belief in an afterlife, so how could his wife possibly suffer heartbreak after her death? It was he, himself, who so hated what he had done. His self-reproach was for accepting the only kind of comfort that could have any effect upon him. He'd been a dazed, frightened man in the first throes of major loss.

"You mean it might have been *all right?*"

Christine insisted that it had all been her fault; she had led him on. He'd been in such anguish she could not bear to see him suffer. And she knew it would be all right with her husband. Hadn't he given her express permission?

"No," protested Corin, "we both have to take the blame."

"Blame or responsibility?" I asked. "Are you to be blamed for being human?"

"Got you," said Corin. "We should take responsibility for what we have done, but do not have to blight the rest of our lives and be apart, out of, well, guilt."

Christine interjected, "But your dear wife and that promise. And quite honestly I feel it's all a bit unfair to my old man as well. So soon after, and everything"

"What do you think we should do?" I was asked again.

"I am not a priest," I said. "But if I were, I would say: take some time. Respect your dead. Absolve each other."

Our time was up.

Now what would have been the point in pestering them about their potty training or their Oedipus complex? Off they went, hand in hand, into the happy sunset of their lives, one hopes.

APPENDIX I

The opening paragraphs of Edward St Aubyn's novel, *Mother's Milk*:

Why had they pretended to kill him when he was born? Keeping him awake for days, banging his head again and again against a closed cervix; twisting the cord around his throat and throttling him; chomping through his mother's abdomen with cold shears; clamping his head and wrenching his neck from side to side; dragging him out of his home and hitting him; shining lights in his eyes and doing experiments; taking him away from his mother while she lay on the table, half-dead. Maybe the idea was to destroy his nostalgia for the old world. First the confinement to make him hungry for space, then pretending to kill him so that he would be grateful for the space when he got it, even this loud desert, with only the bandages of his mother's arms to wrap around him, never the whole thing again, the whole warm thing all around him, being everything.

The curtains were breathing light into their hospital room. Swelling from the hot afternoon, and then flopping back against the French windows, easing the glare outside.

Someone opened the door and the curtains leapt up and rippled their edges; loose paper rustled, the room whitened, and the shudder of the road works grew a little louder. Then the door clunked and the curtains sighed and the room dimmed.

"Oh, no, not more flowers," said his mother.

He could see everything through the transparent walls of his fish-tank cot. He was looked over by the sticky eye of a splayed lily. Sometimes the breeze blew the peppery smell of freesias over him and he wanted to sneeze it away. On his mother's nightgown spots of blood mingled with streaks of dark orange pollen.

"It's so nice of people . . ." She was laughing from weakness and frustration. "I mean is there any room in the bath?"

"Not really, you've got the roses in there already and the other things."

"Oh, God, I can't bear it. Hundreds of flowers have been cut down and squeezed into those white vases, just to make us happy." She couldn't stop laughing. There were tears running down her face. "They should have been left where they were, in a garden somewhere."

The nurse looked at the chart.

"It's time for you to take your Voltarol," she said. "You've got to control the pain before it takes over."

Then the nurse looked at Robert and he locked on to her blue eyes in the heaving dimness.

"He's very alert. He's really checking me out."

"He is going to be all right, isn't he?" said his mother, suddenly terrified.

Suddenly Robert was terrified too. They were not together in the way they used to be, but they still had their helplessness in common. They had been washed up on a wild shore. Too tired to crawl up the beach, they could only loll in the roar and dazzle of being there. He had to face facts, though: they had been separated. He understood now that his mother had already been on the outside. For her this wild shore was a new role, for him it was a new world.

The strange thing was that he felt as if he had been there before. He had known there was an outside all along. He used to think it was a muffled watery world out there and that he lived at the heart of things. Now the walls had tumbled down and he could see what a muddle he had been in. How could he avoid getting in a new muddle in this hammeringly bright place? How could he kick and spin like he used to in this heavy atmosphere where the air stung his skin?

Yesterday he had thought he was dying. Perhaps he was right and this was what happened. Everything was open to question, except the fact that he was separated from his mother. Now that he realized there was a difference between them, he loved his mother with a new sharpness. He used to be close to her. Now he longed to be close to her. The first taste of longing was the saddest thing in the world. [Edward St Aubyn, 2006, pp. 3–5]

. . . .

He was an inconsolable wreck. He couldn't live with so much doubt and so much intensity. He vomited colostrum over his mother and then in the hazy moment of emptiness that followed, he caught sight of the curtains bulging with light. They held his attention. That's how it worked here. They fascinated you with things to make you forget about the separation.

Still, he didn't want to exaggerate his decline. Things had been getting cramped in the old world. Towards the end he was desperate to get out, but he had imagined himself expanding back into the boundless ocean of his youth, not exiled in this harsh land. Perhaps he could revisit the ocean in his dreams, if it weren't for the veil of violence that hung between him and the past.

He was drifting into the syrupy borders of sleep, not knowing whether it would take him into the floating world or back to the butchery of the birth room.

"Poor Baba, he was probably having a bad dream," said his mother, stroking him. His crying started to break up and fade.

She kissed him on the forehead and he realized that although they didn't share a body any more, they still had the same thoughts and the same feelings. He shuddered with relief and stared at the curtains, watching the light flow. [*ibid.*, p. 6]

* * *

The Anglo-American poet Thom Gunn wrote the following poem in 1976.

Baby Song

From the private ease of Mother's womb
I fall into the lighted room.

Why don't they simply put me back
Where it is warm and wet and black?

But one thing follows on another.
Things were different inside Mother.

Padded and jolly I would ride
The perfect comfort of her inside.

They tuck me in a rustling bed
—I lie there, raging, small and red.

I may sleep soon, I may forget,
But I won't forget that I regret.

A rain of blood poured round her womb,
But all time roars outside this room.

> [Thom Gunn, from *Three Songs* in *Jack Straw's Castle* (1976), republished 1993 in *Collected Poems*, p. 247, my italics]

APPENDIX II

Lines from Kahlil Gibran's poem *The Prophet* on the subject of marriage:

You were born together, and together you shall be for evermore.
You shall be together when the white wings of death scatter your days.
Aye, you shall be together even in the silent memory of God.
But let there be spaces in your togetherness.
And let the winds of the heavens dance between you.

Love one another, but make not a bond of love.
Let it rather be a moving sea between the shores of your souls.
Fill each other's cup but drink not from one cup.
Give one another of your bread but eat not from the same loaf.
Sing and dance together and be joyous, but let each one of you be alone.
Even as the strings of a lute are alone though they quiver with the same music.

Give your hearts, but not into each other's keeping.
For only the hand of Life can contain your hearts.
And stand together yet not too near together:
For the pillars of the temple stand apart,
And the oak tree and the cypress grow not in each other's shadow.

[Kahlil Gibran, 1926, *The Prophet*, pp. 18–21]

Useful addresses

This is not an exclusive listing of organizations or professional bodies offering couple therapy or representing couple therapists, but they should be able to put you in contact with trained and accredited therapists.

British Association for Counselling and Psychotherapy (BACP),
BACP House
15 St. John's Business Park
Lutterworth LE17 4HB
Tel: 0870 443 5252
Fax: 0870 443 5161
Email: bacp@bacp.co.uk
Website: www.bacp.co.uk
For accredited therapist listings see:
www.bacp.co.uk/seeking_therapist/index.html

British Association for Sexual and Relationship Therapy
Tel: 020 8543 2707
Email: info@basrt.org.uk
Website: www.basrt.org.uk

Harley Street Private Counselling (including couples)
1–7 Harley Street
London W1G 9QD
Tel: 020 7307 8748
Email: info@HarleyStreetCounselling.co.uk
Website: www.harleystreetcounselling.co.uk

Institute of Family Therapy (IFT)
24–32 Stephenson Way
Euston
London NW1 2HX
Tel: 020 7391 9150
Fax: 020 7391 9169
Email: clinical@instituteoffamilytherapy.org.uk
Website: www.instituteoffamilytherapy.org.uk

Relate
To find the contact details for your local Relate branch centre see
your "Yellow Pages" phone directory
Website: www.relate.org.uk

Society of Couple Psychoanalytic Psychotherapists (SCPP)
Tel: 0870 902 4878
Website: www.couplepsychotheraphy.co.uk
The Couple Psychotherapy Service
Tel: 0870 902 4878
Website: www.couplepsychotherapy.co.uk/cps

Tavistock Centre for Couple Relationships (formerly the Tavistock
Marital Studies Institute)
Tavistock Clinic
120 Belsize Lane
London NW3 5BA
Email: counselling@tccr.org.uk or psychotherapy@tccr.org.uk
Website: www.tavistockcentreforcouplerelationships.org
Psychotherapy & Consultation Clinic
Tel: 020 8938 2372
Relationship Counselling for London
Tel: 020 8938 2431
Email: info@counselling4london.com

United Kingdom Council for Psychotherapy (UKCP)
2nd Floor, Edward House
2 Wakley Street
London EC1V 7LT
Tel: 020 7014 9955
Fax: 020 7014 9977
Email: info@psychotherapy.org.uk
Website: www.psychotherapy.org.uk

GP practices
Occasionally GP services have short-term counselling on offer, which may or may not include working with couples. This service is very patchy indeed across the country.

Private practitioners
It has become common practice for therapists offering couple and individual counselling to advertise in Yellow Pages phone directories under "counselling" or "psychotherapy". Make sure they are properly qualified and if you are unhappy—leave!

The author cannot take responsibility for the quality and type of counselling received by any individual reader. Always check that your practitioner is accredited by BACP or registered with UKCP.

In North America readers may contact:

American Association for Marriage and Family Therapy
112 South Alfred Street
Alexandria, VA 22314–3061
Tel: (703) 838–9808
Fax: (703) 838–9805
Email: central@aamft.org
Website: www.aamft.org

American Psychological Association—Psychoanalytic Division (Division 39)—Couple and Family Section (Section VIII)
750 First Street, NE
Washington, DC 20002–4242
Tel: (800) 374–2721 or (202) 336–5500
Fax: (202) 218–3599
Email: division@apa.org
Website: www.apa.org

Ackerman Institute for the Family
149E 78th Street
New York, NY 10075
Tel: (212) 879–4900 ext. 100
or (212) 879–4900 ext. 122 (for appointments)
Fax: (212) 744–0206
Email: ackerman@ackerman.org
Website: www.ackerman.org

American Family Therapy Academy
1608 20th Street, NW
4th Floor
Washington, DC 20009
Tel: (202) 483–8001
Fax: (202) 483–8002
Email: afta@afta.org
Website: www.afta.org

The Institute of Family Living
3080 Yonge Street
Suite 5062, Toronto
Ontario M4N 3N1
Tel: (416) 487–3613
Fax: (416) 487–2096
Email: ifl@interlog.com
Website: www.ifl.on.ca

Aurora Family Therapy Centre
University of Winnipeg
515 Portage Avenue
Winnnipeg
Manitoba R3B 2E9
Tel: (204) 786–9251
Fax: (204) 772–2547
Website: http://aurora.uwinnipeg.ca

In Australasia readers may contact:

Australian Institute of Family Studies
Level 20, 485 La Trobe Street
Melbourne
Victoria 3000
Tel: (03) 9214 7888
Fax: (03) 9214 7839
Email: library@aifs.gov.au
Website: www.aifs.gov.au

REFERENCES

Albee, E. (1964). *Who's Afraid of Virginia Woolf?*. London: Vintage.

Balint, M. (1968). *The Basic Fault: Therapeutic Aspects of Regression*. New York: Brunner/Mazel [reprinted London: Routledge, 1992].

Beck, A. T. (1988). *Love Is Never Enough*. New York: Harper & Row.

Colman, W. (2005). 'The intolerable other: the difficulty of becoming a couple', *Psychoanalytic Perspectives on Couple Work*, no. 1, pp. 56–71.

Eliot, T. S. (1950). *The Cocktail Party*. London: Faber and Faber.

Fisher, J. V. (1999). *The Uninvited Guest: Emerging from Narcissism towards Marriage*, London: Karnac.

Forster, M. (2007). *Over*. London: Chatto & Windus.

Freud, S. (1933a). *New Introductory Lectures on Psychoanalysis. S.E., 22*. London: Hogarth.

Gibran, K. (1926). *The Prophet*. London: William Heinemann [reprinted London: Pan, 1991].

Grier, F. (Ed.) (2005). *Oedipus and the Couple*. London: Karnac.

Gunn, T. (1976). Baby Song, from *Three Songs*, in *Jack Straw's Castle* [republished in *Collected Poems*, London: Faber & Faber, 1993].

Hinshelwood, R. D. (1991). *A Dictionary of Kleinian Thought*. London: Free Association.

Hinshelwood, R. D. (1994). *Clinical Klein*. London: Free Association.

Jung, C. G. (1934). Individuation. *C.W.*, 7: 171–239. London: Routledge & Kegan Paul (1980).

Luepnitz, D. A. (2002). *Schopenhauer's Porcupines: Intimacy and Its Dilemmas*. New York: Basic Books.

Rubenfeld, J. (2006). *The Interpretation of Murder*. London: Headline Review.

St Aubyn, E. (2006). *Mother's Milk*. London: Picador.

Shreve, A. (1999). *The Pilot's Wife*. London: Abacus.

Skynner, A. C. R., & Cleese, J. (1983). *Families and How To Survive Them*. London: Methuen.

Swift, G. (2007). *Tomorrow*. London: Picador.

Winnicott, D. W. (1971). *Playing and Reality*. London: Tavistock.

BIBLIOGRAPHY

Axline, V. M. (1964). *Dibs: In Search of Self*. Harmondsworth: Penguin.

Bandler, R., & Grinder, J. (1982). *Reframing: Neuro-Linguistic Programming and the Transformation of Meaning*, Moab, Utah: Real People Press.

Berne, E. (1970). *Games People Play*, Harmondsworth: Penguin.

Berne, E. (1973). *Sex in Human Loving*, Harmondsworth: Penguin.

Bowlby, J. (1969, 1973, 1980). *Attachment and Loss*, vols. 1–3, London: Hogarth Press. (Reprinted 1980).

Carter, S., & Sokol, J. (1993). *He's Scared, She's Scared: Understanding the Hidden Fears That Sabotage Your Relationships*, New York: Dell Publishing.

Clulow, C. F., & Mattinson, J. (1989). *Marriage Inside Out: Understanding Problems of Intimacy*, Harmondsworth: Penguin.

Clulow, C. F. (1990). (Ed.) *Marriage: Disillusion and Hope*, London: Karnac.

Clulow, C. F. (1993). (Ed.) *Rethinking Marriage: Public and Private Perspectives*, London: Karnac.

Clulow, C. F. (1995). (Ed.) *Women. Men and Marriage: Talks from the Tavistock Marital Studies Institute*, London: Sheldon Press.

Clulow, C. F. (1996). (Ed.) *Partners Becoming Parents: Talks from the Tavistock Marital Studies Institute*, London: Sheldon Press.

Clulow, C. F. (2001). *Adult Attachment and Couple Psychotherapy*, London: Brunner/Routledge.

Crawford, T., & Ellis, A. (2000). *Making Intimate Connections: 7 Guidelines for Great Relationships and Better Communication*, Atascadero, California: Impact Publishers.

Crompton, S. (2007). *All About Me: Loving a Narcissist*, London: Collins.

De Board, R. (1998). *Counselling for Toads: A Pyschological Adventure*, London: Routledge.

Dicks, H. V. (1967). *Marital Tensions: Clinical Studies towards a Psychological Theory of Interaction*, London: Routledge and Kegan Paul.

Donovan, J. M. (1999). (Ed.) *Short Term Couple Therapy*, New York: Guilford.

Eichenbaum, L., & Orbach, S. (1982). *Understanding Women: A Feminist Psychoanalytic Approach*, Harmondsworth: Penguin.

Eichenbaum, L., & Orbach, S. (1983). *What Do Women Want? Exploring the Myth of Dependency*, London: Michael Joseph.

Erikson, E. H. (1950). 'Eight Ages of Man' in *Childhood & Society*, New York: W. W. Norton; London: Imago Publishing [revised edition New York: W. W. Norton; London: Hogarth Press; Harmondsworth: Pelican 1965, reprinted Vintage, 1995].

Friday, N. (1979). Marriage: the return to symbiosis. In: *My Mother My Self* (pp. 380–423). London: Fontana [reprinted 1994].

Gerhardt, S. (2004). *Why Love Matters: How Affection Shapes a Baby's Brain*. London: Routledge.

Goleman, D. P. (2006). *Social Intelligence: The New Science of Human Relationships*. London: Hutchinson.

Gomez, L. (1996). *An Introduction to Object Relations*. London: Free Association.

Grant, J., & Crawley, J. (2002). *Transference and Projection: Mirrors to the Self*. Buckingham: Open University Press.

Graves, R. (1960). *The Greek Myths, Vol. 1*. Harmondsworth: Penguin.

Grier, F. (Ed.) (2001). *Brief Encounters With Couples: Some Analytical Perspectives*. London: Karnac.

Hill, D. (2006). *The Adoption*. London: Headline Review.

Holmes, J. (1993). *John Bowlby and Attachment Theory*. London: Routledge.

Holmes, J., & Holmes, R. (1993). *The Good Mood Guide: How to Embrace Your Pain and Face Your Fears*. London: J. M. Dent.

Housden, R., & Goodchild, C. (Eds.) (1992). *We Two*. Wellingborough: Aquarian.

Huizinga, J. (1949). *Homo Ludens*. London: Routledge.

Jacobs, M. (1988). *Psychodynamic Counselling in Action*. London: Sage.

James, O. (2002). *They F*** You Up: How to Survive Family Life*. London: Bloomsbury.

Johnson, S. M., & Whiffen, V. E. (Eds.) (2003). *Attachment Processes in Couple and Family Therapy*. New York: Guilford.

Jones, E., & Asen, E. (2000). *Systemic Couple Therapy and Depression*. London: Karnac.

Jung, C. G. (1925). Marriage as a psychological relationship. *C.W., 17*: 324–345. London: Routledge & Kegan Paul (1980).

Jung, C. G. (1939). Conscious, unconscious, and individuation. *C.W., 9(i)*: 273–289. London: Routledge & Kegan Paul (1980).

Kahr, B. (2007). *Sex and the Psyche: The Untold Story of Our Most Secret Fantasies Taken from the Largest Ever Survey of Its Kind*. Harmondsworth: Allen Lane.

Katherine, A. (1993). *Boundaries: Where You End and I Begin*. New York: Fireside, Simon & Schuster.

Klein, J. (1987). *Our Need for Others and its Roots in Infancy*. New York: Routledge [reprinted 1995].

Kübler-Ross, E. (1975). *Death: The Final Stage of Growth*. London: Prentice-Hall.

Lachkar, J. (1992). *The Narcissistic/Borderline Couple: A Psychoanalytic Perspective on Marital Treatment*. London: Taylor & Francis.

Laufer, M. (1975). *Adolescent Disturbance and Breakdown*. Harmondsworth: Penguin.

Lubit, R. H. (2004). *Coping with Toxic Managers, Subordinates . . . and Other Difficult People: Using Emotional Intelligence to Survive and Prosper*. Upper Saddle River, NJ: Financial Times/Prentice Hall.

Mahler, M. S., Pine, F., & Bergman, A. (1975). *The Psychological Birth of the Human Infant: Symbiosis and Individuation*. New York: Basic Books [reprinted London: Karnac, 2002].

McDougall, J. (1986). *Theatres of the Mind: Illusion and Truth on the Psychoanalytic Stage*. New York: Basic Books.

McEwan, I. (2007). *On Chesil Beach*. London: Jonathan Cape.

Medical Research Council (2000). Partners can help depressed people beat the blues. See www.mrc.ac.uk/consumption/groups/public/documents/content/mrc002238.pdf based on research by Leffs, *et al.*, in *British Journal of Psychiatry, 177(2)*: 95–100.

Meyers, M. B. (2005). When the holocaust haunts the couple: hope, guilt and survival. *Psychoanalytic Perspectives on Couple Work, 1*: 42–55.

Miller, A. (1981). *The Drama of Being a Child—and the Search for the True Self*. New York: Basic Books [reprinted in paperback, London: Virago, 1990].

Mollon, P. (1993). *The Fragile Self: The Structure of Narcissistic Disturbance*. London: Whurr.

Morris, D. (1991). *Babywatching*. London: Jonathan Cape.

Morrison, B. (1993). *And When Did You Last See Your Father?* London: Granta [reprinted 2000].

Murphy, T., & Oberlin, L. H. (1993). *Overcoming Passive-Aggression: How to Stop Hidden Anger from Spoiling Your Relationships, Career and Happiness*. Upper Saddle River, NJ: Prentice Hall.

Nichols, P. (1981). *Passion Play*. London: Methuen [reprinted in paperback, London: Nick Hern, 2000].

Nicolson, P. (1998). *Post Natal Depression; Psychology Science and the Transition to Motherhood*. London: Routledge.

Norwood, R. (1985). *Women Who Love Too Much: When You Keep Wishing and Hoping He'll Change*. New York: Tarcher.

Parker, R. (1995). *Mother Love/Mother Hate: The Power of Maternal Ambivalence*. New York: Basic Books.

Phillips, A. (1988). *Winnicott*. London: Fontana.

Reibstein, J., & Richards, M. (1992). *Sexual Arrangements: Marriage and Affairs*. London: Heinemann.

Richo, D. (1993). *How to Be an Adult: A Handbook on Psychological and Spiritual Integration*. New York: Paulist Press.

Rowe, D. (1983). Outside the wall: living with a depressed person. In: *Depression: The Way Out of Your Prison* (pp. 162–207). London: Routledge & Kegan Paul.

Ruszczynski, S. (1993). *Psychotherapy with Couples: Theory and Practice at the Tavistock Institute of Marital Studies*. London: Karnac.

Ruszczynski, S., & Fisher, J. (1995). (Eds.) *Intrusiveness and Intimacy in the Couple*. London: Karnac.

Salzberger-Wittenberg, I. (1988). *Psycho-Analytic Insight and Relationships*. London: Routledge.

Scarf, M. (1987). *Intimate Partners: Patterns in Love and Marriage*. New York: Random House.

Schopenhauer, A. (1925). *The Essays of Arthur Schopenhauer*. T. Saunders (Trans.). New York: Willey.

Schuchter, S. (1986). *Dimensions of Grief*. San Francisco, CA: Jossey-Bass.

Sharpe, S. A. (2000). *The Ways We Love: A Developmental Approach to Treating Couples*. New York: Guilford.

Skynner, A. C. R. (1976a). *One Flesh: Separate Persons*. London: Constable.

Skynner, A. C. R. (1976b). *Systems of Family and Marital Psychotherapy*. New York: Brunner/Mazel.

Skynner, A. C. R. (1990). *Explorations with Families*. London: Routledge.

Skynner, A. C. R., & Cleese, J. (1993). *Life and How To Survive It*. London: Methuen.

Solomon, J., & George, C. C. (1999). *Attachment Disorganization*. New York: Guilford Press.

Sophocles (1947). *The Theban Plays*. E. F. Watling (Trans.). Harmondsworth: Penguin.

Sophocles (1953). *Electra and Other Plays*. E. F. Watling (Trans.). Harmondsworth: Penguin.

Stadlen, N. (2004). *What Mothers Do: Especially When It Looks Like Nothing*. London: Piatkus.

Stern, D. N. (1977). *The First Relationship: Infant and Mother*. London: Open Books [reprinted as new edition Cambridge, MA: Harvard University Press, 2002].

Stern, D. N. (1985). *The Interpersonal World of the Infant*. New York: Basic Books.

Storr, A. (1960). *The Integrity of the Personality*. Oxford: Butterworth-Heinemann [reprinted Oxford: Oxford Paperbacks, 1992].

Storr, A. (1972). *The Dynamics of Creation*. London: Secker & Warberg [reprinted New York: Ballantine, 1993].

Symington, N. (1993). *Narcissism: A New Theory*. London: Karnac.

Tanner, D. (1991). *You Just Don't Understand: Women and Men in Conversation*. London: Virago.

Verrier, N. N. (1993). *The Primal Wound: Understanding the Adopted Child*. Lafayette, CA: N. N. Verrier.

Vickers, S. (2006). *The Other Side of You*. London: Fourth Estate/Harper Collins.

Vickers, S. (2007). *Where Three Roads Meet*. Edinburgh: Canongate.

Viorst, J. (1987). *Necessary Losses: The Loves, Illusions, Dependencies and Impossible Expectations That All of Us Have to Give Up in Order to Grow*. New York: Ballantine.

Welldon, E. V. (1988). *Mother, Madonna, Whore: The Idealization and Denigration of Motherhood*. London: Free Association.

Wetzler, S. (1992). *Living with the Passive Aggressive Man: Coping with Hidden Aggression—from the Bedroom to the Boardroom*. New York: Fireside Books, Simon & Schuster.

Wilson, S. (1997). *Pocket Biographies—Sigmund Freud*. Stroud: Sutton.

Winnicott, D. W. (1965). *The Maturational Processes and the Facilitating Environment: Studies in the Theory of Emotional Development*. London: Hogarth [reprinted London: Karnac, 1990].